MAKING
MONEY TALK

w to Mediate Insured Claims and Other Monetary Disputes

J. ANDERSON LITTLE

AMERICAN BAR ASSOCIATION
Defending Liberty
Pursuing Justice

ABA Section of
Dispute Resolution

Cover design by ABA Publishing.

Printed in the United States of America.

11 10 09 08   5 4 3

Library of Congress Cataloging-in-Publication Data

Little, J. Anderson.
  Making money talk : how to mediate insured claims and other monetary disputes / by J. Anderson Little. -- 1st ed.
      p. cm.
  Includes index.
  ISBN 978-1-59031-825-6
  1. Mediation. 2. Dispute resolution (Law) 3. Negotiation. 4. Compromise (Law) I. Title.

  K2390.L58 2007
  347'.09--dc22

                                                                    2007008604

Acknowledgments

The central ideas for this work took shape in my work as a mediator and mediation trainer, and I have been teaching them to others over the past seven years in a seminar I originally called "The Language of Numbers." Putting those ideas in a written and publishable form was a much harder task than I thought it would be, so I relied upon many generous people to help me bring this book to fruition.

First there is my training partner, Thorns Craven, who patiently endured my obsession with this material for several years as I struggled to understand the dynamics of traditional bargaining and to develop the concepts you will read about shortly. Thorns, I thank you for your patience, your ear, and your encouragement.

My other friends and colleagues at Mediation, Inc. have also been encouraging, but I thank them most for letting me try out my ideas on them. The techniques described in these pages were field tested with my colleagues many years ago and led to the course out of which this volume rose. Several years later, they assisted me in developing the transcripts which appear in Chapter 6 through role play and conversation and assured me that my concepts worked in their practice. I thank you Lynn Gullick, Sydnor Thompson, Frank Campbell, Paul Ross, Lou Bledsoe, and Jim Billings.

My wife, Katie Early, read the early drafts of Chapters 3 and 4 and offered innumerable suggestions for improvement. Katie understands the difference between dictating (which is how I first committed these ideas to paper) and writing. Her skills as an editor and her patience as a partner were important to me throughout this process. Thanks a bunch, Katie; this project's almost over.

Three people read the original version of this volume and offered important suggestions about structure and organization. The first is Jen Wagner, my friend and former staff director, who thoroughly critiqued my organization and presentation. Her insights were invaluable and led to many improvements. I thank her and wish her well in her new career as a lawyer. The second is my friend, Daniel Bowling, who read the earliest version of this volume and suggested changes that have brought it to its current shape. Daniel, I thank you for the time, energy, and care you gave me during this project and for letting me know that there were things on these pages that needed to be said. This book would never have been published without your help and support. I am truly grateful for your encouragement and guidance. The third is my friend, Carol Shumate, who was indispensable in putting this manuscript into publishable form. Her suggestions for changes in the first four chapters of the manuscript and her many editorial suggestions for the remainder helped me tie together many loose ends. I thank you, Carol, for your hard work and encouragement.

My current staff director, Beth Adkins, has handled the many practicalities of formatting, researching, and the like for the past year and a half with dedication and a can-do spirit. As we approach the final stages of publication, I have the advantage of her friendship as well as her hard work. Thank you, Beth.

I thank the Publications Board of the Dispute Resolution Section of the ABA for taking on the work of an "unknown" and giving it their serious attention. It has been my pleasure to work with two capable people during the Board's review and contract process: it's Chair, Nancy Welsh, and the Director of the Section's staff, Ellen Miller. I am thoroughly impressed with their professionalism and commitment to our young profession and look forward to working with them towards publication.

I am also indebted to Arlene Hanks, who generously gave me important legal assistance during contract negotiations for the book; to Stephanie Shipper for making substantive suggestions in the later stages of the manuscript; and to Shirley Ellis for her editorial improvements.

My friends, Mike Collins and Linda Leikin, volunteered to help with the cover design for this book. I am grateful for their professional skill, for their personal interest in my work, and for their friendship.

And finally, I wish to thank the many persons, lawyers, and other professionals who have chosen me as their mediator and who have taken our seminars. You have helped me develop these understandings and techniques by giving me feedback and by seeking my guidance for your own work as negotiators and mediators. I hope that this volume will be an aid to you in the important work that you do.

Andy Little
January 2007

Dedication

To the many teachers who have graced my life thus far, especially my son, Cully.

I make no argument that it contains a statement of the mediation process that should supplant all others known to our profession or that it describes the only valid model for disputes of all kinds. In fact, the thesis implicit in these pages is that there is no single model of the mediation process that is useful in all types of cases. On the contrary, the nature of the dispute itself will dictate much about the process that a mediator chooses to employ.

The audiences to whom I speak in these pages are several. The principal audience is the steadily increasing number of mediators who conduct mediations in civil lawsuits in state and federal courts throughout this country. They understand civil litigation. They are comfortable with the presence of lawyers and adjusters who negotiate on behalf of their clients. They are familiar with a negotiating process that is characterized by positional bargaining and multiple rounds of proposals and counterproposals.

Their ranks are composed primarily of able lawyers and former judges who, despite their competence in the field of civil litigation as advocates and decision makers, often have doubts about their efficacy during the settlement conference process. They start their mediations on familiar ground, as the parties discuss and debate the merits of the case, but they soon feel lost as discussion about the merits of the case fades away and the parties begin a seemingly endless process of proposals and counterproposals.

These mediators often feel that they are on the periphery of the action during those negotiations and wonder whether they have a useful role to play in bringing the parties to closure. In the numerous trainings I have conducted on this topic, these mediators tell me that they often have the feeling of being "just a messenger" as the parties swap proposal after proposal, position after position.

I write primarily for them: to help them better understand the dynamics of money negotiations, to identify the recurring problems presented in those cases, to acquaint and arm them with new tools to handle those challenges, to build a model of the mediation process that will serve as a road map when traditional bargaining is unavoidable, and to describe how they can assist the parties with traditional bargaining in a facilitative, rather than a directive, way.

I write also for the many mediators in this country who do not mediate in the context of civil litigation and who mediate disputes in which the preservation and enhancement of relationships is a major concern. Even the most intensely personal of interpersonal disputes can have the sound, feel, or flavor of money negotiations. In a family financial dispute, for instance, there will be negotiations about money that resist the mediator's best efforts to reframe them into problem-solving discussions. Mediators will find in this volume a nugget or two to serve as a supplement to other approaches that are more appropriate for mediations conducted in family or workplace settings.

And finally, I write to add my thoughts to the national debate about what makes for good mediation. Years ago, Professor Jim Alfini wrote an article raising concerns about the quality of civil trial court mediation in Florida's civil courts in which he posed the question, "Is this the end of good mediation?"[1] Mandatory civil trial court mediation has grown enormously since Professor Alfini's article, and as it has grown, the ranks of its critics have grown as well.

If you believe the critics, civil trial court mediation should not be dignified with the title "mediation." It is, in that view, a highly directive process conducted by aggressive lawyers and former judges who achieve settlement by imposing their opinions on the parties, belittling, berating, or ignoring them and their positions, and engaging in arm-twisting tactics.

I admit that this may describe the conduct of some mediators in some court-ordered mediations. However, I confidently assert that trial court mediation is not necessarily a directive or coercive process. With a better understanding of the dynamics of money negotiations and with an expanded formulation of the mediation process, civil trial court mediators can be facilitative rather than directive in their approach to mediating disputes about money. The problem of being facilitative rather than directive is, after all, not solely the problem of civil trial court mediators. It is the central task of mediators everywhere in all types of disputes.

I write to provide a resounding "No!" to Professor Alfini's question. Good mediation is present whenever mediators properly understand the parties and the nature of the dispute and seek to employ processes and techniques that are facilitative rather than directive. The opportunities for conducting good mediation are as abundant in the mediation of civil trial court cases as they are in family disputes. They are as abundant in disputes dominated by traditional bargaining as they are in disputes dominated by interpersonal relationships.

It has been 15 years since I mediated my first civil case. The vast majority of the 4,000 cases I have mediated thereafter have been personal injury lawsuits based on a theory of negligence that, if successful, are covered and paid for by insurance. I return, then, to the question that plagued and intrigued me in 1992: Is there a formulation of the mediation process that can equip trial court mediators to handle the special problems presented in those cases? And, is there a formulation of the mediation process that can help mediators be facilitators of negotiations, even if those negotiations are characterized by positional bargaining?

To answer that question, let us explore the dynamics of negotiations about money that characterize cases in the civil trial court context. We begin with a case that is representative of the many personal injury cases that populate our courts, a personal injury case I call "The Rear Ender."

Notes

1. James J. Alfini, *Trashing, Bashing, and Hashing It Out: Is This the End of "Good Mediation"?*, 19 FLA. ST. U. L. REV. (1991).

The Case:
The Rear Ender

The mediator was greeted in plaintiff's lawyer Attorney John Smith's waiting room by his paralegal, Jennifer Ormand, who explained that all the parties to the mediation were assembled in the conference room and were ready to begin. The mediator entered the conference room, greeted everyone, and invited the participants to have a seat for the beginning of the conference. In attendance were Attorney Smith; his client, the plaintiff, Jimmy Young; the defense lawyer, Bill Walker; and his insurance claims representative, Joseph Moore. Allen Jones, the defendant, was not present because he had been excused from attending by agreement of the lawyers and the mediator.

The mediator knew little about the case but had worked with lawyers Smith and Walker several times in the past. He noted that fact to all in attendance as he easily slipped into his opening remarks and welcomed all to the conference. His remarks were informative but conversational in tone. They included all of the usual subjects: the purpose of the conference, his role and the role of the lawyers, the costs of the conference, the conference format, the informality of the process, the confidentiality of the process, and statutes covering the inadmissibility of statements made during the conference. His remarks were summaries of the topics he had set out more fully in a pamphlet he distributed to the participants at the opening of the meeting.

The mediator made every effort to attend to all persons in the room, stopping from time to time to involve some of them in short conversations about the case, thus ensuring that his remarks were delivered in an engaging manner. At the end he asked for questions and suggestions about the process. Hearing none, the mediator invited the plaintiff's lawyer Smith to tell the assembled participants what he wanted the others to understand about the case. Smith began:

"My 24-year-old client, Jimmy Young, was driving to work on two-lane NC 101 at 7:30 on a Monday morning in February two years ago. As Young approached a commercial area near the town of Turnersville, he moved into the right-hand lane of the highway that had now widened into four lanes. About four or five car lengths ahead of him was another vehicle that was behind two other cars. The line of traffic ahead of him slowed for the first car to make a right-hand turn. Young slowed also and kept a reasonable distance from the last car in line.

"After the first car turned right, the line of traffic picked up speed without anyone changing into the left-hand lane. Suddenly the car in the front of the line slowed abruptly, apparently considering a right-hand turn at the next intersection. Instead of turning right, the vehicle sped up, slowed down, and then made a sudden turn left across the other lane and into the median crossover. Young and the driver ahead of him came to a quick halt, with plenty of room separating them.

"As he did so, Young heard the sound of screeching tires behind him. He looked into his rearview mirror in time to see a vehicle driven by Allen Jones plow into his rear end. The impact tore loose Young's rear bumper and spare tire assembly at the rear of his truck. The defendant's car came to rest under the rear of Young's frame. Closer inspection showed that the frame was bent and that the bed had damaged the body of the cab as it twisted on impact.

"At the scene, Young complained of neck, back, and left shoulder pain. He also complained of pain in his right knee. The day after the collision he began treatment with Dr. Batson, a well-respected chiropractor in town, and continued treatment for two months. Young's neck, back, and shoulder injuries eventually were resolved with conservative treatment and no permanent disability.

"Two and a half weeks after the collision, Young saw Dr. Angelo, a local orthopedic surgeon, for pain and swelling in his right knee. Dr. Angelo had performed surgery on Young's knee five years earlier to reconstruct the right AC ligament injured in a high school football scrimmage. Records for this recent injury show that Young had suffered swelling and a bruised right knee with pain and tenderness. Dr. Angelo prescribed no physical therapy, only rest.

"Several weeks later, Young sought a second opinion at the urging of his chiropractor. He was referred to Dr. Carlson, an orthopedic surgeon in a nearby town. Dr. Carlson performed arthroscopic surgery on the knee two months after the collision. During surgery, Dr. Carlson discovered sinovitis in the joint, a tear in the meniscus, and a loose AC ligament. Repairs were made and a brief course of physical therapy was prescribed. Young now complains of intermittent pain and swelling in his right knee and says that the injury has completely changed his life. He is no longer able to maintain the unusually high level of physical fitness he was dedicated to before the accident and has gained 50 pounds.

"Dr. Angelo's records from the earlier football injury indicate that Young had pain, a popping sound, and a giving way for a year and a half after the earlier surgery. Similar complaints were reported after this collision, but the records reveal no history of complaints, treatment, or examination for the three and a half years before this injury. Dr. Carlson gave Young a 6 percent permanent disability rating to the knee, although he didn't report any loss of function in the joint. He relates the current condition and disability rating solely to this collision.

"Young's medical bills are $7,400. He has lost wages of $3,000. There is no claim for future loss of wages or medical expenses. In this action, which is set for trial in four months, Young will seek those amounts plus additional damages for pain and suffering and permanent disability. His scarring from the surgery is minimal, and he has elected not to ask for damages due to disfigurement. That's all we have at this time, Mr. Mediator."

The mediator thanked Smith for his comments and invited Jimmy Young to say what he wanted to about the collision or his injuries. Young declined to speak, saying that his lawyer had covered the subject sufficiently; so the mediator reminded him that he could speak later if he wished.

Turning his attention to the defense side of the table, the mediator asked defense lawyer Walker if he wished to give his perspective on the case. Walker spoke briefly, saying to Young directly that his client Allen Jones was sorry that he had been injured in the accident. "We certainly wish that this had not happened, and we have come here today to work hard to settle the claim. Having said that, it's only fair to alert you to the fact that we view this matter a bit differently than you. Mr. Jones's insurance company has hired me to evaluate your claim and I want you to know what I've told them about your case. Principally, I'm drawing on your own records for most of my information and interpretations."

"Now, we're not going to be talking about insurance coverage today. The policy is plenty sufficient to cover the injuries Smith outlined in his settlement brochure. We're also not going to say a lot about liability either, but you should be aware that, if we have to try this case, we'll be talking to the jury about contributory negligence. If the jury finds that you stopped too abruptly or that your stopping constituted a sudden emergency for Mr. Jones, then you won't be able to recover anything for this accident. You and your lawyer can talk about that, but there's a possibility you'll come out of trial with a zero because of the facts of this case.

"It is important to note that the accident was a chain-reaction type of incident. No one's going to get angry with Mr. Jones for his conduct on this occasion. He was driving a late-model sedan on the day of the collision. He had a 9 A.M. appointment with a client at that client's place of business in the next town and wasn't in a hurry. He was driving 20 to 25 mph at the time he applied the brakes. I think every juror who hears this case will believe this to have been an unfortunate occurrence and find that there were really no bad actors here. It was an accident, and accidents happen. Every one of those jurors will have been in Mr. Jones's shoes at one time or another in their driving histories.

"I might add along those lines that Mr. Jones was a model citizen after the accident. He tended to Young at the scene of the accident until the EMTs arrived. He also removed Young's bumper and spare tire assembly from the roadway so no passing motorist would be endangered. He then placed a call for Young to Young's mother, so that she wouldn't worry about her son should she hear about the accident some other way.

"Now, Mr. Mediator, I'm not going to talk much about the injuries in this matter in the general session. You and I can talk more about them in private. But I would note here that there are some previous injuries in the same knee that Mr. Young injured in this accident. We know we owe something for the injuries we caused, but we don't owe anything for what someone else caused. In particular, we don't believe that we're responsible for permanent disabilities arising out of this accident.

"You all have the same records we have, so I won't go over those in detail here. I would point out for your consideration, however, that the first opinion letter Dr. Carlson sent to Mr. Smith in this matter stated that he was assigning the 6 percent permanent partial disability rating 'inclusive of all injuries.' It was only after Mr. Smith's second letter requesting yet another opinion that Dr. Carlson stated the disability was due solely to this accident. We think a jury would find that circumstance interesting in their evaluation of Mr. Young's claims. Now, Mr. Mediator, we're here to talk and negotiate, but we need to be talking within a reasonable range of settlement. Thank you, Mr. Mediator."

The mediator then asked the claims representative whether he would like to add anything. The representative deferred to Walker's presentation. When it was clear that no one was going to say anything further, the mediator asked the parties whether they would like to speak with him in private. All agreed that private sessions would be useful, and so the mediator led the plaintiff's team to another room on the other side of Smith's suite of offices.

In private session, the mediator discussed the merits of the case with Young and his lawyer. He asked probing questions about the plaintiff's case and Smith spoke about how he would handle the arguments and evidence mentioned by the defense in general session. After a lengthy discussion about the value of the case, the mediator asked Smith if they were prepared to make an opening settlement proposal. Smith replied:

"We'd like to hear from them first. They haven't offered a dime in this case."

"Yeah," Young chimed in. "We've been doing all the work. We've given them tons of medical bills and reports; we've answered their picky interrogatories; and I spent the better part of a day being interrogated at a deposition. They haven't done a thing. They don't even care enough to have Jones here. Why should we do all the work!?"

There followed a lengthy discussion about who would "go first" at the settlement conference. When the mediator realized that the plaintiff's team would not make the first move, he proceeded to the defendant's room for a private session. Another discussion about the merits of the case ensued in which the theories of the plaintiff's case were discussed in greater detail than in the general session. After considerable discussion, Walker asked the mediator: "What kind of demand did they make?"

The mediator replied: "Bill, I don't have a proposal from them yet. They want to hear from you first. They want to know what kind of range you're talking about."

Walker retorted: "We haven't given them a number because they've never made a demand."

The claims representative added: "Why are they wasting our time? They know how this is done. We're just not going to bid against ourselves."

The mediator assured the defense team that he understood "the drill" in these cases and that he would convey their sentiments to the plaintiff. He also observed that the plaintiff's position presented an opportunity for the insurance company to set a tone for the negotiation and to establish a range it considered reasonable.

After much conversation about the pros and cons of "going first," the defense team opened with an offer of $7,400, the amount of Young's medical expenses.

When the mediator conveyed the defense's offer to the plaintiff, Young exclaimed, "That's insulting." His lawyer, too, clearly was not pleased with the offer; it was obvious from their reactions that Young and his lawyer had different expectations about what amount of money was acceptable to settle the case.

The mediator conveyed the defense perspectives on some of the issues in the case, noting in particular that the defense was honing in on the differing disability ratings in the two letters from Young's own doctor. Young and Smith finally settled on $85,000 as an opening proposal, but it was a proposal Smith thought was too high. The mediator returned to the defendant's room to relay the proposal.

"That's ridiculous," the insurance representative said. "That knee was disabled before the accident. It's not clear that we owe anything for the surgery or disability."

Walker was frustrated also. "What's Smith trying to do with this case? He knows we're not going to pay that kind of money on these facts. Listen, Mr. Mediator, we've got better things to do than sit around and let some uninformed plaintiff run the show and waste our time! Tell Smith to get control of his client."

The mediator listened for several minutes to the defense lawyer's review of the evidence in the case, and then invited the defense to make a counterproposal. With some reluctance, the defense countered with a new proposal: $10,400, the total of Young's claim for medical expenses and lost wages.

Young threatened to walk out of the mediation when he heard the proposal and it appeared that the negotiations would collapse. But after much consultation and consternation, the plaintiff's team countered with $80,000.

When the defendant's lawyer heard Young's second proposal, he stood up abruptly. "Well, that's it," he said. "We might as well pack our bags and go home. There's no way this is going to settle; he'll never get realistic."

With the mediator's help and encouragement, however, the defense team decided to remain at the table. For hours, the negotiations continued with round after round of proposal and counterproposal, each arrived at with great agony and deliberation.

Slowly the parties inched toward each other in small increments; and eventually, after 12 complete rounds of proposals, the parties settled at $27,500. The mediator then helped them draw up a memorandum of settlement.

This court-ordered mediation took a total of four hours and 36 minutes. The parties met with each other only once for less than 30 minutes. They said nothing to each other beyond their initial, rather formal presentations. The remaining four hours were spent in private sessions with the mediator.

At the end, the participants signed their agreement, wrote their checks, said their goodbyes, and went their separate ways. Their interaction was courteous but stiff. Although an agreement was reached at mediation, no one was particularly happy with the settlement or the difficulty with which it was reached.

This was a once-in-a-lifetime experience for Jimmy Young. He would not have an opportunity to see or speak with the people on the defendant's team again. His relationship with Smith concluded with the settlement of the case and he would not seek the services of a lawyer until age 40 when he inherited some money, bought a house, and made a will.

The members of the defense team were professionals. For them, this was just one more automobile accident, one more claim, and one more negotiation.

Welcome to the world of civil trial court mediation.

The Realities of Negotiations about Money

1

"The Rear Ender" tells the story of settlement of an insured claim based upon a theory of negligence. It is representative of the majority of cases in our trial courts, and its mediation is representative of civil trial court mediation that occurs on a daily basis throughout our land.

There are, of course, other types of civil lawsuits in our courts: business cases, corporate disputes, real estate and construction matters, employment issues, and civil rights and discrimination cases. They present mediators with opportunities for creative problem solving that generally do not exist in negligence cases; and, for that reason, I will return to them in Chapter 8.

However, they share with negligence cases an important characteristic that is the subject of this book—their settlement is achieved through the negotiation of an amount of money that is paid by one side to the other.

■■■■■

The majority of civil lawsuits, whether they are state or federal claims, will be settled through the payment of money. The currency of settlement in these cases is cash, and civil trial court mediators must come to grips with this fundamental reality.

Most of the people who mediate civil trial court cases have spent a professional lifetime trying, negotiating, and settling hundreds, even thousands, of insured claims. However, as mediators, these former litigators and judges frequently are frustrated by the challenges negligence claims present, and they long for tools to understand them and facilitate their settlement.

Complicating the situation is the fact that most mediators trained in this country have been taught to use a problem-solving approach in their work and to reframe position-based bargaining into problem solving. Mediators trained to use a problem-solving approach carry perceptions into the mediation process that collide with the realities of negotiations about money. To them, the mediation in "The Rear Ender" may look, sound, or feel strange indeed.

This volume was developed from an advanced mediator training course I've conducted for the past six years, and it is designed to help you become more confident and effective as a facilitator of the positional bargaining that occurs in civil trial court mediation. I begin this chapter with a description of the realities of negotiations about money and the perceptions mediators often have that stand in sharp contrast to them. In Chapters 2 through 7 I describe a model of the mediation process and a set of tools that will equip you to deal effectively with the challenges money negotiations present.

Chapter Synopsis: The Realities

- Lawyers perform a valuable role in mediation by helping their clients understand the realities of their case.
- The mediator's "clients" are the disputants and their legal and financial advisers.

- The parties to position-based bargaining tend to withhold information.
- The parties want private sessions so they can talk about private information.
- The first topic the parties want to talk about is the case and its value.
- Proposals made by the parties are monetary in nature.
- The parties will make multiple rounds of monetary proposals and spend the better part of the mediation doing so.
- The parties become frustrated and angry with each other as they swap proposals.
- Movement from one proposal to another stops before the parties reach their best numbers.
- One of the most important things a mediator can do is to help the parties move through their negotiating ranges when they are inclined to stop in frustration.

Perception: Lawyers Are Disruptive in the Mediation Process

Reality: Trial Lawyers Perform a Valuable Role for Their Clients

The participation of lawyers may not be the most important characteristic of money negotiations—in fact, most automobile claims are negotiated and settled by insurance companies and claimants before lawyers are involved—but this prominent feature of civil trial court mediation screams for attention.

When I first took mediation training at our local dispute settlement center in 1988, I was the only lawyer in a group of 24 would-be mediators. During the training, I detected several undercurrents about lawyers and the courts that surprised me. The flavor of the communication was that courts are bad and lawyers are worse. That message has been reinforced in the literature, advertising, and language of mediation for several decades and is one of the reasons that mediation was not well received initially in the legal community.

This message about lawyers and the courts has been an unfortunate feature of the mediation movement. Mediation has been sold in this country as an alternative to a supposedly inadequate form of dispute resolution called litigation. Courts, lawsuits, and lawyers have been demonized in a steady diet of negative advertising in the mediation community.

Of course, lawyers themselves have not enjoyed wide acclaim and affection in our society for reasons that are of our own making. We are often aggressive, condescending, combative, greedy, and dismissive. As one Internet joke sent to me recently stated, "Ninety-nine percent of lawyers give the rest a bad name." I am fully aware of that reputation and know that we create much of it ourselves through our own behavior.

Lawyers, as you might expect, have a much different view of themselves and their function in society, and it is a much more positive one than I have just painted. We believe that we are guardians of the rule of law. We vindicate, affirm, and preserve individual rights and liberties. We right wrongs; we protect and defend; we rescue the powerless from the tyranny of the powerful.

Those who represent plaintiffs in personal injury cases see themselves as representing the underdog in a commercial society, the wrongfully injured person who, but for the hard-fought and courageous efforts of the plaintiff's lawyer, is at the mercy of powerful insurance companies. Those who represent insurance companies often feel as strongly about their clients. They defend the wrongfully accused; they root out fraud and abuse; they bring clearheaded decision making to a tort system gone amuck.

Both views are a bit misleading when one considers the role of lawyers in representing litigants in personal injury lawsuits. From a practical point of view, lawyers perform an important, if less idealized, role for the parties.

■■■■■

In functional terms, lawyers help their clients analyze the value of their case and help them realize that value in settlement negotiations.

Mediators who do not have an appreciation for the positive role lawyers play in negotiations may want to review the thinking of Fisher and Ury in their landmark book, *Getting to Yes.*[1] Fisher and Ury's book is frequently cited to explain the importance of identifying disputing parties' needs and interests in mediation. Their thinking on that subject has been incorporated into the problem-solving model of the mediation process and receives much attention in the literature of mediation.

Another equally important observation in *Getting to Yes* is the notion that negotiations are enhanced when the parties have a firm grasp of their "Best Alternative to a Negotiated Agreement" (BATNA). A negotiator's BATNA is what he or she will do if agreement is not reached in a negotiation. Fisher and Ury suggest that negotiators clearly define their BATNA in order to provide a foundation for their negotiations.[2] This insight has not received as much attention in the literature of mediation as their insight about "needs and interests," but it is an especially useful one in the negotiation of claims for money.

What lawyers do positively for their clients in mediation is to help them analyze their BATNA and negotiate on the basis of it. They help their clients understand the value of their case and use that value as a benchmark for their negotiations. Stated in the most positive terms, lawyers want what is best for their clients, and they describe what is best for them in terms of what the case is "worth." They then negotiate on behalf of their clients to make sure their clients get what the case is worth, the case's value.

Mediators in civil trial court cases—lawyer and nonlawyer mediators alike—would do well to find a positive place for case analysis and a positive place for the participation of lawyers in their model of the mediation process. Otherwise, mediators may react negatively to lawyers who tend to dominate discussions and who are inclined to talk about the merits of their cases rather than the needs and interests of their clients.

Perception: The Disputant Is a Single Individual
Reality: The Disputant Is a Team of People

To be useful and successful in the mediation of civil trial court mediation, mediators should confront their own preconceptions

about lawyers and broaden their understanding of who "the disputant" is in the mediation of a civil trial court claim. I have found
it helpful to think of the "client" or "disputant" in these cases as a
team of people rather than as a single person who is the plaintiff
or defendant in a lawsuit.

■ ■ ■ ■ ■

I have put aside the notion that the individual party "should"
have center stage or that the parties "should" be talking to
each other without lawyers, as is sometimes suggested by critics of civil trial court mediation. Instead, I have cultivated the
notion that the client in civil trial court mediation is a team of
people who sit on one side of the controversy or the other. It
includes the plaintiff or defendant, the lawyer, and any other
advisors of the parties such as claim representatives.

Insurance Claims Representatives

Insurance claims representatives are frequent participants in
efforts to settle civil claims, because most civil claims are insured
by a policy of liability insurance. One of the important features of
most liability policies is a provision that gives the right to settle
the case to the insurance company. Most defendants in personal
injury lawsuits are not aware that they do not have control over
the outcome of their case. Indeed, quite often neither the defendant nor the plaintiff understands that the defendant's insurance
company has the deciding vote as to what is offered in the case.
Although most insurance companies do not want to ignore their
policyholders' opinions about liability or damages altogether, it is
clear that the insurance company has the right to settle the case
based on its own evaluation of the law and the facts.

While most lawyers try to prepare and educate their clients
about this reality, a mediator should be prepared to encounter litigants who don't understand that the "real party in interest" on
the defense side of the table is often the insurance company. In
cases involving automobile collisions, the insurance company's
representative is the ultimate decision maker who will write the

check for a settlement if it occurs. Mediators who are not lawyers would do well to observe multiple civil trial court mediations to get a feel for the way in which the participants who are professionals interact with each other and contribute to or control the decision-making process.

Defendants

Notice that in "The Rear Ender," one of the parties named in the lawsuit, the defendant, was not present for the mediation even though the rules governing court-ordered mediation required the presence of all parties. Under North Carolina rules, a person who is required to attend may be excused from attending by agreement of the parties and the mediator. Although it is not my preference to excuse the attendance of anyone required to attend, I often agree to the request of the parties to excuse a defendant in an automobile, personal injury case. My reasoning is that policies of automobile liability insurance give the insurer the right to settle the insured's (defendant's) case and that the defendant's involvement may not be necessary.

Many of the defense lawyers I work with, however, require that their insured clients attend the settlement conference even though the plaintiff might agree to excuse them. They know the plaintiff may be provoked by the absence of the defendant; they know that the defendant may supply useful information that others did not anticipate would be needed or supply an apology or word of sympathy that may soften the plaintiff's position; and they know that the defendant may be excused after the opening session if that seems appropriate.

Plaintiffs

The plaintiff in our case, Jimmy Young, is in a different position. No settlement agreement can be reached without the plaintiff's consent and signature. More importantly, it is usually the plaintiff who is the decision maker on his or her side of the table. No matter how many times one may hear from a plaintiff that "I'm leaving it all up to my lawyer," it is seldom true that the plaintiff takes a completely hands-off role in the mediation. In most mediations, the plaintiff has great expectations of recovery from the suit and is offended by the defense's remarks and view of the case. The plaintiff's views, concerns, questions, irritations, and expectations are important factors to be dealt with in the settlement of the case and, therefore, the plaintiff's presence and participation are important.

While mediators who are not lawyers may need to become familiar with the positive role lawyers play in civil trial court mediation, mediators who are lawyers may need to learn to pay more attention to the parties whose case is the subject of the mediation. Lawyer-mediators should remember that we are used to running the show, being the boss, and talking with fellow professionals to the exclusion of others. We may need to remind ourselves that the "team" on one side of the table includes the people in the room who are not lawyers or claims professionals.

We would also do well to remember that people (I'm now thinking mostly of plaintiffs in personal injury cases) do not make decisions to settle cases based solely on case analysis and case value; they often make decisions based on personal considerations, relationships, and needs and interests. Mediators should look for opportunities to engage nonprofessionals in conversation about their real needs, to pay attention to the personal comments parties make about themselves and others, and to mark and attend to those palpably emotional moments that are often turning points in the settlement of disputes of all kinds. (More on this subject will be covered in Chapter 8.)

Perception: Litigants Are Eager to Discuss Their Cases
Reality: The Parties (Teams) Tend to Withhold Information

When I began mediating civil trial court cases, I expected that the parties would welcome the opportunity to engage in conversation with each other about the merits of the case. In reality, the parties, both the lawyers and their clients, were reluctant to talk with each other when they had the opportunity to do so in general or opening sessions. Given the opportunity to talk about their case directly with the other side, the participants made only broad, general comments about the matter without revealing many of the details they spent months accumulating through the process of discovery.

The opening session in "The Rear Ender" was realistic in terms of its length and amount of detail the parties were willing to discuss. However, in many mediations I conduct, the opening remarks are more like the following:

> "Mr. Smith, what would you like for us to know about your client's case?"

> "Thank you, Mr. Mediator. Jimmy Young was injured in a rear end collision that occurred because of Mr. Jones's negligence and without any fault of Young's own. Although he recovered from most of his injuries, he had to have surgery on his knee and now has a permanent disability. We're here to see if we can settle the case."

> "Anything else Mr. Smith, or Mr. Young?"

> "I don't think so now; we may have a few things to talk about with you in private session."

> "All right, Mr. Walker, what would you like for us to know?"

> "Thank you, Mr. Mediator. This was a routine accident, but everyone came through it pretty well. I think we've got a lot to talk about at trial. Mr. Jones's actions weren't heinous, so a jury's not going to want to punish him. Besides that, we're not sure Mr. Young wasn't negligent himself on that occasion. On damages, I'd just say that the knee had as much permanent disability before the accident as now, so I don't think we owe anything for disability. We'll have a lot to talk about at trial, if this case goes that far. Thank you, Mr. Mediator."

> "Anything else you'd like us to know about the case or about your client?"

> "I don't think so just now, but we might have a few things to talk about in private session."

Much of the literature of mediation and mediation training is devoted to developing skills to enhance communication among the parties. This makes sense in light of the fact that many disputes arise because of failures of or difficulties in communication. Coming from this background, one can easily get the impression that the "ideal" in mediation is mediator-assisted, face-to-face conversation among the parties.

However, opening conversations like the one above are commonplace in automobile negligence cases. Even in longer opening sessions like the one in "The Rear Ender," one detects reluctance on the part of the lawyers to engage in an in-depth discussion of the case. Notice Walker's comment, for instance, when he said to the mediator, "You and I can talk more about them in private." That was Mr. Walker's way of signaling that he wasn't going to show his entire hand during the opening session and that he wanted to discuss the facts further in private session.

■ ■ ■ ■ ■

The parties to civil litigation and their lawyers are reluctant to talk openly with each other and with the mediator in general session. To mediators who have been trained exclusively to facilitate face-to-face communication, this can be a maddening reality.

Lawyers Discourage Conversation

Unfortunately, the "ideal" in mediation, that the parties will talk directly to each other, does not take into account the fact that lawyers discourage conversation. Civil trial court mediators quickly learn that free and open conversation isn't going to occur regularly when the disputants are teams of litigants and their legal representatives. Contrary to the popular notion that lawyers, by temperament and training, are apt to be aggressive, hostile, and disruptive during negotiations, lawyers are generally the participants in mediations who keep a lid on open conversation.

There is a positive side to this phenomenon. Lawyers not only keep a lid on conversation, but they also keep a lid on the disruptive tendencies of their clients. Because of that fact, I seldom experience problems with disruptive behavior in the mediations I conduct. My experience is that there are more instances of disruptive, insulting, and interruptive behavior in family or community mediations than in civil trial court mediations. Consequently, mediators in a civil court setting do not have to pay as much attention to what I call "crowd control" as do their colleagues who mediate other types of disputes.

Many lawyers believe that disruptive behavior and insulting speech are nonproductive and not likely to be conducive to settlement. They do not let their clients give vent to all they have to say, because they fear that it will irritate the other side and make it more difficult to settle the case. So, lawyers often put a lid on conversation in the belief that they are aiding the cause of settlement.

Lawyers Protect Strategic Information

Lawyers also discourage conversation in general sessions for strategic reasons that have to do with gaining, or not giving up, an advantage at trial if mediation does not bring about settlement. In most civil cases, lawyers and their clients withhold information from each other in order to gain the advantage of surprise at trial, in spite of the fact that rules of discovery were enacted to prevent trial by ambush.

■ ■ ■ ■ ■

Springing information on an opponent during the course of a trial has a dramatic impact on the course of litigation and is a pretrial fantasy of most trial lawyers.

In the dispute resolution process known as litigation, information is power. Those who know the facts have an advantage over those who don't. Those who know the facts sooner rather than later have the opportunity to think about how those facts can be spun and shaped in order to fit the picture of the case they want the judge or jury to have. Therefore, parties to litigation tend to guard the information they possess with great care and are reluctant to divulge it at mediation if they think the case will not settle and, thus, go to trial. The general rule for lawyers is that the less said to the other side about the evidence in the case, the less chance there is of giving away important information and, thus, an advantage.

Because they are never sure what their clients will say in an unrehearsed mediation, lawyers generally instruct their clients to say very little. That keeps their clients from revealing strategically advantageous information or making damaging admissions in the presence of their opponents.

Lawyers tend to put a lid on conversation during civil trial court mediations and appear that they have nothing important to talk about. In fact, they have plenty to say and will demonstrate it as soon as they are cloistered with the mediator in private session. In a confidential setting, the parties and their lawyers will convey to the mediator much of what they believe is important about the case. Mediators of civil litigation need to recognize the parties' need for privacy when they discuss the evidence in the case; and that fact is an important backdrop for much of the discussion in the following sections.

Perception: Mediation Will Be Conducted in Joint Sessions
Reality: The Parties Prefer Private Sessions

One of the most striking characteristics of civil trial court mediations is the extensive use of private sessions. Most of the mediator's time is spent shuttling back and forth from one team's breakout room to another. This procedure may sound foreign, and even offensive, to mediators who work with clients in other kinds of disputes. In the community center where I took my first mediation training, private sessions were considered extraordinary interventions to be used only when the parties could not occupy the same room without getting into a fight.

Private sessions are used so much by civil trial court mediators that other mediators think we believe that is the "proper" way to conduct mediations. In truth, we do use a lot of private sessions and we teach, by example at least, that private sessions are desirable in civil case mediations. However, no one I know who trains trial court mediators believes that the only way, or the proper way, to conduct mediation is with the use of private sessions.

The private session is a tool mediators use to achieve a goal or to solve a problem. We use private sessions for a particular purpose—and the purpose in civil trial court mediation is to deal with the phenomenon discussed in the previous section, the parties' need for privacy.

> ■ ■ ■ ■ ■
>
> Frequently, the most important factors influencing settlement are those that are withheld. Those factors include: the strengths and weaknesses of the case and the lowest or highest number to which the parties will move to settle the case. A party's assessment of those factors is strategic information.

It is information that, if known by the other side, would jeopardize that party's bargaining power and position. Therefore, when the parties are trying to develop or respond to proposals, they need private sessions to discuss these strategic matters openly. The type of information the parties need to discuss, assess, and consider is private and confidential and should be honored as such by mediators.

Be aware that the parties may express the desire to go into private session in subtle ways. They may signal a need for private sessions by simply not responding when the mediator asks for additional comments. They may also signal that need in the way Walker did in "The Rear Ender" ("You and I can talk more about them in private.") Walker was saying to the mediator, "I've got some things I want to talk about but I don't want to talk about them in general session. So, don't ask me about them."

It is ironic, however, that what lawyers think is strategic information often turns out to be information that, if they did convey it to the other team, would help settle the case. Knowing this, mediators may be tempted to push the parties in general session to talk in greater detail about the case than the parties initially discussed. I suggest that mediators resist this impulse and respect the parties' need for privacy. The private session might be the vehicle they need to assess the risks of exchanging information; and as a result of that private assessment, they may change their minds about the strategic value of the information and decide to divulge it to the other side.

As in the choice of any tool we use as mediators, the use of private sessions has its downside. If the parties remain in private sessions for most of the conference, the parties do not talk to each other directly. As all good mediators know, communication will not occur as clearly or completely with the mediator shuttling back and forth between the parties as it would if the parties were talking to each other directly.

In order to enhance the opportunities for clear and complete communication, civil trial court mediators should always be mindful that the opportunity to reconvene in general session, or in a meeting of the parties' representatives, exists throughout the mediation; and they should inquire from time to time whether the parties think such a meeting would be beneficial. Such meetings can be useful during the conference to foster greater communication and greater trust between the parties or to make the exchange of technical information more efficient.

Perception: Mediation Will Focus on Needs and Interests
Reality: The Participants Will Focus on Case Value

The major topic of conversation in both the general session and the first private sessions with the parties will be "the value of the case"—the result of the case if it is tried to a judge or jury. Conversation about the value of the case involves a discussion of the evidence likely to be admitted at trial, the law governing the controversy, verdicts in similar cases, the costs of prosecuting the case, the skills of the advocates, the tendencies of the judge who will be presiding over it, and many other factors.

■ ■ ■ ■ ■

Conversation about case value will dominate the parties' early discussions in their settlement efforts, whether or not mediators are involved in the process. While no lawyer claims to be able to predict with scientific certainty the outcome, and therefore the value, of a case, lawyers attempt to evaluate their case based upon their own knowledge and experience and the knowledge and experience of their colleagues. The working assumptions of the professionals in the room are:

- that the dispute is about what the claim is worth; and
- that the discussion is about the factors that make up that value.

We will come back to this topic in the next chapter, but I suggest that one of the useful things mediators can do in civil trial court mediations is to help the parties conduct a thorough case, or risk, analysis—more accurately, to help them clarify their own evaluations of the case. Since the evaluation process involves an assessment of the strengths and weaknesses of the case, and since those assessments are private information, the work of the mediator in this regard generally will be conducted in private sessions.

Lawyer-mediators will feel comfortable with the language, concepts, and subject matter of evaluation in civil trial court mediations. I should quickly add, however, that because of their substantive expertise, lawyer-mediators are tempted to inject their own evaluations, opinions, and beliefs into case evaluation. Mediators who inject their own opinions run the risk of turning a legitimate mediation into a neutral evaluation and imposing their opinions and solutions upon the parties.

Mediators who are not lawyers may feel uncomfortable with conversation that is focused on case value, particularly if the professionals in the room are talking more than their clients. They may too quickly conclude that the lawyers are doing nothing more than posturing and that the litigants' interests are getting lost in the shuffle. Nonlawyer mediators may need to reassess their understanding of the importance of "case value" to the process of traditional bargaining, in order not to discount the important work that professionals do in evaluating their client's claims.

The mediator in "The Rear Ender" met with Jimmy Young's team in private session when the parties ran out of things they were willing to talk about together. Smith immediately started talking about the evidence in the case.

As the session moved along, the mediator learned that, while Smith believed the need for surgery was well documented in the medical records, he worried that some jurors might question the close relationship between the chiropractor and Dr. Carlson. He also learned that Smith was not concerned about a defense of contributory negligence, because Walker was unable to articulate any acts of negligence on Young's part.

The mediator heard a lot in this session about Smith's evaluation of the case. What he thought most important, however, was the fact that Young expected more money out of the case than Smith thought it was worth. It was obvious that the lawyer and the client were not on the same page regarding case value, and, as a result, the mediator left the plaintiff's private session with a first proposal that was higher than the lawyer wanted to start with—$85,000.

Perception: The Parties Will Engage in Creative Problem Solving

Reality: Proposals Are Monetary in Nature— The Process Is Traditional Bargaining

One of the most important characteristics of mediations in the civil trial court context is the fact that proposals for settlement are generally monetary in nature. Mediators of civil cases quickly learn that the opportunities for creative problem solving that appear in other types of controversies are rare in the mediation of insured claims. The subject matter of these disputes does not lend itself to settlement in terms other than money.

In addition, the parties themselves are usually strangers to each other. The lawyers and claims representatives may have worked together many times, but the parties have had few, if any, contacts prior to the mediation and will have none after the mediation is concluded. They attend the mediation to settle a monetary claim, and their negotiation is about how much money one side will pay to the other.

Mediators of civil cases quickly learn that they are being asked to facilitate a process of position-based bargaining or, as I like to call it, traditional bargaining. I can tell you from 15 years of experience with these cases that everything you have heard about position-based bargaining is true. It's hard to reach settlement by arguing over positions. It's hard to get the process started; it's hard to keep making concessions; it's easy to get mad or discouraged along the way and want to stop; and it's hard to reach settlement if it appears that a gap will exist between the parties' positions at the end of the process.

Mediators who are schooled solely in a problem-solving orientation to the mediation process may experience a great deal of frustration with this type of process. They may try, as I did at first, to convert this bargaining to a problem-solving process. They will rarely succeed. (In Chapter 8, I describe when and how the problem-solving model can be useful in the mediation of a claim for money.)

■■■■■

Because the settlement of claims for money is inherently a traditional bargaining process (and, I would submit, an inherently evaluative process), some mediators do not believe that facilitated negotiations in this context are possible.

Some assert that the process found in trial court mediations should not be dignified with the title "mediation" and suggest that it is neutral evaluation in disguise.

It is my hope that such conclusions will be unnecessary by the time one finishes this volume and the reader will conclude that negotiations dominated by traditional bargaining are as susceptible to the facilitative intervention of a mediator as any other form of dispute.

Perception: Case Analysis Will Dominate Settlement Discussions
Reality: Case Analysis Gives Way to Multiple Rounds of Monetary Proposals

The negotiation in "The Rear Ender" started with a proposal of $7,400, the amount of Young's medical expenses. It was countered with a proposal of $85,000. The parties exchanged 12 complete rounds of proposals before finally concluding an agreement at $27,500. Every one of those proposals was monetary in nature.

In my early work as a civil trial court mediator, I envisioned my task primarily as one of assisting the parties with case analysis. As a lawyer, case analysis came easily to me, as it did to the lawyers and claims adjusters I worked with. My struggle in the early years was to learn how to do case analysis in a facilitative rather than in a directive way.

Most of us approach settlement conferences expecting to spend a lot of time discussing the case and "what it is worth." "Hashing, bashing, and trashing the case"—this is what Professor Alfini called case analysis in the early days of civil trial court mediation. Although bashing and trashing should never be a part of our work as mediators, "hashing the case" will always be an important part of any civil trial court mediation. It is case analysis pure and simple.

■ ■ ■ ■ ■

However, my experience with a small personal injury case in 1993 started a process of exploration that radically changed my thinking about my job as a mediator. It was a personal injury case in which the plaintiff's first proposal was $10,000 and the defense's counter was $2,500. Twelve rounds later, the case settled at $4,700. During part of the negotiation, the parties were moving toward settlement in $50 and $100 increments.

This was a frustrating experience for all concerned. The lawyers became irritated with each other as the increments of movement became smaller and smaller. The parties became upset as the negotiations dragged on and the mediation began to feel like a used-car sale. And I, the mediator, grew increasingly frustrated as the lawyers continued to talk numbers to the exclusion of either the merits of the case or the needs of the parties.

Throughout the process, I encouraged the lawyers to meet with me without their clients to see if we could cut through their difficulties. On many previous occasions they had taken me up on my offer and settled their case. This time they did not, and to my amazement the case dragged on and on through many more rounds of proposals. I had no explanation for this course of events and wondered on many occasions thereafter why this simple case produced such protracted negotiations.

Several years later, I conducted a pre-litigation insurance claim that went on for 19 complete rounds of offers and counteroffers. The claimant started at $125,000 and the defense countered at $95,000. It was settled on the nineteenth round at $115,000 after five hours of negotiations. Again, I was amazed and puzzled. I wondered why it had been so difficult for the parties to reach a number that could settle the case.

In studying my notes from this last case, I became aware of a new wrinkle in the mediation of claims for money. I realized that the parties discussed the claim thoroughly in the beginning of the conference but seldom mentioned the merits of the case after the second round of proposals. For three and a half hours and for 17 rounds of proposals, the parties were consumed with reacting to each other's proposals and deciding whether, or how, to respond with a proposal of their own. I was mystified.

I mention these two experiences, first, because they were landmark events for me in my development as a mediator. They alerted me to an important aspect of civil trial court mediation that I had not trained for or understood. Secondly, I mention them because they highlight a phenomenon that is present in every negotiation about money I encounter.

■ ■ ■ ■ ■

Although case analysis does and should play a major role in civil trial court mediation, it will at some point in the mediation fade into the background. At some point in their negotiations, the parties will engage in purely position-based bargaining. That stage of the negotiations has its own dynamics and problems and calls for a new range of skills and techniques from civil trial court mediators.

Many participants in civil trial court mediation have commented negatively on this phase of the mediation. Many of them have called it "a used-car sale." Sometimes they say it in jest;

most of the time they do not. To an injured plaintiff, the process of traditional bargaining feels exactly like a used-car sale. They are not happy about it because it feels demeaning. When the professionals haggle over what their injuries and losses are worth, it discounts the impact of those injuries on their lives. It just feels bad to the individuals involved.

I will speak more in later chapters about how to handle situations during the mediation when a party is angry with the mediator because the process is experienced as demeaning. For now, however, I want to make an important point.

■■■■■

The used-car sale, and the parties' negative reaction to it, does not represent a failure on the part of the mediator or herald the arrival of a directive approach to the mediation. On the contrary: the used-car sale is an integral part of all negotiations about money. When money is the only currency of settlement, there will be round after round of proposal and counterproposal until the case settles or the parties can move no more. At some point in the mediation, the settlement process will look, feel, and sound very much like a used-car sale.

We mediators cannot change this dynamic. It is inherent in the negotiation of a claim for money. What we can do is study this phenomenon, ponder it, and develop skills and techniques that will help the parties work through this challenging stage of their negotiations.

After the parties made several rounds of proposals in "The Rear Ender," Jimmy Young said to me angrily, "They just don't seem to understand that this wreck changed my life!" With the patient work of his lawyer and the mediator, Jimmy Young did not walk out of the negotiation or quit making proposals. Slowly, he began to understand that the only resolution he could get for his injuries was a monetary one. He stayed, made additional offers to settle, and eventually reached agreement with the insurance company based upon his lawyer's case analysis and risk assessment.

Perception: Mediation Will Improve Working Relationships

Reality: The Parties Become Angry with Each Other as They Swap Proposals

■■■■■

The interesting thing to me about the used-car stage that dominates the settlement of civil litigation is that I rarely "just" walk back and forth between the parties delivering proposals. I rarely do that because the parties frequently become angry when they receive a proposal from the other side; they debate with great vigor and intensity whether or not to respond to it; and they have difficulty formulating a proposal to send in return. There is much for a mediator to do during this stage of the mediation.

In "The Rear Ender," for example, Jimmy Young reacted to the defense's first offer with visible and audible emotion. Young got up from his seat and stomped around the room saying, "That's insulting! I'm not even going to respond to a number like that." Other negotiators have literally packed their bags, put on their coats, and left the negotiations, all the while making disparaging remarks about the other side's character and legal abilities.

■■■■■

It is fascinating to me that people can attend a settlement conference and conduct themselves with great dignity, even politely discussing legal issues about which they strongly disagree—until they hear a proposal from the other side that they don't like.

These outbursts occur even though the parties have no personal animosity toward each other. They are not hostile toward each other during the general session; they negotiate from separate rooms; they do not curse each other or make disparaging remarks about each other's kinfolk. They do not even speak English sentences to each other. The only thing that occurs is that one side conveys to the other a monetary proposal that the other doesn't like.

I remember clearly the first time I encountered this phenomenon. I was mediating an injury case in which the plaintiff's lawyer was a relatively inexperienced but well-prepared lawyer and the defendant's lawyer was an older, experienced litigator. When I announced the plaintiff's opening proposal to the defense team in private session, the older lawyer let loose with a stream of invectives and criticized the character of the other lawyer. I was taken aback by his reaction and chalked it up to his well-known vitriolic nature. Finally, his diatribe abated and he gave me a small proposal to take back to the plaintiff.

Years later, I look back upon this experience with amusement, because I had wrongfully assumed that the lawyer's reaction was solely attributable to his fiery nature. I now know that most negotiators of an insured claim will react with at least annoyance, if not outright hostility, to a proposal from the other side that they consider to be unrealistic or "out of the ballpark" of settlement.

Through the years, I have discovered that much of the work I do as a mediator in civil trial court cases is to help the parties who react negatively to the other side's proposals work through their reactivity and then invent, consider, and make additional proposals of their own—instead of shutting down the negotiations and walking away.

Perception: Proposals Will Flow until Settlement Occurs or Best Numbers Reveal an Impasse

Reality: Movement Stops before Best Numbers Are Reached

■■■■■

In theory, movement will stop in a negotiation about money when the parties have reached their bottom or top lines, their best numbers. But movement often stops before the parties have reached their best numbers.

The parties will also stop moving when they get angry or frustrated with the other side's movement. They will walk out, refuse to move, or make meager changes in their positions in reaction to the other side's proposal. Something like that happened in "The Rear Ender" when the defense heard Young's second proposal of $80,000, a drop of only $5,000 in the face of the defense's move to $10,400.

Mr. Moore, the claims representative, commented that Young would "never get realistic." Mr. Moore was discouraged about the prospects of settlement. He thought Young's proposal signaled that the ranges of settlement for the two sides were too far apart for settlement to occur.

This phenomenon poses some intriguing questions to the mediator of civil litigation. When the parties, or one of them, announce that they are not going to move any more, are they doing so because they are angry at the other side, because they've reached their best numbers, or because they do not believe their movement will lead to settlement?

When a party makes a small move in comparison to his previous moves, is that party slowing down because he is nearing his best number, because he is reacting negatively to the other party's last move, or because he believes that the case won't settle? The mediator of civil trial court litigation spends much time and effort trying to answer those questions and working with the parties to respond to and develop proposals in spite of their frustration or discouragement. I will have more to say about best numbers in Chapter 7 and about how to help the parties develop proposals in Chapters 3 and 5.

Perception: A Mediator Is Useless When the Parties Are Exchanging Numbers

Reality: A Mediator Can Do Much to Help the Parties Overcome Their Reactivity and Move Through Their Negotiation Ranges

After the parties have swapped several rounds of proposals, the numbers may begin to flow rather quickly. At this stage, the parties are bidding on the price of the lawsuit. Mediators often find themselves spending little time in either room as a proposal is delivered and discussed and a counterproposal formulated. It is at this point that the mediator may begin to doubt his or her utility and may begin to feel somewhat useless. Mediators tell me that they feel like little more than a messenger when this happens. A friend of mine calls this part of the process "toting bones."

It is important for mediators to remember that as the messenger totes proposals from room to room, he or she nevertheless may be useful to the negotiation process. The feeling of being "just a messenger" is a phenomenon that sometimes is experienced when the parties are negotiating well and do not need much assistance from the mediator. I like to say that mediators at that moment are guardians of the process.

We may be doing nothing obvious, but we are doing it alertly— kind of like the cat that does nothing as it sits alertly outside the mouse's door. We are watching and listening for kinks in the process, missteps that may occur, or problems that may develop in what is otherwise a smoothly running negotiation. To mediators with this experience, I say, "Relax. They're doing exactly what you want them to do: negotiating well. Believe me, when they reach settlement, they'll turn to you and congratulate you for the fine job you did."

■■■■■

Some mediators, however, complain about being "just a messenger" whether the parties are negotiating well or not. They feel useless during the entire time that the parties are swapping proposals. Some of these mediators are uncomfortable with the position-based bargaining that goes on in this "used-car sale" phase of the negotiation. They are not equipped with an understanding of the problems associated with this phase of the negotiation or with tools that can help them help the parties through it. These mediators do not know what to do once the negotiation goes beyond case analysis.

In the position-based bargaining that goes on in civil trial court mediation, the mediator's chief aim is to help the parties overcome their reactivity, refrain from stopping prematurely in reaction to the other side's proposals or in reaction to their own pessimism about the prospects of settlement, make thoughtful rather than reactive proposals, and continue moving through their ranges until they reach their best numbers or are sure that their best numbers will not settle the case.

The reality of negotiations in civil trial court mediation is that settlement will occur most frequently through a process of position-based or traditional bargaining. The reality for most mediators is that the model of the mediation process we have been trained to use, the problem-solving model, is inadequate to meet the challenges traditional bargaining presents. In the chapters that follow, I will articulate a model of the mediation process that civil trial court mediators will find helpful to assist the parties through negotiations dominated by case analysis and reactive monetary proposals.

Summary of Chapter 1

- Lawyers perform a positive role in mediation by helping their clients understand the realities of their case and what may happen if the case does not settle.
- Litigants depend upon lawyers to provide information, case analysis, and recommendations for settlement. As a result, the mediator's "client" is a team of people that includes the litigant, the lawyer, and other advisors.
- The details of a party's case analysis are strategic and, therefore, private information. Parties to litigation tend to withhold information from each other in fear of giving up bargaining advantage.
- The parties do not want to discuss private information with the other side. Private sessions, then, are an important part of the mediation process and meet the processing needs of the parties.
- Lawyers tend to talk about "the case" instead of the needs and interests of the parties. This focus is an important part

of the process of settling civil litigation, because it helps litigants understand the realities of their claims, and become more realistic and practical during their negotiations.

- The proposals made in the settlement of civil litigation are usually monetary in nature. Mediators are stuck with position-based bargaining. This volume is devoted to that fact and to the task of equipping mediators with understandings and tools to help the parties overcome the many pitfalls of traditional bargaining.

- Conversation about case analysis recedes into the background as the parties try to fashion their proposals. The parties engage in multiple rounds of proposals and counterproposals and spend the majority of their time in mediation doing so.

- As the parties swap proposals, they become frustrated and angry with each other. They react negatively and emotionally to proposals they don't like and, thus, formulate their responses reactively.

- As a result of the parties' frustration with the apparent inadequacy of their opponents' positions, the parties tend to stop or slow movement within their negotiating ranges and avoid approaching their bottom or top lines. This is a hallmark of the process we call position-based, or traditional, bargaining.

- There is much a mediator can do to help the parties overcome their reactivity and move toward settlement. With a model of the mediation process that makes a place for traditional bargaining, an understanding of the dynamics of negotiations about money, and a set of tools to assist with the parties' frustrations, a mediator can help the parties develop a plan for their negotiations and make thoughtful rather than reactive proposals.

Notes

1. Roger Fisher and William Ury, Getting to Yes: Negotiating Agreement Without Giving In (New York: Penguin Books, 1983).
   2. *Id.* at 18.

Making a Place for Traditional Bargaining among the Models of the Mediation Process

2

The Need for a New Approach

■■■■■

Much of the literature in the field of mediation over the past three decades articulates a problem-solving model of the mediation process. That model is a useful tool for many disputes, but it has limited utility in civil trial court mediation where money is the only currency of settlement.

In the settlement of claims for money, negotiations will be conducted as position-based bargaining and will resist the efforts of mediators to reframe them as opportunities for joint problem solving. This is a fundamental fact of life for mediators who operate in the civil trial court arena: We are stuck with disputes that will be settled through traditional bargaining.

Civil trial court mediators need a model of the mediation process that helps them deal with the realities of negotiations about money. The model I describe in this chapter does just that, and it consists of three ways that mediators can make traditional bargaining more productive for the parties:

1. Facilitate the flow of information.

2. Facilitate case or risk analysis.

3. Facilitate movement.

The first two of these are discussed below. The third, facilitating movement in traditional bargaining, is important and novel enough to warrant chapters of its own: Chapters 3–7.

Facilitate the Flow of Information

Withholding information about their case is an established reflex of litigants and their lawyers in civil litigation. Guarding against the possibility that the case may not settle, they hold tightly to the information they've developed in order to spring it on the other side at trial, thus creating a dramatic and favorable impact on the judge or jury.

This is an important factor for mediators in the trial court context to remember and take seriously. Information that one side has and the other side doesn't is a valuable commodity, so negotiators don't take the decision to release information lightly. Mediators should remember that lawyers and their clients will be making important strategic decisions about information during their negotiations that will have an impact on the prospects for settlement.

Mediators are trained in the skills of uncovering information and they know that the development of information is an important factor in the successful resolution of conflict. Many mediators, therefore, have an ideological or professional bias toward openness and candor in the mediation process. Mediators must be careful about this subject.

■ ■ ■ ■ ■

We must learn to blend our instincts for openness with the realization that the parties and lawyers in civil litigation consider information to be a valuable commodity and the release of information to be a strategic decision. Mediators need to give the parties' decisions to release or swap information the same importance as their ultimate decision to settle the case.

An Example of the Strategic Importance of Information

A dramatic example of the strategic importance that information has in civil trial court mediation involves the existence of surveillance tapes. These are video or film recordings that the defense makes of an allegedly injured person in an effort to show that the claimant is not as injured or disabled as he claims. At mediation, the defense may be unsure whether the tapes should be shown to the plaintiff during mediation or held for trial where they can be shown to the jury in the presence of a surprised opponent.

Many years ago, I mediated a case in which the plaintiff was injured by the perpetrator of a bank robbery. The plaintiff was shot during the hold-up and was suing the bank for not following stated security procedures during the robbery. It was revealed to me by the defense in a private session that, during the robbery, a bank camera had taken photographs that the plaintiff did not know existed. Those pictures showed the robbery in progress and captured the images of a clock on the wall of the bank lobby. They conclusively demonstrated that the plaintiff was wrong about the length of time that it took for the robbers to complete the crime, and, thus, they had the potential to completely undermine the plaintiff's case.

I spent several hours in a series of private conversations helping the defendant's team decide whether or not to show these pictures to the plaintiff's team. The defendant in that case struggled with whether or not some strategic advantage would be given up by showing the plaintiff the taped evidence at mediation instead of "springing it" on him at trial. On the positive side, releasing the information might lead to settlement. On the negative side, it might give the other side a chance to regroup, find additional evidence, and develop arguments to minimize the impact of the apparently damning information.

Ultimately, the defendant's team decided that it had little to lose by showing the tapes and much to gain if doing so would lead to settlement and avoid trial. The pictures were shown and the plaintiff's team and I discussed their impact on the case. The case settled several weeks later as a result of this exchange of information at mediation.

When mediators work with parties in these discussions, it's important to be facilitative rather than directive. Mediators should never try to sell disclosure as the best or right decision. Lawyer-mediators are often accused of practicing directive mediation in this type of situation and, indeed, in mandatory civil trial mediation as a whole. This does not have to be true. If the mediator truly believes that the decision to withhold or convey information is the clients' to make, he or she will do everything possible to help the parties make thoughtful and informed decisions and will not insist that information be exchanged.

The mediator can develop a process of thoughtful decision making by asking such questions as the following:

- What does the tape actually show?
- What activities does the tape show the plaintiff engaging in?
- Are those activities similar to the types of activities that the plaintiff claims are now limited by the injuries?
- What factors suggest that it would be useful to show the tape? What factors suggest otherwise?
- How likely is it that the plaintiff will discover the tape before trial begins even if the tape is not shown at mediation?

The Importance of Providing Legitimacy

Lawyers do not always understand the importance of developing and sharing information in the process of settlement. Like anyone else in a dispute, lawyers make bold and assertive claims about what is right, what is proper, what is correct, or what is true. They often act as if the other side should rely on their word alone in judging the truth of their assertions. What they sometimes forget is that the development and sharing of information from other sources can provide a sense of legitimacy to their claims that their mere assertions do not provide.

"Of course Jimmy Young has been permanently disabled by this collision," says the plaintiff's lawyer to the defense. The defense, however, doesn't see it that way. They want to see the medical records from before the incident and after. They want to see a doctor's statement that there is permanent disability and not assume that disability exists simply because the plaintiff had surgery. They want to see some kind of documentation for the assertions that the plaintiff makes.

This notion of legitimacy is important to negotiators and mediators alike, and it was first defined and described by Roger Fisher and Bill Ury in *Getting to Yes*.[1] My way of framing their notion of legitimacy is to say that legitimacy answers the question children ask when a conflict arises on the playground. One child asserts, "My daddy's stronger than yours!" "Who says?" asks the other rhetorically. Negotiators do the same thing. "My case is worth $85,000!" says the plaintiff. The defendant wants to know "Who says?"

In an injury case, "Who says?" Does the doctor say so? Do you have the medical records? Do you have the medical bills? In a property damage case, "Who says?" Do you have estimates for the repair of the vehicle? Do you have appraisals before and after the storm damage for that property? The question "Who says?" needs to be answered if assertions about the value of the case are to be taken seriously by the other side.

■ ■ ■ ■ ■

I have said previously that the decision to divulge information is a strategic decision for the parties. The flip side of that coin is that developing and divulging information from outside sources may be crucial to the settlement process. A mediator can help the parties think through the positive effects of divulging information, which a party may not have considered, thus providing legitimacy to his claim.

The Timing of an Information Exchange

The timing of an information exchange is important as well. Many lawyers, particularly on the plaintiff's side of the negotiation, do not understand the need for providing information before their efforts to settle the case. As a consequence, problems develop during mediation because the plaintiff's lawyer has not conveyed important information, such as medical and billing records, to the defense lawyer in a timely fashion.

In "The Rear Ender," the defense lawyer said during the general session that his side would be hard-pressed to pay any amount of money to the plaintiff for lost wages, because he had no documentation of the fact that Young had lost wages as a result of the accident. "I have no statement from the doctor that Young was ordered out of work. I have no statement from his employer showing his rate of pay or the hours or days he was out of work. I have nothing to justify paying money for that part of Young's claim."

What is it that keeps lawyers from conveying important information to their opponents, other than the natural reluctance of adversaries? One reason is that trial lawyers typically respond to deadlines; and they don't consider the deadlines associated with mediation as important to meet as those for trial. Another reason is that they don't understand the need for the other party to have information in a timely way. This reason is associated with one of the "cultural differences" that exist between the plaintiffs' bar and the defense bar.

The plaintiffs' bar typically views medical records and medical expenses as a given in the case. The defense does not. The defense scrutinizes medical records and medical expenses carefully. They discover things in the record that plaintiffs have not bothered to review. The defense frequently will refer records to consulting doctors and nurses for help in analyzing medical treatment and expenses.

Defendants comb through medical expenses with much greater care than plaintiffs. They total the numbers. They look for duplications. They look for unrelated charges. Thus, they need time to process the information that plaintiffs provide through discovery before deciding what value they will give the case. If they don't get basic claims information well in advance of the settlement conference, they will not be able to make informed decisions and negotiate a settlement. Plaintiffs' lawyers often fail to take this need into consideration as they approach settlement discussions and, unwittingly, thwart their hopes of reaching settlement.

Resolving Informational Problems before the Conference

Mediators in the civil trial court context would do well to keep the parties' need for information in mind before the mediation conference is convened. In court-ordered mediation, the mediation process begins long before the parties convene to negotiate their differences. The administrative tasks of scheduling and picking a location for the conference present mediators with many important mediation moments and opportunities.

During these times we can inquire about the readiness of the parties to negotiate. We can discover whether the parties, or one of them, need additional information before they can negotiate intelligently. We can help the parties agree to a process that will gather necessary information.

■■■■■

If the parties do not have necessary information, we can continue a scheduled mediation or seek additional time from the court within which to schedule it. In doing these things, we help the parties understand the needs of the other and understand how those needs affect the prospects of settlement. Mediators who understand the importance of information and the timing of its development make a major contribution to the parties' settlement efforts.

Unfortunately, we are not always able to ferret out problems associated with the exchange of information before the settlement conference is convened. The mediator may discover at the conference itself that the parties lack important information. Occasionally, the parties are able to negotiate without that information, by making educated guesses about what the information would reveal if discovered. At other times, however, the parties will be unable to proceed with negotiations. In that event, the mediation may become a mediated discovery conference in which the parties outline their discovery needs and develop a process that will produce the necessary information and make a productive negotiating experience possible when the settlement conference is reconvened.

Facilitate Risk Analysis: Become Grounded in the Realities of the Case

Every trial lawyer knows that information is the key to effective litigation. The discovery of a single fact can completely change one's legal analysis and, ultimately, the outcome of the case. The information one has about a case is the basis for determining its likely outcome, and therefore its value, so much of the discussion that occurs in the mediation of civil litigation concerns the "value" of the case. It concerns what evidence supports or does not support one's opinion about the likely outcome of the case at trial.

Many lawyers and their clients are well prepared to articulate their case analysis when they show up for mediation. They have thoroughly conducted discovery of their case, the lawyer has formed an opinion about the value of the case based upon the evidence and his or her legal analysis, and the lawyer and client have formed a common understanding about the case and have decided upon an appropriate range of settlement.

These folks are a joy to work with. They don't huff and puff about their case and grandstand for the mediator or their opponents. They are typically quietly confident about their claim and are able to clearly articulate the basis for their optimism. These folks do not need a mediator to facilitate case analysis; they have done that for themselves and can quickly formulate initial proposals. Information that they learn about for the first time at mediation will need to be factored into their analysis, of course; but, with that caveat said, these folks are ready to get down to business.

■ ■ ■ ■ ■

Mediators need to approach the subject of case analysis with a great deal of care, because the risk of deeply offending lawyers is great.

With folks who are well prepared this is doubly true. They sometimes consider the mediator's questions a waste of time, and they sometimes are offended by the implication that they are trying to negotiate without being prepared.

One lawyer said to me years ago when our court-ordered mediation program was in its pilot phase, "I don't like this mediation process, because it assumes that lawyers have not done their jobs. I'm here to tell you that I do, and I resent being treated as if I don't." He went on to say, "And my case analysis is my own. The other side doesn't need to know my strengths and weaknesses. We're not going to engage in a whole lot of discussion about that." I would say that his view of the mediation process in our civil courts was, and is, atypical, but it does highlight two important points.

The first is the assertion I've made throughout this book that the thinking of the parties about the strengths and weaknesses of their case is private information. The lawyer in this scenario was content with negotiating the numbers and saving his "ammunition" for the courtroom in the event the case did not settle. The second important point is that some lawyers may find a discussion about case analysis offensive in and of itself, or offensive in the way the mediator conducts it. Mediators need to be careful about what subjects we choose to discuss or inquire about and we need to listen closely to the clues our clients give us about what they are unwilling to say or do.

However, regardless of how good a lawyer is or how well prepared he or she may be, mediators and litigators must reckon with an important fact of litigation that affects the ability of the parties to be fully prepared. Most of us cannot think of everything that could possibly go wrong with a case or of every interpretation of the facts or law that cuts against our own view of the case.

The adversary system itself ensures that the other side will find facts and interpretations of the law that differ from our own simply because it's their job to do so. They have a vested interest in coming up with interpretations that are favorable to them; we do not. For that reason, some new fact, case, statute, or interpretation will come to light when opposing parties sit together and discuss their case. And for that reason, almost no one in civil trial court mediation is fully prepared. Opportunities to help the parties with case analysis will probably arise even when they believe they are well prepared.

Most lawyers understand their case reasonably well before beginning negotiations and they have tried to help their clients understand the strengths and weaknesses of the case. However, many lawyers and their clients are unsuccessful in reaching a common understanding of the case's value.

■■■■■

In a civil trial court context the mediator should be aware of some cultural differences. It has been my experience in civil cases, particularly those that involve insured claims, that the defense team is better prepared than the plaintiff's team for negotiations. I am not referring to the preparation of the lawyers at this point. I am referring to the ability of the team to achieve a shared understanding of the case and negotiate on the basis of it.

The climate on the defense side of the table is strongly influenced by the fact that defense lawyers and their clients, insurance claims adjusters, are repeat litigators. Claims representatives are engaged in the settlement of claims as professionals. Each and every day they evaluate, negotiate, and settle negligence claims similar to the claims that wind up in litigation. They are experienced clients, and they strongly believe that they are in control of the decision making in the case. They write the checks; they make the decisions.

In addition, the defense culture typically involves lawyers and clients who have worked with each other on numerous cases. They often know each other well. They tend to communicate frequently about the case and its discovery prior to settlement efforts. The claims representative often requires the lawyer to keep him or her abreast of discovery developments. The claims representative, for example, may require the lawyer to write and send memos summarizing the evidence discovered when depositions are taken and answers to interrogatories are received. The defense team tends to be more unified in its approach to the case and to its negotiation by the time mediation is commenced.

In contrast, plaintiffs are usually first-time litigants. They have little understanding of how claims are evaluated or settled, and they have little knowledge of or experience with the outcome of similar cases at trial. They are not familiar with the way in which the court system works and how the value of a case can change by the evidentiary rulings that judges make during trial. They often rely upon the advice and counsel of their lawyers and do not engage actively in the discovery process.

What plaintiffs typically bring to the experience of litigation and its settlement is their subjective experience of pain, turmoil, and disruption that the accident or injury has caused in their lives. Those are obvious and important factors in the mediation, but they are factors that take a backseat to the hard-nosed risk or case analysis lawyers and insurance companies are used to conducting. Plaintiffs are so aware of their own traumatic experience that they have little appreciation for how anyone else (meaning members of a jury) would not immediately relate positively to it. For those reasons, plaintiffs typically come to the settlement process with different, and usually higher, expectations for their case than do their lawyers.

This is not to say that plaintiffs' lawyers do not work with their clients to help them understand the value of the case—or, to be more accurate, the value of the case as they see it. Lawyers are often accused of inflating the value of the case for their clients and of being extremely litigious. Quite frankly, that has not been my experience. Plaintiffs' lawyers generally work hard with their clients to help them understand the possibilities and the pitfalls of their case. They try diligently to help their clients understand that juries often do not return the kind of verdicts that injured parties expect.

■■■■■

Conversations about case value are difficult for any lawyer to have with a client, but especially for plaintiffs' lawyers. There exists in the lawyer/client relationship a thin line of confidence that the lawyer can cross inadvertently. If the plaintiff's lawyer dwells too harshly or too long on the negatives of the case, the plaintiff sometimes begins to think, "This guy's not on my side. Maybe I should find somebody else to handle the case." The client can quickly lose confidence in a lawyer and doubt whether the lawyer will earnestly prosecute the case. The plaintiff's lawyer's job is to develop the evidence, analyze it objectively, and discuss it honestly with the client. That job is harder than the general public thinks.

The lawyer/client relationship can also become strained on the defense side as well. Sometimes claims representatives base their case analysis solely on the paper that has been generated in the case and do not take into consideration the impact that witnesses will have in a jury trial. A live, face-to-face settlement process can help the defense team understand those intangibles. Despite that fact, claims representatives, ignoring the advice of their lawyers on this point, may seek to be excused from attending the conference in person and may ask, instead, to be allowed to attend by phone.

Some years ago, a lawyer asked me prior to the settlement conference if his insurance adjuster could be excused from attending the conference in person. I asked him about the circumstances that led him to make this request and got a very surprising answer. The lawyer blurted out:

"You know, I really hope—don't tell anyone else this—I really hope you deny this request. I had to make it because my insurance adjuster told me to. She didn't want to travel from Chicago, and that's understandable, but, you know, I've been trying to get her to pay attention to this plaintiff ever since we've had the case; and she just won't do it. This is a dangerous case for our side and she needs to understand that. And the only way she can understand it is to see the plaintiff and her family and to listen to their story. I think if she does, she will come to understand, as I understand, that this case has some dangerous aspects to it. My client needs to be here; and I hope you deny this request." Tensions between lawyer and client, then, may be experienced on both sides of the table.

■ ■ ■ ■ ■

Case analysis, or risk analysis, is fundamentally important in a traditional bargaining situation, for both the claimant and the defense. Very simply, case analysis provides a framework within which one will negotiate and beyond which one will not settle. In other words, the value of the case provides the touchstone for the party's negotiation. Without good case analysis, the negotiator has no compass with which to navigate the process; he or she is lost.

If I value my case at $85,000 and the best and final offer of the defendant is $7,400, why would I accept such a proposal? The best offer of the other side is far lower than what I can get at trial. So the outcome of the case, or the value of the case, provides a touchstone for the negotiation. It's how people become grounded in the negotiation. If I don't know the value of my case, I don't know when to accept an offer and when not to accept an offer. I don't know what kind of offers to make.

So it's important for people who are negotiating the settlement of claims for money to understand the value of their claim. Valuing a case is not an exact science, but the job of lawyers prior to mediation is to learn about the case, compare it with similar cases that have produced settlements and verdicts, and reach a conclusion about its value (more accurately, the range of value into which the case will fall).

Mediators Can Facilitate an Inherently Evaluative Negotiation

Some commentators on the process of mediation criticize mandatory civil trial court mediation for being inherently evaluative and directive. In fact, the negotiation of an insured claim is inherently evaluative, because the negotiation itself is about value. If the parties are doing their jobs well, they will be evaluating their claim and discussing their evaluations with each other.

When I say that the mediation and negotiation process is inherently evaluative, I do not mean to imply that the mediator should be directive within that process. We are not aided in understanding that point by the fact that there is in our current language about mediation an unfortunate identification of the words "evaluative" and "directive." Many people say that a mediator should not be evaluative when what they really mean is that a mediator should not be directive.

■■■■■

Stated in another way, mediators can facilitate an inherently evaluative process like traditional bargaining without being directive. This volume is dedicated to that proposition and is designed to equip mediators with tools to facilitate an inherently evaluative process. The mediator facilitates the parties' process of evaluation primarily by asking questions about probable outcomes and by helping the parties bring their evaluation to a conscious and verbal level.

That is what happens every day of my working life as I conduct civil trial court mediations. I help litigants assess case value and negotiate based on that value. I do so using the tools employed by mediators everywhere regardless of case type or process model: open-ended questions, listening, understanding, summarizing, and reframing. These are the tools of facilitators.

Case, or Risk, Analysis

I'm not really breaking new ground here. The notion of evaluating one's claim is at least as old as the work of Fisher and Ury in *Getting to Yes.* The same people who brought us the powerful concept of needs and interests and helped us expand the problem-solving model of the mediation process also brought us the powerful concept of BATNA, the Best Alternative to a Negotiated Agreement.

Fisher and Ury believe that it is important for negotiators to identify their best alternative in the event a negotiated settlement is not reached. Understanding their BATNA grounds negotiators in the realities of their situation, provides a measure by which they determine an appropriate range of settlement, guides them in formulating and responding to proposals, and empowers them to improve their bargaining position.

I was first introduced to the concept of BATNA in a community center training in 1988. The use of the concept there now seems rather quaint and unsophisticated. When the BATNA question was asked in the context of a dispute between neighbors, it was answered frequently with, "Well, I'd have to go to court." The implication was that going to court is a bad thing and that, therefore, the disputants needed to get serious about settlement. My reaction as a trial lawyer was very different. To me, going to court is not a bad outcome for the person who needs to vindicate an important right or who is being taken advantage of by a more powerful person.

■■■■■

In the context of civil trial court mediation, the BATNA question is really a series of questions that form the basis of an adequate case analysis:

1. What do you get if you go to court? That is, what is the likely result in monetary terms?
2. What are your chances of obtaining that outcome?
3. What does it cost you to get that outcome?
4. What are your chances of collecting a judgment if you obtain one as a result of trial?

In legal parlance, these questions can be translated into questions about damages, liability, costs, and collection. These are the four fundamental case evaluation questions that lawyers wrestle with as they assess case value. A reminder here from our earlier discussion of the realities of mediation in the civil trial context: Discussion of case analysis should be undertaken by the mediator in private sessions, because it involves strategic and private information.

Damages: What Will You Get If You Win? If I were to direct the discussion about case analysis entirely (which I do not for reasons discussed next), I would start with the subject of damages. It has been my experience both as a mediator and litigator that the damages aspect of civil litigation is more undeveloped than the liability aspect. Left to their own devices, lawyers will begin discussing the value of their case by first addressing the issue of liability.

Plaintiffs exhibit this tendency more so than defendants. It seems to be in the nature of things that plaintiffs are concerned with "who did me wrong." I have heard many a plaintiff go on and on about how badly the defendant was driving or how callously the defendant behaved even after the defense had admitted liability and stated that the only issue for the settlement conference was the amount of damages to be paid.

Mediators should be aware that a discussion about damages will probably help the plaintiff, in particular, focus on an important and frequently neglected area of his or her case. The timing of that discussion in private sessions will depend heavily on what the parties have on their minds. Sometimes I delay conversations about damages because the parties want to talk about other issues in the case first.

When a mediator works with the parties in the first few private sessions, he or she has two important tasks. One is to establish rapport with the participants so that they will respond to the mediator's important and penetrating questions. For this purpose, I seldom have an agenda when I walk into a private session for the first time. I like to open with either a question to the client about his injuries or an innocuous question to the lawyer, such as:

M: Well, Smith, are you going to be able to get this case settled today?

or

M: Is there anything you want me to know that you didn't tell them in general session?

The point of questions like these is to encourage the parties to talk, so that I can listen and discover what they think is important about the case. What the parties say first, say the loudest, and talk about the longest will reveal something about what they like and don't like in their case. If they start with damages, then we talk about damages. If they start with liability, then we talk about liability. The point is to start with what they think is important, not what I think is important. By doing so, I am less likely to be directive, to waste their time, and to insult their assessment of the case.

The second task of the mediator at this stage is to frame questions that encourage the participant to think more completely about the case. One of the ways I have found to accomplish that difficult task is to take the material the other side has given me in either a general or private session as the basis for my inquiry. I often say things like:

M: They seem to think you've got a problem linking these damages to this collision. What's your thinking on that subject?

or

M: The defense is telling me that you may have a problem with the fact that you asked for a second letter from Dr. Carlson. How do you evaluate that issue?

■■■■■

If I am true to my intention to be facilitative rather than directive, I won't argue with the lawyer's answer to my questions. I may ask follow-up questions that encourage him or her to consider additional facts or theories, but my intent is to evoke the team's own thinking about the issue at hand, not mine. My inquiries and their answers will help the team articulate and clarify their thinking about the case.

I like to have a significant discussion about the damages in the case with the plaintiff's team before they give me a proposal. Such a discussion helps ground the plaintiff's team in the realities of their case. As a result, the plaintiff's team is more likely to formulate an opening proposal that resembles its case analysis and is less likely to make an outrageous demand that generates an equally outrageous counterproposal.

Liability: How Often Will You Win and Why? One can be awarded damages only if he or she proves a basis for liability in both law and fact. Put in practical terms the question of liability is a question of probability. "If you tried your case 10 times, how many times would you win? Seven times out of 10? Five times out of 10? Three times out of 10?"

I use questions about probabilities in discussions about the case as a whole and about discrete issues within the case to help the parties clarify their chances of succeeding at trial. An example of the latter is a question about the likelihood of a trial judge admitting a statement of one of the parties into evidence if the case goes to trial.

When I ask questions about case value, I am asking a team to articulate what may be only vague notions or impressions. By talking about the evidence and law with me, the members of the team will clarify or change their evaluation of the case. Generally, they will broaden their negotiating range as a result of that discussion and make proposals that are more realistic and more in line with a thoughtful analysis of the case.

It is worth repeating here that you should not ask for proposals from the parties before you have given them a chance to talk about the evidence supporting their case analysis. If you ask for proposals before the parties have clarified their thinking, you will not get realistic and thoughtful proposals that will encourage realistic and thoughtful responses from the other side.

Correlating Analyses of Damages and Liability The relationship between one's assessments of damages and liability is not always understood by negotiators. Assuming for example that the plaintiff's assessment of damages is $80,000 (that's the amount of money he or she would be awarded if victorious at trial) and that his or her chances of winning at trial are only 50/50 (that's the likelihood of winning based upon the evidence in the case), then how does that analysis affect case value?

Statisticians say that a 50/50 chance of winning an $80,000 case reduces its settlement value to $40,000. Many people with such a case are offended to hear an offer of $35,000, because they have the number $80,000 firmly fixed in their consciousness. In reality, $35,000 approaches what a careful analysis of the claim reveals is the value for that case ($40,000) with all the risks of and problems with the case taken into consideration.

A careful review of the probabilities of winning and losing the case can make an enormous difference in the range a team thinks is appropriate for settlement and an enormous difference in the way the team negotiates its case. And a mediator who guides them through that process can add enormous value to the negotiation process.

Costs: Monetary and Nonmonetary A discussion of the value of a case is not complete without considering the costs involved in prosecuting it. If a case is worth $40,000 at settlement, given all of the risk factors previously mentioned, a litigant may still have unreimbursed costs to factor into his or her calculations. Those are the costs involved in taking the case to its conclusion at trial, which can vary from several hundred dollars in a simple case to several hundred thousand dollars in a complex one.

■■■■■

You should remember that we mediators bring up the subject of costs because identifying costs is a part of the process of valuing a case. We should not treat a discussion of costs as a way of talking someone into settlement.

For that reason, you should keep two things in mind about costs. The first is that some of the costs typically incurred by a party are recoverable from the losing party. Certain expert witness fees, court reporter fees, and other costs of court may be taxed to the losing party depending upon the law in the state where the case is tried. Mediators who lead discussions about costs should remember this point in an effort to have an honest discussion about the subject.

■ ■ ■ ■ ■

Secondly, the timing of a discussion about costs is important. In my experience, initiating a discussion about costs early in the mediation invariably conveys the impression that you're "trying to make them settle" and, therefore, is viewed as manipulative. You can avoid this interpretation by saving questions about costs until the subject is brought up by a party or the party has received a best offer from the other side.

For example, if the plaintiff is told by the defense that $35,000 is their last, best, and final offer, you can introduce the subject of costs as the plaintiff's team discusses all the risk factors in the case. You want the plaintiff to see and hear what amount of money he or she would actually clear from the settlement if the offer were accepted and how that net figure compares to a net figure resulting from trial.

Those are interesting discussions to be a part of, assuming that the team will allow you to be a part of them. Some lawyers will invite you out of the room, so that the team can make their calculations in private. One of the reasons for that request has to do with another little-known fact about lawyers, and that is they often offer to reduce their fees as an inducement to settlement. Here's how that works.

Suppose the lawyer has a contingency fee agreement with the client that sets her fee at one-third of the amount recovered. If the lawyer decides that the case should be settled and, therefore, decides to reduce her fee from one-third to one-quarter of the settlement proceeds, she can change the amount of money going into the client's pocket at the end of the case. In the following example, the parties' best proposals were $40,000 by the plaintiff and $35,000 by the defense. Ask the team to do the math.

Three-quarters (the net after lawyer's fees) of $35,000 (the amount offered) is $26,250 (the net to the plaintiff). Two-thirds (the net after reducing the lawyer's fees) of $40,000 (the value of the case as determined by the plaintiff's team) is $26,666 (the net to the plaintiff). Thus, the parties are only $416 apart. The offer of the insurance company at the settlement conference now looks and sounds a lot more attractive after the reduction in fees than it did when it was first offered. If we ask the team members to do the math, their perception about the adequacy of the other side's offers may change, making settlement a more likely possibility.

A word of caution here: Never ask a lawyer to reduce his or her fee either in or out of the presence of the litigant. And never do so indirectly by asking the team to calculate costs using a lower lawyer fee than the one agreed to by the team members. You will put the lawyer in a terrible position with his or her client if you do so and you will lose a client for life. Simply leave the amount of the fees unspoken and ask them to subtract "lawyer's fees" from their estimated recovery as they calculate all costs in the case.

■■■■■

As you lead a discussion about costs, do not forget the many types of costs associated with litigation that may not be obvious to the litigant. These include the loss of business opportunities that inevitably accompanies the process of preparing for and conducting litigation.

Some well-placed questions about the loss of income a litigant might suffer during his or her absence from business for the two weeks it takes to try the case may alter the litigant's perception about the adequacy of an offer.

Mediators should also be aware that many nonmonetary costs are experienced by litigants in the form of the uncertainty, anxiety, and disruption that accompanies the process of litigation and, where appropriate, mediators should help the parties identify them. A litigant may decide to accept a proposal his or her lawyer believes is below the value of the case for these many not-so-obvious reasons.

A party might even accept a proposal that is far below the value of the case because of the many monetary or nonmonetary costs associated with litigation. For that reason, mediators should pay as much attention to the needs and interests of the parties involved as they do to the case analyses of the lawyers and claims representatives. Litigants make decisions based not only upon the value of the case but also upon the needs, goals, and objectives of their lives.

In a personal injury case I mediated many years ago, the plaintiff's lawyer advised his client that the low end of the case's value was $45,000 and that she should not accept the insurance company's final offer of $32,500. At some point soon thereafter, I pulled the plaintiff's lawyer aside for a private conversation:

M: I'm not trying to get into your business, but I just want you to know that in the past hour I've heard your client say three times that she can't afford to continue with this suit if she loses one more day's work because of it. I wasn't sure you heard that.

L: You're kidding! She said it how many times?

M: Three. (Pause) Would you like a few minutes alone with her?

L: Sure I would. Thanks.

After a 30-minute private discussion between the plaintiff and her lawyer, the case settled at $32,500.

Can You Collect If You Obtain a Judgment? It's an axiom to lawyers that three legs are needed for a tripod to stand and three things are needed to have a lawsuit with value: liability, damages, and a defendant who can pay a judgment. If a lawyer doesn't have all three, he or she should think about not taking the case in the first place. So, case analysis is not complete without an assessment of the defendant's ability to pay a judgment if a judgment is awarded at trial.

It is generally the defendant who injects the subject of collectibility into the discussion.

D: They really ought to consider this offer seriously, because they won't have anything if they proceed to trial and get a judgment. I just won't be able to pay it; I'll be forced into bankruptcy.

The subject of bankruptcy and insolvency appears frequently in state and federal court cases and is often a surprise to the plaintiff's team. In most instances, the defendant has given no notice to the plaintiff that insolvency will be a factor in the settlement discussions, and the plaintiff has not done an asset check to alert him or her to the problem. Cases are difficult to settle under those circumstances, because the plaintiff has no objective information with which to evaluate the defendant's claim of insolvency.

When the plaintiff is able to make an educated guess about the reliability of the defendant's claim of insolvency, he or she may continue the settlement discussions based upon the probabilities that the defendant is telling the truth. More often than not, however, the element of uncertainty interjected into the negotiation by the defendant's claim will make the case impossible to settle at that session of the mediation.

At that point, the parties may be inclined to quit the negotiation altogether or adjourn the session due to a lack of information. You should be aware that this situation presents a wonderful opportunity to help the parties make progress when they think none can be made. By shifting the subject of the discussion from settling the case to negotiating the discovery needed to assess the defendant's claim of insolvency, you may save the parties time, money, and energy and help them engage in a cooperative discovery process.

Also be aware that the negotiation about the issue of insolvency can result in surprising emotional conversations between the parties. To assess the defendant's true financial condition, the plaintiff will probably want to review sensitive financial documents in the defendant's possession such as tax returns, loan applications, balance sheets, and the like. The defendant, on the other hand, may initially resist revealing that kind of private information. At a minimum, the defendant will want assurances that his or her financial condition will not become public knowledge.

■ ■ ■ ■ ■

You may want to shift your own thinking and your process model at this point in the negotiation, because this is one of the few issues in the negotiation of a claim for money that lends itself to an application of the problem-solving model of the mediation process. More on that subject will be covered in Chapter 8.

Litigation Risk Analysis™

By the time I began mediating the settlement of civil litigation, I had litigated in the courts of my state for many years. Like most trial lawyers, I knew how to navigate through the process of discovery, prepare and put on documentary evidence, and examine and cross-examine witnesses. And, like most lawyers, I thought I knew how to evaluate cases.

It was not until I stumbled upon a course taught by Marc Victor called Litigation Risk Analysis™ that I began to understand that the way I evaluated cases was lacking in many respects. In 1996, my colleagues and I took the one-day version of Marc's course and came away with a better understanding of the evaluation process and with a wider array of tools to help us help others evaluate their cases.

When Marc was an MBA and law student at Stanford University in the 1970s, he conceived of applying an analytic tool he had learned in business school to the evaluation of litigation for settlement purposes. He has since made a career for himself helping lawyers analyze their cases for discovery and settlement purposes and teaching lawyers across the country how to incorporate this tool into their practice and decision making.

The tool is a "weighted probability" or "decision tree" analysis. It involves identifying the important variables that affect the outcome of litigation (the points at which value can change depending on the occurrence or nonoccurrence of an event or decision), determining the probability of each variable occurring, and calculating the probabilities of the various outcomes for the case. In one sense, Litigation Risk Analysis™ is about using the arithmetic of probability theory to quantify one's judgment calls about litigation and settlement strategies. More important, however, it's about learning how to become better at:

- identifying important defenses, theories, factual uncertainties, and damages;
- uncovering significant relationships between issues;
- brainstorming factors that might influence decision makers on each issue;

- arriving at realistic verdict ranges that one can have confidence in; and

- communicating evaluation results unambiguously to clients and advisors.

Litigation Risk Analysis™ was helpful to me in many ways in my development as a mediator and I highly recommend it to you. Most importantly, it helped me understand how a mediator can assist in the process of case evaluation by doing something other than giving opinions, and that is by framing powerful case evaluation questions that help negotiators give more objective assessments of probabilities than they are used to giving. I will have more to say in Chapter 5 about the importance of using questions to facilitate case analysis.

Summary of Chapter 2: Facilitating Traditional Bargaining: A Process Model

- Facilitate the flow of information.

Lawyers often do not understand how important it is to provide information to the other side prior to the mediation session. Mediators can help the parties prepare for negotiations by inquiring about their informational needs and helping them swap information prior to the mediation session.

Because lawyers believe that information is power, they are reluctant to disclose information they believe their opponents do not have. Mediators can help the parties make thoughtful, rather than reflexive, decisions about the exchange of information that may occur during the session itself.

- Facilitate case analysis by the use of well-framed questions.

One of the most important things a mediator can do during the mediation of civil litigation is to help each team assess the value of their case and achieve a common understanding of that value among team members. Case analysis consists of determining:

- what one gets if he wins the case (damages),
- the chances of succeeding at trial (liability).
- the costs (monetary, nonmonetary, and loss of opportunity) of conducting litigation, and
- the likelihood of collecting a judgment (collections).

■ Facilitate movement.

Problems of movement from position to position in traditional bargaining are so prevalent, important, and understudied that the next several chapters will be devoted to them. Mediators can assist the parties in making proposals and counterproposals by helping them create thoughtful, rather than reflexive, proposals and by helping them develop a plan for their movement from position to position.

Notes

1. ROGER FISHER AND WILLIAM URY, GETTING TO YES: NEGOTIATING AGREEMENT WITHOUT GIVING IN (New York: Penguin Books, 1983), at 18.

Facilitating Movement: Understanding the Problems of Movement in Traditional Bargaining

3

The most interesting phenomena I've observed in the mediation of civil trial court cases are those associated with the problems that parties experience when they negotiate in a position-based bargaining format and try to navigate through the many rounds of proposals and counterproposals that characterize this form of negotiation.

When parties try to settle money disputes through traditional bargaining, they find the process difficult at best. They have a hard time starting the process; they have a hard time keeping it going when they find their ranges diverge widely; and they grow discouraged and resentful as they make concession after concession.

> ■■■■■
>
> This was the surprise for me in the mediation of civil trial court cases. I had expected to spend most of my time with the parties facilitating case analysis. Instead, I found that I spend the majority of my time helping them to get over their negative reactions to the other side's proposals and to develop appropriate responses that would keep negotiations moving.

There are many excellent negotiators in the civil trial court arena. They research their cases, discover the facts, communicate with their clients, determine tentative walk-away numbers, and choose realistic starting numbers. However, when it comes to the task of making offers and counteroffers, even experienced negotiators often fail to recognize that they have not planned their negotiation as well as they have the rest of their case.

Instead of having a plan for their movement, negotiators react reflexively to the other side's movement by walking away, demanding that the other side bid against themselves, and throwing low- and high-ball proposals. More often than not, they react in ways that impede the progress of negotiation and make settlement impossible.

What causes the parties to stop making proposals when they have room to move? What causes them to react with anger and frustration when the other side sends them a proposal? What causes them to slam their books into briefcases and head for the door when they hear proposals they don't like? And what can mediators do to help the parties overcome these reactions and move through their negotiating ranges?

Chapter Synopsis

- Recognize the signs of impending disaster in traditional bargaining: low- or high-ball proposals, walking away from the table, or putting the other side in a position of bidding against themselves.

- Understand that monetary proposals are a form of communication.

- Understand that the subject of the parties' communication is the range in which settlement can take place. Since this information is private information, the parties will talk about their ranges indirectly through monetary proposals.

- Because they communicate indirectly, the parties miscommunicate and inadvertently mislead each other as to their intentions.

- The parties will be discouraged or encouraged to move by their perception of the other side's proposal. The perception of movement from one side breeds movement from the other.

- Many cases will settle if the real gap between the parties is known. That gap is the one between the parties' best numbers.

- The parties will be reluctant to continue movement if they believe that, by moving to their best numbers, the case will not settle.

- The parties react to the other side's proposals because they have no plan for moving from position to position throughout the negotiation.

Negotiators React Negatively to Their Opponents' Monetary Proposals

The parties to civil litigation usually use position-based bargaining in an attempt to settle their case and, thus, they face many challenges as they attempt to settle. As I observed in Chapter 1, negotiators often become surprisingly emotional as they swap proposals. One of the things that civil trial court mediators ought to be aware of is that the parties express that emotion through the proposals they send to one another.

■■■■■

As the parties to traditional bargaining react in frustration or anger to the proposals they receive from the other side, they do one of a number of things that stall or end the negotiations, and make them more difficult to conclude. Mediators need to be able to spot these reactions and understand why they occur.

In response to a proposal they don't like, negotiators will pack up and walk away; put the other party in a position of bidding against themselves, or deliver a low-ball or high-ball proposal in return. All of these behaviors have a deleterious effect on negotiations and make it hard for their opponents to generate additional proposals. Chapters 3 and 4 identify these behaviors, explain why the behaviors occur, and describe things that mediators can do or say to help the parties keep moving toward settlement.

When the parties pack up and leave, curse at the other side, or send low- or high-ball proposals in retaliation against proposals they think are unacceptable, it is safe to assume that they are communicating something with their behavior. In fact, the parties' own words tell us much about what they are trying to do with their behavior. In many of the court-ordered mediations I conduct, someone inevitably will say,

"I want to send them a message!"

or

"Don't they get the message?!"

■■■■■

I achieved breakthrough insights about money negotiations when it occurred to me that position-based bargaining—the money proposals parties typically exchange during civil trial court mediation—is a form of communication. The tip-off for me was the oft-recurring theme of the "message" that I hear in the language of lawyers and parties alike in settlement conferences in which traditional bargaining abounds.

Communication is a topic mediators know something about. One of our roles as mediators is to foster and enhance communication among the parties, and we clearly see the opportunities to perform that role in mediations about interpersonal disputes. Is there such a role in mediations in which position-based bargaining dominates the negotiating process?

The answer is "yes" and most obviously so in that portion of the mediation that is concerned with case evaluation. In civil trial court negotiations, we seek to enhance the parties' communication about the value of the case and the basis for reaching a conclusion about value. In conversations about case value, we try to achieve not agreement, but understanding. And in doing so, we try first to ensure that the communication about case value is accurate and complete.

Are there also opportunities for the mediator to help the parties communicate better in the bargaining stages of the settlement process? Absolutely! A mediator doesn't have to be "just" a messenger during the proposal-swapping stage of traditional bargaining. A mediator can become an aid to better communication between the parties by:

- helping them clarify the messages they want to send with their proposals and
- helping them develop proposals that will convey those messages to each other accurately.

The Parties Communicate Indirectly through Monetary Proposals

The subject of the parties' communication is the range in which settlement can take place. In order to reach settlement in traditional bargaining, the parties have to communicate about the number that will settle the case. They have to communicate about their bottom and top lines.

However, the negotiating range of the parties, or more specifically their top and bottom numbers, is private information. This is precisely what they will not speak to each other about directly for fear that the other side will take advantage of the information. Mediators should take this fact seriously; and what we learn about the parties' best numbers should be treated as confidential information whether the parties ask us to keep it confidential or not.

■■■■■

Why do the parties communicate indirectly about their best numbers and their bottom and top numbers? They do so for the simple reason that each wants to maximize his or her monetary outcome in the negotiation. The plaintiff wants as much money as he can get, and the defendant wants to pay as little as possible. Neither wants to give up the possibility of settling the case for a number that represents a really good outcome for the negotiation. Neither one of them wants to start the negotiation with their bottom or top numbers, because that is the least desirable outcome of the negotiation. I'm describing a simple fact of human nature. In any negotiation about money, negotiators want to get as much as they can get.

I should quickly add that the parties could communicate directly about their real range of settlement if they wanted to. They could say to each other, "Here's my best number; take it or leave it." I've mediated negotiations like that. They are what I call "one-and-only-one number" negotiations. It's perfectly OK to negotiate in that fashion, but I would never recommend that a negotiator take that approach at mediation. It simply infuriates the folks on the other side. Better in that situation to write opposing counsel and propose the "best number" before the mediation than to waste everyone's time getting ready for and anticipating a negotiation that will never take place.

In an effort to get more or pay less than the very bottom or top number in their range of settlement, negotiators will sneak up on their best numbers hoping that they will not have to go to those numbers to settle the case. Negotiators will open with a number that, if accepted, would maximize their return. When that number is rejected, they will move to a less favorable number that is still higher than their best numbers. Only when it is absolutely necessary to do so to settle the case will they go to their bottom or top number.

■■■■■

Thus, negotiators communicate their range of settlement indirectly, through the publication of proposals. Over a series of moves, they gradually let the other side know where they can and cannot settle the case. The position of the parties and their movement from one position to another are communications about that number, range, or ballpark of settlement.

The Parties Communicate Indirectly and, as a Result, They Often Miscommunicate

Consider this example:

> The plaintiff begins the negotiation at 100, having decided that 50 is probably his "homerun verdict," and sets 35 as his absolute bottom number.
> The defendant, having evaluated the case at 15 to 30, thinks 100 is "ridiculous" and counters at 2.
> The plaintiff gets angry at the defendant's "low ball" and counters at 98.

What has happened in this scenario? The plaintiff wanted at least 35. The plaintiff's lawyer's case analysis is that 50 is his best day in court. But on the theory that "you can't get it unless you ask for it," he went for a much bigger number than was justified by his own case analysis.

The defendant then hears the "message" that the ballpark of settlement is much higher than he can or will pay and reacts negatively to the plaintiff's proposal. (We'll talk more about the parties' emotional reactions in just a moment.) In an effort to tell the plaintiff he's "out of the ballpark" and that he needs to get into the defendant's ballpark, the defendant sends a "low-ball" proposal.

The message the plaintiff receives, however, is different from what the defendant intended. What plaintiff hears is, "We're not going to pay anywhere near what this case is worth." Based on that message, the plaintiff then reacts in frustration and thinks, "This damn insurance company is playing their silly games again and not bargaining in good faith. They don't want to settle for what this case is worth, so I'll just have to tell them to get serious." He then tells the mediator, "Tell them my next number is 98."

■■■■■

Many observers of this exchange will interpret the interaction of the parties in interpersonal terms—the parties are engaging in a contest of wills or egos. That may well be true, but the analysis does little to help us understand how to assist these negotiators. A more useful frame for this scenario is the language of communication. The parties have tried to convey a message and have failed to get their messages across. Instead of making moves that are consistent with their theory of the case, and thereby sending signals about where they can really settle, the parties have sent messages that will be misinterpreted.

The source of that miscommunication lies in the fact that they have formulated their counterproposals out of anger and frustration and in reaction to the other's proposal. When the parties formulated their counteroffers reactively, they failed to convey accurately the range in which they are willing to settle. In this example, the range that each side thinks will work for the other is much different than the range the other party actually has in mind.

It is not the anger or frustration of the parties I am concerned about at this point. Rather, it is the fact that they will formulate their proposals while angry or frustrated and, as a result, develop proposals that do not convey clear and accurate messages. They make reactive and inaccurate proposals instead of thoughtful and accurate ones. If they continue to send inaccurate messages, they will quickly quit the negotiation in the mistaken belief that there is a vast difference in their best numbers. This is a hallmark of traditional bargaining.

In our example, the parties' case analysis reveals that, if they each stretched to reach their best numbers (the plaintiff's bottom number and the defendant's top number), their real gap is only five, the difference between 35 and 30. If they had not been misled by each other's proposal, the negotiation may have played out much differently.

Let's examine the parties' communication in our example in more detail. The plaintiff, wanting as much money from the negotiation as he can get, starts with a high number that is not in line with his analysis of the case. The defendant, not liking the plaintiff's proposal, acts reflexively and gives a number that is probably lower than he would have given if the plaintiff had been "reasonable." The plaintiff, not liking the defendant's proposal, acts reflexively and gives a number higher than he would have if the defendant had not "low-balled." As the negotiation unfolds, the parties say to the mediator at every stage, "I want them to get the message."

■■■■■

Did each party have a clear message? And did each party communicate in such a way that the other got the message? The answer is both yes and no. The parties did convey accurately to each other that they didn't like the other side's number and the range of settlement that the other side's proposal signaled. However, the parties did not convey accurately the range within which they could settle the case. This is crucial. The messages the parties sent and received about the range of settlement were mixed, and therefore inaccurate and misleading.

From the plaintiff's first number, the defendant probably thought the plaintiff would settle between 50 and 100. Given the defendant's own case analysis, that range is too high. The plaintiff's second number, sent in reaction to the defendant's low ball, communicated a settlement range of maybe 80 to 100, even higher than the defendant had thought. Likewise, hearing the defendant's first proposal, the plaintiff probably thought that the defendant's range was up to 10, maybe 15. In reality, the defendant's range was 15 to 30.

Because they sent inaccurate signals about their range of settlement, both parties restricted the movement they were willing to make in their next proposals. Without an intervention on the part of the mediator, these parties likely will quit their negotiation in the belief that they have no chance of reaching an agreeable number and that they "are wasting their time."

Miscommunication occurs in several ways during the proposal-swapping stage of a money negotiation. One occurs when a party makes a change in the rate of his or her movement. Let's say that the plaintiff has been dropping in $10,000 increments but is still a long way from his bottom number. The plaintiff hears a number from the defendant he doesn't like and says, "They don't seem to be getting the message that we can't go there. Let's shorten up on our moves. Maybe then they'll get it. Let's drop only $5,000 this time."

The defendant certainly will understand that the plaintiff is unhappy about the defendant's position. But the defendant will also get the message that the plaintiff is approaching his bottom number. That's what shortening up usually signals—"I'm getting close enough to my bottom number that I am going to change the rate of descent." Unfortunately, that's inaccurate in this instance. The plaintiff, in reducing his rate of movement, has sent a message that is inaccurate (that he is nearing the bottom of his range) and it will probably have an adverse effect on the negotiation.

It is no wonder, then, that the parties easily reach impasse. They don't communicate directly and, therefore, they miscommunicate about their intended range of settlement. As a consequence, the parties begin to slow their movement toward settlement and, eventually, quit negotiating altogether.

The central question for us as mediators, then, is how we can help the parties keep negotiating when they want to quit. What can mediators do to assist the parties at this point? The first thing that we can do is to help them define the messages they are trying to send about their range of settlement. The second thing we can do is to help them develop positions that will accurately convey those messages. I will have more to say about these suggestions in the two sections that follow.

Movement Breeds Movement

The parties' proposals will have an impact on the other side. The parties will be encouraged to make a good move or they will be discouraged from doing so. The greatest motivation of the parties to settle is the perception that the case can settle. And the greatest impediment to settlement is the perception that the case will not settle.

Proposals Will Have an Impact on the Other Side

Mediators often hear the parties say, "They aren't getting the message that I'm serious." What this means is that the negotiator is not happy with the other party's movement and wants to send his next number in such a way that the other party will be inclined to make a move that he likes. Negotiators do in fact believe that their movement will have an impact on the other side's movement. They most certainly are right: The proposals negotiators make will either encourage or discourage the other party regarding movement.

However, negotiators in traditional bargaining generally behave as if they believe that the way to encourage the other party to move closer is to make no movement at all or to make a very small move. An example of this frequently occurs at the beginning of negotiations. In reaction to the plaintiff's opening proposal that the defendant thinks is unrealistic and in an effort to get the plaintiff to "get realistic," the defendant may say,

> "That's ridiculous! Tell them I'll give them a number when they get real."

> or

> "I can be as ridiculous as they can! Take a hundred dollars to them" (a pitifully low number compared to the defendant's highest number).

Another example: After several rounds of proposals, the defendant thinks the plaintiff's numbers are still too high. In an effort to get the plaintiff to "get realistic," the defendant may say,

> "They're just not getting into the range to settle this case. We increased our number $10,000 last time; this time we'll increase it by $2,000. Hopefully they'll get the message."

The negotiator in this example wants the plaintiff to quit negotiating "in the stratosphere." He wants the plaintiff to drop substantially, because the case won't get settled if he doesn't. Negotiators generally try to create an impact on the other side by slowing their rate of movement or making no movement at all. Usually the result they desire is the complete opposite of the result they get.

The negotiator's attempt to get the other party to move into his range by making a smaller move will signal to the other side that his range of settlement is lower than previously thought. In an effort to send a message that he can't go that low, the plaintiff also will change his proposal by a smaller increment than before. In many negotiations, this action and reaction will result in a cessation of movement and eventually in impasse, because the parties mistakenly conclude that the best numbers of each side are too far apart.

If one studies the behavior of negotiators, as mediators have the opportunity to do, discernible patterns emerge. One of them is that minimal movement on the part of one negotiator will produce a small move from the other. Conversely, a move that one side perceives as substantial will often motivate the other to make a significant move himself. The solution to getting better movement, then, is counterintuitive. The way to get movement is to make movement. If a party wants movement from the other side, he or she should make movement of his or her own.

Get the Next Number

A move by one party will motivate the other party to also make a move and to keep the negotiation moving. If a party senses that the case has a chance of settling, or at least that the other side isn't approaching a quitting point, the party will be motivated to make another move. That move in turn will motivate the other side, and so on until the parties approach their best numbers.

■■■■■

Among the many things a mediator should be aware of, then, is the need for the parties to have the experience of movement toward settlement. Thus, one of my goals as a mediator during a negotiation about money is simply to get the party's next number. To do so, I often have to help him overcome his reflex to quit or slow down and help him develop positions that will encourage the other party to keep making substantial movement themselves.

A word of caution is appropriate here. Parties quit moving for several reasons. Sometimes they quit moving because they have reached their walk-away numbers. More often than not, however, they quit, or slow down, because they are reacting to their perception that the other side is "out of the ballpark." The mediator may not know the real reason a party is "slowing down," because the parties often leave us with the impression that they have gotten to their best number. Only later do we discover that they had more room to move and were slowing down in reaction to a proposal that they didn't like.

> Example: "Well, Andy, we're just not going to put more money on this case. They're being too unrealistic."

This is an intriguing statement. The first sentence suggests that the speaker has reached the end of his negotiating range. The last sentence is ambiguous and leaves us puzzled. Has the speaker reached the end of his range or does the speaker want to quit because he doesn't like the range the other side is showing?

If the speaker has reached his best number, we should take that seriously. We should not be asking someone to change his or her case analysis (i.e., alter his walk-away number) just to get a settlement. Our goal is not to get a settlement at any cost. We are in the business of helping the parties negotiate within a range they, not we, deem acceptable. Mediators should take seriously statements that suggest the party has reached his best number.

■■■■■

But, I also know from experience that parties who slow down or want to quit, and who say they've reached their best number, will often move toward settlement when conditions on the other side of the table have changed. So, one of the mediator's tasks is to ferret out whether the party has truly reached his best number or, instead, is simply reacting to the other side's minimal movement.

If it's the latter, then we can help him develop an alternative to quitting or slowing down. We can help him formulate a proposal that will convey accurate messages about his range of settlement, which will then serve as encouragement to the other side to make additional movement. I have included many examples of these interventions in Chapter 6.

Find Out What the Real Gap Is between the Parties' Best Numbers

Most cases will settle if the parties reach their best numbers during the mediation. One of my aims as a mediator is to get the parties to continue moving through their acceptable ranges of settlement until they get to their best numbers. If I can get one party to make movement, I can usually get the other party to respond by making movement of his or her own. Over a period of time I can help the parties get to the lowest and highest numbers within their acceptable ranges of settlement.

More frequently than not, there will be a gap between their best numbers at the end of the negotiation process. Generally, the plaintiff's lowest number and the defendant's highest number will not be the same; their ranges will not overlap.

■■■■■

Don't despair! You have helped them through the toughest and most time-consuming part of the negotiating process. You have helped them assess, plan, and communicate effectively. You have helped them get to their best numbers, and the real differences between them have been revealed. That's real progress.

Don't quit! Now they can think about bridging that gap. (More on that will be covered in Chapter 7.) Perhaps the greatest aid in their doing so is the fact that the gap has been clearly stated. And surprisingly, the gap is often much narrower than the parties first thought. That fact, and that fact alone, is great motivation for the parties to continue their efforts toward settlement.

So, while movement breeds movement, proximity of the parties' best numbers breeds settlement. Parties who get to their best numbers often discover they are not far apart. When they discover that, they see the negotiation in a new light. Parties whose best numbers are not far apart will reassess their case to decide whether the small gap existing between them is worth the fight. They will be motivated to review the costs of litigation in terms of time, energy, money, and lost business opportunity. They will compare the current gap between the parties, a certain outcome, to a contingent outcome, something they might get in the future as the result of a trial. Parties who are not far apart at the end of their negotiations will reassess their case in ways that were not possible or relevant before their best numbers were known.

In a high percentage of cases in which the parties reach their "best numbers" or "bottom lines," the parties will come to some unexpected settlement. The plaintiff may settle on the defendant's best number. The defendant may settle on the plaintiff's best number. They may move somewhere in between. Be flexible and be prepared! The negotiation process will take more time and considerable effort on everyone's part, but settlement is now a real possibility. It may happen today. It may happen tomorrow. It may happen next week. In a high percentage of cases, if the real gap between the parties is known, they will find an amount of money that settles the case.

Developing a Plan for Movement: The Neglected Aspect of Traditional Bargaining

Most negotiators act reflexively. They develop their next proposal in reaction to the other side's last proposal. If they like it, they move. If they don't like it, they don't move. If one thinks in more detail about this habit of operation, one may conclude that it is counterproductive to achieving settlement. This reactive approach can be outlined as follows:

- I don't like how they moved.
- I want them to move closer to me and get into my range of settlement.
- So, I will make a small move myself to show them I'm serious and that they need to come toward me.

As we have discussed, the impact of that small move on the other side is to discourage movement toward settlement, not to encourage it. The irony of money negotiations is that a party has to make movement toward his opponent in order to get his opponent to move toward him.

Most of us do the reverse; we hold back in an effort to get the other side to come to us. That's our instinct; that's our reflex. We reflexively think about how to formulate our proposals. We say to ourselves, "How much will I move in relation to their move?" This type of inquiry keeps our focus on the other side's movement rather than on our own case evaluation and our own plan for negotiation.

■■■■■

There you have it. The crux of the problem is that most negotiators never get beyond case analysis to develop any plan for movement during the negotiation. They simply develop proposals in reaction to the other side's proposals. They are reactive rather than proactive. They focus on the other side and the movement the other side is making, rather than on their own goals and the movement within their range of settlement that they're able to make.

What do I mean by having a plan for negotiations? I mean first of all answering the following questions:

After I have reviewed my case,

After I have decided what I get on a good day and on a bad day in court,

After I have factored in all of the costs and contingencies,

After I have conducted a thorough case analysis,

After all of that,

> At what number will I start the negotiation?
>
> At what number will I walk away from it? and
>
> How will I move from number to number in between?

This sounds simple, and it is. Surprisingly, the majority of negotiators I work with give little thought to this kind of planning. This is particularly true for the plaintiff's team in personal injury cases. Plaintiffs and their lawyers often are not on the same page about value in general, so they are not able to develop a plan for negotiations. Fortunately, the mediation process itself helps clarify that team's thinking about case value and, thus, provides a starting point for their negotiation.

Plaintiffs typically start much higher than their own case analysis supports. Defendants often have a best number in mind, but start low in reaction to the plaintiff's high starting number. Neither has a plan for what happens next and the rest is predictable. Left to their own devices, the parties typically quit the process after swapping a few proposals, believing that their best numbers are very far apart and that the case won't settle.

Much of my time in the first private session with the plaintiff's team is spent helping them get on the same page with each other about their case analysis. If such a session produces an opening proposal, I also spend time with them discussing how their proposal relates to their case analysis and how their proposal will affect the other side.

■ ■ ■ ■ ■

True story: Early in my career, I mediated a personal injury case in which the plaintiff's lawyer engaged willingly and openly with me in a discussion about the merits of his case. At the conclusion of that discussion he told me, "On my best day in court, $80,000 is the best that I will ever do with this case." I asked him if they were ready to make a proposal. He quickly said yes and gave me $125,000 as his starting proposal. Instantly I knew that the negotiation was in trouble.

I told this lawyer that I didn't understand the rationale for starting with a number that was more than 150 percent of his best-case scenario. He told me he understood my concern but had decided to start at $125,000 because "I can't get $80,000 if I don't start higher than $80,000." This lawyer had certainly thought about the relation between his analysis and his starting number, but he had not clearly thought through what kind of impact his number would have on the other side. Since he didn't change his mind as a result of our discussion, I carried his number to the defense team. They blew up, slammed their notebooks into their briefcases, put on their coats, and headed for the door. (For a fuller discussion of this situation, see Scenario #3 in Chapter 6.)

In my experience, starting numbers that can be clearly supported by case analysis are received better than those that cannot. A number at the top of the plaintiff's verdict range may be no more acceptable to the defense than one that is 150 percent higher. However, the defense's reaction to it and their willingness to negotiate in realistic ranges themselves is much different and more positive. Thus, I frequently ask one side or the other to consider how their starting number relates to their case analysis and how the other side, as a consequence of that relation, will react to it.

Based on those thoughts, I believe that plaintiffs should not start their negotiations with a number higher than their own case analysis. I made that statement to a group of plaintiffs' lawyers at a seminar some time ago and received an interesting response. Some of the participants took it to mean that I was criticizing them for starting their negotiations with inflated numbers. One lawyer who handled high-dollar, personal injury cases, said: "But how are we supposed to know what a catastrophic case is worth? How do we know what's too high?"

I had, and still have, no useful answer to that question. The plaintiffs" lawyers who handle high-end cases often don't know what their case is worth. In many of those cases, there's no "blue book" of similar cases to suggest what juries will do with those facts and those injuries. I sympathize with those lawyers. They will have to guess what the top of the verdict ranges will be and generally err on the high side. I would do the same.

However, my assertion was addressed to an entirely different phenomenon, and that is the circumstance in which the lawyer has conducted an analysis and has decided that the case is worth, as in our previous case, $80,000 tops. In that situation, most plaintiffs will be well served not to start with a number they cannot support with their case analysis. They should think about how that number will affect the other side's movement. The impact generally will be negative if they start with a number that is higher than their "best day in court."

Similarly, the defense often starts with a number that their case analysis doesn't support. They justify it with a different rationale—that is, that the plaintiff's proposal is too high and we need to send him that message—but the result is the same. They start with a low number in reaction to the plaintiff's high one. Their number bears little relationship to their case analysis and generally is much lower than they would have started if "the plaintiff had come in with a realistic proposal."

One of the questions I often ask the defendant's team in this circumstance is,

> "What would have been a reasonable number for the plaintiff to begin with?"

A frequent follow-up question is,

> "Where would you have started if they had been reasonable?"

These questions often lead to a discussion about the defendant's plan—or lack of one—for the negotiation. As a result of that discussion, defendants sometimes develop a format for their movement that is less dependent on the plaintiff's movement and more related to their own case analysis.

Since few negotiators have a plan for their negotiations, you may be wondering what a plan for movement would look or sound like. There are as many possibilities as one's imagination can create, and all of them have advantages and disadvantages.

> ■■■■■
>
> Much of my work as a mediator during the proposal-swapping stage of a money negotiation is directed toward helping the parties create a variety of proposals, identify their advantages and disadvantages, and choose the most effective one for that round of the negotiation. Many of the mediation transcripts I have included in Chapter 6 are examples of that inventing and evaluation process during discrete moments in the mediation.

The same is true for helping the parties develop a plan for their negotiations. I help them invent options and evaluate their advantages and disadvantages. Many negotiators have never thought of developing a plan and need help with the concept of a plan itself. Here is one option I sometimes throw out for consideration (in which the party's highest evaluation is $100,000 and their walk-away number is $50,000, for a negotiating range of $50,000):

_____	100,000_____
_____	75,000_____
_____	62,500_____
_____	57,500_____
_____	53,750_____
_____	51,875_____
_____	50,937_____
_____	50,468_____
_____	50,234_____
_____	50,117_____
_____	50,000_____

This plan assumes that the team has already determined their starting and ending numbers, both of which have been derived from their case analysis. It proceeds through the party's range by dividing the available range by one-half on each move. It proceeds faithfully through the range in that manner until the case settles or the plaintiff announces 50 as his best number.

In evaluating this plan, litigants frequently tell me that it has the advantage of creating movement, particularly in the difficult, first stages of negotiation. It also allows the party to arrive at a new proposal without wasting a lot of time and energy reacting to the other side. And, it does not leave the other side guessing about the intentions of the party. It clearly communicates the range of settlement.

On the negative side, the parties often tell me that the first move gives up too much ground too quickly. They also say that the message to the other side about their lowest number is too clear. It telegraphs the ending number and thus eliminates the possibility of settling at a number higher than the party's best number. Because of this plan's deficiencies, it is rarely chosen by negotiators with whom I work.

A second plan I often describe is one that attempts to keep the advantages of the previous plan while eliminating its negatives. It proceeds by dividing up the available range for negotiations into a number of equal increments. It proceeds increment by increment through the range rather mechanically until the party gets near the end of the range. The positions of the parties are then reevaluated and, if it appears that it would be beneficial to keep negotiating, the available range is redivided into smaller equal increments to signal that the party is approaching its best number. The negotiation of the previous case using this format might look like this:

100,000

(Now divide the available range of 50,000 by 8 moves to give you equal increments of 6,250. The number 8 is completely arbitrary and will vary from negotiation to negotiation.)

_____93,750_____

_____87,500_____

_____81,250_____

_____75,000_____

_____68,750_____

_____62,500_____

(Reevaluate and divide the available range of 12,500 by 8 moves to give you equal increments of 1,562.)

_____60,938_____

_____58,356_____

_____56,508_____

_____55,242_____

_____53,680_____

_____52,118_____

_____50,546_____

_____50,000_____

This format creates a sense of movement, gives the plaintiff a chance to get more than 50 if the defendant's willing to pay it, gives a clear signal when the end of the range is in sight, but hides the negotiator's final number through the beginning rounds of proposals. This type of movement is one way that the negotiator can continue to make reasonable movement and, at the same time, safeguard his or her bottom line.

If the parties are receptive to a discussion about developing a plan for their negotiations, they often opt for this one because it is an efficient way to negotiate. They are able to move quickly, carefully, and effectively through their range and avoid the many agonizing discussions that occur when they attempt to create proposals solely in reaction to the other's movement.

Summary of Chapter 3: A Guide to Facilitating Movement

The Problem: The parties react negatively to each other's proposals and stall or quit the negotiation before they reach their bottom lines. They do this by packing up, walking away, refusing to respond with a proposal, responding with low-ball or high-ball proposals, or putting the other side in the position of bidding against itself.

The Keys to Understanding Movement in Money Negotiations

- Monetary proposals are a form of communication.
- The subject of the parties' communication is the range in which settlement can take place.
- The parties communicate indirectly and, as a result, they often miscommunicate.
- Movement breeds movement. The parties' proposals will have an impact on the other side; they will be encouraged to make a good move or they will be discouraged from doing so. The greatest motivation of the parties to settle is the perception that the case can settle. And the greatest impediment to settlement is the perception that the case will not settle. Mediators should concentrate not on settlement but on eliciting well-thought-out proposals that encourage movement.
- Most cases will settle if the parties reach their best numbers during the negotiation. Get the parties to their best numbers and find out what the real gap is.
- The parties seldom have a plan for their negotiations and simply react to the other side. Help them develop a plan that does not depend on the other side's proposals.

Facilitating Movement: Helping Negotiators Overcome Their Negative Reactions to the Other Side's Proposals

4

Chapter Synopsis

Mediators Can Facilitate Movement If They:

1. Understand the reasons a party reacts negatively to the other side's proposal.

   - Parties experience differences as criticisms.
   - An unacceptable proposal seems like a waste of time.
   - Parties resist being dragged into an unacceptable range of settlement.

2. Communicate that you understand the party's negative reaction.

3. Use the insights of control theory to focus the party's attention on forming thoughtful proposals rather than on the inadequacy of the other's proposals.

4. Help the parties to develop a plan for their negotiations rather than making proposals in reaction to the other side's proposals.

Understand the Parties' Negative Reactions

At many points in the negotiation of a claim for money, the parties become frustrated or angry and lash out verbally in private sessions with the mediator. They will then respond to the other side's proposal by packing up, refusing to make another move, or by making minimal movement—all in the name of "sending them a message."

Negotiators will react with hostility and with snide or offensive comments to a proposal that is unacceptable to them. Occasionally, they will even call the mediator's effectiveness into question when they don't get the response that they want from the other side. If mediators do not understand what motivates the parties to react in such a negative manner, they may get caught up in negative reactions of their own.

When a negotiator becomes irritated with the mediator, the mediator may also become reactive and do some un-mediator-like things. She may find herself chastising the offending party. She may begin to lecture the party about how wrong and unproductive he is to react in such a manner. She may get into an argument about the character of the opposing party. She may become defensive about her own conduct and competence. None of these reactions communicate neutrality, and they all compromise the mediator's effectiveness and credibility. If we react to the reactions of one of the parties by becoming defensive, judgmental, or pedantic, we will add an additional level of difficulty to an already difficult negotiation.

■ ■ ■ ■ ■

The key to avoiding detours into a judgmental and directive approach at this stage of the mediation is to concentrate on understanding the cause of the party's reaction. It is important that mediators think about the frustrations of the parties and the causes of their anger in the context of a negotiation about money. As we become acquainted with the interior world of the reactive party, we will then be able to construct ways of communicating effectively with him and helping him develop a thoughtful response.

What is it, then, that flips one side into a reactive, even hostile, mode when they hear the latest proposal of the other side? What was it about that proposal that sets them off? It's really rather odd; the parties have no real history with each other. They are not in the same room when the offending communication occurs. No one actually "speaks" to the other in an insulting or derogatory way. No one calls the other names or calls their heritage into question. All one side does is convey a money proposal to the other side.

However, the communication—that is, their proposal—is taken personally.

"Do they think I'm stupid?!"

"That's insulting!"

"Who do they think I am?!"

"Is that what they think my mama's worth?!"

In the communication that is delivered in the form of a money proposal, the receiving party hears something that is personally offensive. What makes that so? There are at least three explanations.

1. **There is a tendency in human experience to treat differences of opinions as personal criticisms.**

   This is especially true on the plaintiff's side of a personal injury or wrongful death lawsuit. The plaintiff typically translates a low money proposal by the defendant as a message about his value as a human being. A low-ball proposal is demeaning of his experience as an injured person or as one who has lost a beloved relative.

"That's all they think my arm's worth?"

Even when the defense conveys a proposal that it believes accurately reflects the verdict range of a case that has legally problematic features, it is heard, felt, and seen by the plaintiff as reflecting on the value of his life. The plaintiff, therefore, is personally insulted.

Sometimes the defense is "insulted" as well. The proposal of the plaintiff is experienced as a comment on the intelligence of the claims representative. The defense is insulted for a slightly different, but important, reason.

"Do they think I'm stupid enough to consider that proposal?!"

The professional negotiator may experience the other's proposal as a negative comment on his competence or intelligence and, then, may react with an insulting proposal of his own.

2. **Proposals that appear to be out of the ballpark of settlement indicate to the other side that the case won't settle.**

Upon receiving a proposal that he believes to be "out of the ballpark of settlement," a party may conclude that it will be a waste of time to continue negotiating. He will actually say,

"They're wasting my time!"

This response may be given by either side to the negotiation but it is given most often by the defense. The defense team believes that: they know their business; they know this case; they've got a lot to do back in the office; and they don't want to waste their time. Plaintiffs who aren't negotiating in a "reasonable range" are wasting their time. The response on the part of the defense is less "That's insulting" and more:

"I've got better things to do than sit around and let some inexperienced, uninformed plaintiff waste my time!"

3. Negotiators resist being pulled into an unacceptable range of settlement.

A proposal from one side to another is an implicit suggestion, expectation, or demand that the receiving party move into the sending party's range. If the sending party's range is perceived by the receiving party to be unacceptable, the receiving party will resist being pulled into that range. When people perceive they are being dragged somewhere they don't want to go, they reflexively resist being dragged. And they generally do so with more force than is necessary.

"So they want me to go to 50 or 75? No! In fact, hell no! I was going to move 5; but just to be sure they get the message, I'm only going to move 2!"

The adverse reaction of one side to the other's proposal is often an overreaction to a perception that the opposition is trying to get them to do something they don't want to do.

Communicate Your Understanding to the Reacting Party

■■■■■

It is our challenge as mediators to help the parties respond to each other in a thoughtful rather than in a reactive fashion. In order to help them move from a reactive to a thoughtful state, we must understand what prompted their reactions and communicate effectively to them that we understand. If the reacting party truly believes that we understand them, they will entertain our questions, thoughts, and suggestions.

The active listening skills we learned in mediation training will hold us in good stead in our work with civil case negotiators.

When we listen actively, we pay attention to the words, gestures, tone, volume, and cadence of the parties' communication. We form a hypothesis about what the party is trying to say. And we test that hypothesis by using a summary statement.

A summary statement captures the essence of the party's communication and reflects it back to the speaker in the form of a question. With the summary statement, we're trying to determine whether we've properly understood the party's reaction. If they let us know we got it right, we can move on to consider how to help them think about the problem in a different way. If we didn't get it right, they will let us know, and we can listen and try again.

When a mediator fully understands a party's reaction, it frees that party to construct and consider thoughtful proposals. If they don't believe the mediator understands them, they will resist the mediator's best efforts to settle the case. The reactive party's experience of being understood is the foundation upon which thoughtful, rather than reactive, proposals are created.

As you already know, there are as many ways to construct a summary statement as the imagination will allow. I discuss the use of summary statements in Chapter 5, and you will find examples of their use in the settlement conference transcripts I've set out in Chapter 6. As I mentioned a moment ago, the defense team often reacts negatively to the plaintiff's first proposal. A typical summary statement for me in that situation is:

"So, they're wasting your time with that kind of move?"

If they let me know I was right in my conclusion, I then proceed to the task of helping them create a number of proposals to convey in return. Until I've correctly understood their reaction, I will have a hard time helping them come up with a proposal that will encourage the other side to move.

Help the Parties Construct Thoughtful Proposals by Employing the Insights of Control Theory

The thinking of William Glasser, the American psychologist and author of the book *Control Theory*,[1] has been helpful to many of us who mediate in the context of traditional bargaining. *Control*

Theory is, in part, a discourse on human motivation and a critique of the theories of motivation that many of us learned in Psychology 101.

Traditional theories of human motivation are derived from the work of Pavlov, who demonstrated that animals can be trained to perform tasks by conditioning their responses. The theory is that animals, human animals included, can be motivated to perform in certain ways by rewarding desirable behavior and punishing undesirable behavior. Behavior can be shaped and molded and conditioned by external stimuli.

Glasser's formulation of human motivation is based upon the notion that human behavior is directed by the internal needs of individuals as opposed to the influence of external stimuli. He believes that, after the satisfaction of the basic need for food and shelter, we are motivated to satisfy our own internal needs for belonging, fun, freedom, and power (competence). True, strong, and lasting motivation is created through the satisfaction of those needs, not through response to external stimuli.

We are motivated by and will stay engaged in activities in which our needs are met. Conversely, we are not motivated by and will not stay engaged in activities that do not meet those needs. Glasser's insights about human motivation have sparked a change in the way psychologists think about influencing human behavior in family, school, and workplace settings.

■ ■ ■ ■ ■

People who lack motivation or who tend to blame others for their difficulties are often helped by those who employ the insights of control theory. Control theory techniques work by focusing a person's attention and energy on his or her own internal processes and resources. Control theory is not concerned with achieving control over other people. Rather, it is concerned with fostering and enhancing the power that people have to control their own destiny and to effect change in their own lives. Glasser points out what is in reality an obvious fact: We can control only what is in our power to control. We can control only our own behavior.

Glasser's work has been useful to me in the mediation of lawsuits that are negotiated and settled through traditional bargaining. During the proposal-swapping stage of traditional bargaining, reactive parties hurl epithets, engage in name-calling, and blame the other side for not getting the case settled. Out of a reactive state, they engage in behavior (make outrageous counterproposals) that drives the other side away and makes the result they give lip service to (settlement) harder to achieve. It is important for us to remember that, when negotiators react reflexively by slowing their movement or stopping movement altogether, they have lost control of their own creative processes.

■■■■■

Control theory encourages us to focus parties on what they, as opposed to the other side, can do to make progress toward settlement. In the settlement of civil litigation, the parties have control over some things and no control over others. For instance, litigants cannot:

- control the behavior or decisions of judges.
- control the decisions of juries.
- control the movement their opponents make in negotiations.
- keep their opponents from evaluating the case differently than they do.
- keep their opponents from opening negotiations with low-ball or high-ball proposals.
- keep their opponents from moving slower than the litigants wish they would.

Litigants can control:

- their own case evaluation.
- their own negotiating ranges.
- their own movement at any point in time.
- their own stopping point at the end of their bargaining range.

One party cannot make the other do anything. Most importantly, one party cannt make the other go beyond the range he or she thinks is appropriate to settle the case.

When I first employed the insights of control theory in civil trial court mediations, I discovered an amazingly simple phenomenon: The party to a money negotiation who becomes reactive to the other's proposal has lost control. He has lost the ability to see the many options he has at his disposal to encourage the other side to make significant movement. Having lost control, he puts forth a proposal that succeeds only in driving the other side away and making it impossible to accomplish his own objective, which is to settle the case.

Not surprisingly, a mediator can play a useful role at this point by understanding why the parties are reacting negatively, by helping them invent and assess alternatives to their reflexive behavior, and by helping them formulate proposals that communicate clearly and accurately. In short the mediator can help parties regain control over their own destiny.

■ ■ ■ ■ ■

A conversation between a mediator and a negotiator who is reacting negatively to the other side's movement can be constructed using the principles of control theory. The mediator's side of that conversation consists primarily of questions, and the structure of the mediator's inquiry goes like this:

1. What do you want?
2. What are you doing to get it?
3. Is that working?
4. If not, what can you do differently to make it happen?

A word of caution is necessary here. Mediators will have to formulate and time their questions so that they do not appear to be conducting an interrogation in which the mediator controls the process and, in fact, has all the answers. People on the receiving end of such conversations may feel manipulated and deceived during the process. The mediator using this structure will have to work hard to avoid sounding pedantic and condescending.

In the mediation of a personal injury lawsuit in which the defendant thinks the plaintiff's proposal is "ridiculous" and wants to send the mediator back to the plaintiff's room to get a "realistic" number, a conversation that is constructed using the principles of control theory may reveal the following information:

What do you want?

- I want to negotiate within the range I believe is appropriate.
- I want to save some money if it's possible.
- I want to send the message that the other side's proposal is too high.
- I want to signal that I'm still moving and still working.
- I want the other side to move to a range that I can negotiate in.

What are you doing to get it?

- I am refusing to give him another proposal until he "gets realistic."

Is that working?

- Yes, in the sense that I've communicated that he's not in the ballpark of settlement.
- But probably not, in the sense that he'll say I'm making him bid against himself and he won't give me a proposal in return.

If not, what else could you do?

- I could say that my last number is my best number.
- I could move a teensy bit to show how frustrated I am.
- I could shorten up on my increments.
- I could ignore his pitiful number and just move through my range in increments that I determine are appropriate.

The final phase of such a conversation would involve an evaluation of each of these options to determine which of them comes the closest to meeting the party's objectives.

We can assist the reactive party, then, by helping him regain a sense of his own power and control, helping him generate new options to further his goals, and helping him choose the option that advances his goal of a settlement within an acceptable range.

■ ■ ■ ■ ■

A conversation that is structured in this way will gradually focus the party on what he can do in the situation and away from what the opposition has done or should do. It focuses the party on his own goals and objectives and nudges him toward creating options to meet those goals. As a result of this process, the party regains a sense of control in the negotiation and takes action to make things happen.

I note here that the structure of this conversation bears a resemblance to two stages of the problem-solving model of the mediation process, the options-generation and evaluation stages. Parties in conflict lose a sense of control in the situation and get locked into one way of dealing with it. One of the benefits of the mediation process is that it helps the parties step back and invent new ways of looking at the problem and solving it. The problem-solving model of the mediation process does in a macro sense what control theory does in the moment. It focuses the party on his own goals and objectives and creates an environment in which he can invent, evaluate, and choose new options.

To make the principles I've discussed in the last two chapters more understandable, I present 25 situations in Chapter 6 that occur repetitively during the course of traditional bargaining that threaten the course of productive negotiations and present challenges and opportunities to discerning mediators.

These scenarios occur during the proposal-swapping stage of traditional bargaining and are examples of negotiators making outlandish proposals of their own in reaction to proposals they perceive as outlandish from the other side. In each, I describe the dynamics of the parties' interactions that give rise to the reaction. In many, I include a verbatim transcript of a possible mediator intervention to help the parties achieve a thoughtful rather than reactive state and make proposals that keep the negotiation moving.

Before proceeding to those scenarios, however, let us take a brief detour into the practicalities of making those interventions work. In Chapter 5, I review the tools that mediators may use in the context of traditional bargaining to bring about the thoughtful, rather than reactive, process I've been describing in the past two chapters.

Summary of Chapter 4:
A Guide to Facilitating Movement

The Problem: The parties react negatively to each other's proposals and stall or quit the negotiation before they reach their bottom lines. They do this by packing up, walking away, refusing to respond with a proposal, responding with low-ball or high-ball proposals, or putting the other side in the position of bidding against itself.

How to Overcome Negative Reactions to Proposals

- Understand the source of the parties' negative reactions.
- Communicate that understanding through summary and reframing statements.
- Help the parties construct thoughtful proposals by employing the insights of control theory:
  - Identify communication goals for the proposal.
  - Invent an array of proposals.
  - Evaluate and choose the proposal that sends a well-formed communication.
- Help the parties develop a plan for their negotiations.

Notes

1. WILLIAM GLASSER, CONTROL THEORY: A NEW EXPLANATION OF HOW WE CONTROL OUR LIVES (Harper & Row, 1985).

Tools of the Trade: The Skills of a Mediator

5

There are moments when I wonder how important the debate is in our profession about the proper way of framing and describing the mediation process. In those moments, I suspect that it would be more productive for us to devote our energies to developing benevolent and nonjudgmental attitudes and the practical skills to help us handle the many specific interactions that occur in mediation. The important subject of developing a nonjudgmental attitude will have to wait for another book and another author. My attention in this chapter is on the tools we use to facilitate settlement of disputes involving traditional bargaining.

Chapter Synopsis:
Tools Available to the Mediator

- Questions
- Summary Statements

- Brainstorming
- Observations and Suggestions

Frame Powerful Questions

I start my thinking about tools with a subject that is familiar to all of us but is somewhat underdeveloped in the literature of mediation—the use of questions. The use of questions is generally covered in basic mediation trainings in which students learn the advantages of asking open-ended, as opposed to leading, questions. My experience as a mediator confirms what I was taught in training—that questions are important and that open-ended questions are better than leading ones.

■ ■ ■ ■ ■

My experience also tells me that the most creative thing we do as mediators is to frame questions. We inspire and prompt people to give pause and thoughtful reflection to the realities of their case and their lives by the way we construct and deliver questions. As a result, they become open and receptive to new information and new perspectives.

There is some good news in that thought for lawyer-mediators. In our training as students and in our work as advocates and problem solvers, lawyers learn to ask good questions. Lawyers develop skills in the study and practice of law that are immediately transferable in a positive way to the mediation process.

Many of us, however, still have to work hard to make asking questions a routine part of our conversation. To illustrate this point in mediation training, I often invite my students to make a mental survey of the conversations they are a part of or listen to for one day. I ask them to become aware of the percentage of normal conversation that is comprised of interrogatory statements, questions. Typically they discover that few people make asking questions a habit in daily life.

After we have learned the utility of asking questions and have become good at framing open-ended inquiries, we learn some of the subtleties of their use. One of my early learnings about the use of questions is that they are often experienced as intrusive. This is particularly so when the mediator asks an endless stream of questions without summarizing or commenting on the clients' responses. I will be discussing summary statements in a moment, but suffice it to say that the coupling of summary statements with well-framed questions is an important strategy for mediators. Statements that summarize the speaker's communication transform an interrogation into a lively conversation.

Timing

Another early learning of mine about the use of questions is that the timing of questions can be very important. The use of questions in a general session in civil trial court mediation can be tricky. As a rule, questions should be used in general sessions only to discover general topics of common knowledge. Questions that go to the case analysis of the parties are best reserved for private sessions.

■■■■■

Since most civil trial court mediations involve private information about case analysis, the use of questions in a general session may be counterproductive. I have found that it is better to wait until private sessions to ask questions about case evaluation. And, in general sessions, it is better to ask questions about the topics I'm interested in after all the parties have had a chance to speak.

There are at least two reasons for doing so. The first is that, by delaying my questions, I can avoid stealing the thunder of one or more of the parties. Suppose, for example, I become interested about the issue of contributory negligence based upon the plaintiff's initial presentation in general session. If I ask a number of questions of the plaintiff at the end of his presentation, I run the risk of stepping on the

> presentation of the defense about that same issue. Inadvertently, I may diminish the impact of the defendant's presentation and create a situation in which the "airtime" of the parties is out of balance. The second reason I delay asking my questions is that I have fewer questions to ask if I postpone asking them. In most instances, my questions are answered by the presentations of the other parties.

Delaying Questions to Avoid Taking Control

Questions about case analysis come easily for lawyer-mediators, because we are used to such discussions as litigators. We do case analysis all the time with partners, clients, and other lawyers in the community. A couple of things about the use of questions during private sessions, however, are worth mentioning to those who would transition from advocacy to facilitation as mediators.

Beginning mediators often feel responsible for settling the cases they mediate. As a consequence, they often take charge and direct conversations in private sessions. Beginning mediators usually develop an agenda of topics they want to discuss with the parties. They have a lot of information gaps to fill, so they act to satisfy their own needs for clarity and information.

> ■■■■■
>
> The problem with having an agenda of issues to talk about in private sessions is that it encourages mediators to take charge and move in directions the parties have no need to travel. We are not necessarily meeting the needs of the parties when we forge ahead with our own questions about the case. In my own development as a mediator, I have tried to check this tendency to direct discussion by formulating questions that are designed to place the "conversational ball" in the parties' court.

When I go to the plaintiff's room for a first private session, for instance, the conversation might sound like this:

M: Well, John, what would you like for me to know that you didn't feel comfortable talking about in general session?

P: Andy, there's not a thing we have that they don't know about. But I just don't think they've got a chance of making that contributory negligence argument stick. This was a rear end collision, you know.

There were a lot of things that I wanted to talk about with Jimmy Young and his lawyer in "The Rear Ender," but I let those go in favor of discussing the issues with which they were concerned. Young and his lawyer wanted to talk about the issue of contributory negligence raised in general session by the defense and to tell me how absurd that notion was to them. After hearing the statement of the plaintiff's lawyer, I dropped what I wanted to talk about and went with the issue of contributory negligence. After we discussed that subject, I followed up with a question like this:

M: John, what do you think the defendant needs to worry about the most in this case?

Again, I'm trying to bounce the conversational ball back to the participants and find out what they think is most important about the case. This type of question has several benefits. It keeps the focus of the conversation on what they think is most important and thereby keeps my tendency to control the agenda at bay. It also has the benefit of arming me with information that will be useful in formulating questions in the defendant's room. The plaintiff is going to tell me the weaknesses of the defendant's case by talking about his own strengths, and vice versa.

I also use what I call a "throwaway question" to start private sessions, particularly in the first private session. As I enter the plaintiff's room for a first private session, for example, I might say:

M: Well, John, are we going to get this case settled?

What kind of question is that? It's a throwaway. It's designed to take me out of the lead and put the conversational ball in the plaintiff's team's court. Most of the time, I'll hear something like:

P: Well, Andy, I hope we're not wasting your time here today. I'm not sure this thing's got any chance of settling. The defendant has been acting like this is a soft tissue case when we have a case of documented surgery.

M: They're not taking it seriously, huh? [That's right.] What have they told you about the surgery? Are they claiming that it was unnecessary or not caused by the collision? What's their story on that?

■■■■■

I have found that my early sessions with the parties go much better if I give them a chance to take the lead. Mediators with an inclination to favor closure and completeness over open-endedness will have to train themselves to give up control of the agenda in these private conversations. As a trade-off, however, we can take comfort in the reality that we will get positive results by giving the parties more control over the conversational process and that we can always return to the questions we have at a later time in the mediation.

The use of questions is extremely important when the conversation is about case analysis. I use questions to bring to a conscious level the factors that make up and can change case value. During the proposal-swapping stages of traditional bargaining, however, I also use questions to focus the party's attention away from how bad the other side's proposals are and toward a consideration of what the party himself can do to further the negotiation. In Chapter 6, the reader will find examples of questions I use during that stage.

■■■■■

Case Analysis Questions. The importance of questions may be demonstrated at any point in the discussion where case analysis is the subject. The goal in asking case analysis questions is to provide an opportunity for the parties to clarify their own thinking about an issue or to consider new information or perspectives on an issue.

Consider the example of a personal injury case in which the plaintiff exited a parking lot and started to cross two travel lanes of a four-lane road to get into the two travel lanes moving to her left. She was struck by the defendant who was crossing from the opposite side of the highway to get into the two travel lanes moving to his left. They hit head on just before the plaintiff entered the center turn lane. She alleged that the defendant was speeding and not keeping a proper lookout. The defendant's lawyer said that she had more time than the defendant to see the potential for disaster and was, therefore, either solely negligent or contributorily negligent and should recover nothing. In private session, the plaintiff appeared unwilling to consider this as a factor in reducing the amount of her demand. I asked her lawyer the following question:

M: David, if you were writing the script for this trial, where would you like to place the point of impact? Here [pointing to the actual point of impact on the accident report]? Or, here [pointing to a point past the center lane and into her intended lane of travel]?

L: Oh, I'd much rather have the point of impact closer to the defendant's original side of the road, so that he couldn't argue we had the better chance to avoid the collision.

That exchange prompted a discussion between the plaintiff and her lawyer about how a trial involving a claim of negligence unfolds and what kind of evidence it takes to prove the case. It also provided an opportunity for them to discuss how evidentiary problems in the case might lead the plaintiff to consider taking less in settlement than the amount considered previously.

Consider the example of a personal injury case in which the defendant's lawyer can't or won't articulate the weakness of his case for a defendant who will be exposed to a jury verdict greater than his insurance coverage if the case goes to trial. In private session with the defendant's team, I asked the lawyer and the claims representative to hypothetically place themselves in time immediately after the jury renders a verdict against the defendant. I then asked the following question:

M: Joe, I know that you don't think this is possible, but suppose they render a verdict against you after a well-tried case. You ask each of the 12 jurors why they voted against your client and each of them gives you a different answer. What reasons might each of them have, one by one?

This type of question is designed to provide cover for a lawyer who has been unable to share bad news with his client. In this format, he is able to distance himself from his own evaluation of the case. In answering, he tells us what each juror might have thought about the case; thus, he can talk about his evaluation as if it were not his own. It is important to create this emotional distance for the lawyer, because it often prompts a lawyer to talk about subjects that are unpleasant to talk about—such as, that the jury might not like the client for one of a variety of reasons.

One way to ask a case analysis question is to fold into it an idea the opposing side has identified as a strength of their case or a weakness of the team I'm working with. A question like that might go as follows:

> M: Joe, opposing counsel seems to think that you're going to have a tough time with your loss of wages claim, because certain types of income didn't show up on your tax returns. Have you and opposing counsel had a chance to talk about that aspect of their claim?

■■■■■

These questions are nominally addressed to the lawyers in the room. However, they are framed in such a way as to stimulate discussion between the lawyers and their clients in the hope that litigants will better understand the strengths and weaknesses of their case and make more informed, and more realistic, decisions.

I am greatly indebted to Marc Victor in my thinking about the framing of questions to help lawyers with their own case analysis. The example of the mediator asking the lawyer to give the jurors' perspective is a specific creation of his that I have used in hundreds of cases.

The implementation of a weighted probability analysis, which is at the heart of Litigation Risk Analysis™, is not a mechanical process. It involves articulating the probability of a host of things happening throughout the course of litigation that lawyers have identified as key points or nodes in the case. The assessment of probabilities by lawyers who are invested in one side or another is greatly enhanced by the use of both visual and verbal devices. Verbal devices, like the questions set out above, give those lawyers emotional distance from their investment in the case and make their assessments of probability more objective.

I am also indebted to those who work and train in the area of neuro-linguistic programming in my thinking about how to frame questions. In particular, the use of presuppositions in the framing of questions has been helpful to me as a way to add power to the already-potent tool of asking questions. I will define the term "presupposition" and have more to say about its use later in this chapter when I discuss reframing and making suggestions.

Use Summary Statements

Mediators who work in the civil trial court arena have to listen no less, and no less well, than mediators in other contexts. So, the skills of active listening should occupy a prominent place in the mediator's toolbox. The part of active listening I want to concentrate on here is the restatement of the speaker's communication by the mediator.

Commentators on the art of active listening generally concentrate on the verbal aspect that is known as the "reflective response," which was developed as a therapeutic technique by the psychologist Carl Rogers. The reflective response is a verbal summation of the emotional content of the disputant's communication made by the mediator for a number of reasons, but primarily to check out whether the mediator has heard the disputant correctly.

It has been my observation, however, that there is in the speech of disputants far more cognitive than emotional content. And, it has been my discovery that one can summarize the cognitive content of the disputant's communication and achieve many of the benefits achieved by the use of the reflective response. People want others to understand their message, whatever form it takes. Therefore, I make extensive use of summary statements to reflect both the cognitive and emotional content of the speaker's communication. They are effective and powerful tools to facilitate understanding and communication.

■■■■■

Summary statements produce benefits for the participants in civil trial court mediation. Summary statements:

- give the mediator a chance to get the message right.
- give the disputant a chance to correct the message.
- give the other disputant a chance to absorb the message.
- demonstrate that the mediator has understood the speaker.
- build rapport between the mediator and the disputant.
- keep the conversation from becoming an inquisition.
- handle effectively interruptions by the participants.

I recommend the use of summary statements throughout mediations conducted in the civil trial court context. For lawyers, the use of summaries may not come as naturally or easily as the use of questions. Framing summary statements takes concentration and attention as well as creativity. In addition, it is sometimes difficult to formulate and use a summary statement so that it does not sound trite, canned, or condescending. For that reason I seldom start off a summary with the familiar phrase, "So, I hear you saying . . . ." Some of the phrases I use to begin summary statements in civil case mediations include:

- So, you want them to know that contributory negligence isn't a risk in your view?
- So, what I need to convey to them is your sense that . . . ?
- So, the most important factor in your damage estimate is . . . ?
- So, you're thinking the jury verdict range in this case is . . . ?

You can drop the "So," in these formulations if it doesn't fit you. I use it because it helps me slow down and concentrate on capturing the important elements of the communication. What works for me may not work for someone else. Each mediator has to find ways to formulate summary statements that feel natural to him or her and that accurately summarize the speaker's communication. Examples of summary statements can be found in the transcripts in Chapter 6.

Use Reframing Summaries

■■■■■

A reframing of something is a reconstruction of it. When one reframes something, he gives that something a new shape, a new sound, or a new feel, thereby changing its purpose, understanding, or impact.

Mediation is often helpful because it reframes the process of negotiation from traditional or position-based bargaining to joint problem solving. Mediators are reframers of the negotiation process. That's a statement about process.

On the level of skills and techniques, mediators can add to their toolbox the device also known as reframing, or as I call it, a reframing statement. A reframing statement is a specialized form of a summary statement. It is a summary of the disputant's statement in which its content is recast in such a way as to give it a new meaning. The purposes of a reframing statement are at least twofold.

The first purpose is to achieve a greater level of understanding of the speaker's message. In this sense, it is used like any other summary statement. An example is a summary statement that eliminates demeaning, derogatory, or insulting language from a disputant's statement. The mediator summarizes the content so that its message is not lost in the negative language in which it was conveyed by the disputant.

The second purpose is a bit more suggestive. A reframing statement can also be a summary that directs the disputant's attention to how his content fits into a larger or different context. In a custody dispute, for instance, the mediator may summarize information about the details of the child's or family's life and, in so doing, link those details to the best interests of the child or the needs and interests of the parties.

I use reframing statements in both senses. When a disputant in a civil case mediation talks about the other party and, in doing so, calls the other insulting names, I summarize the speaker's information, feelings, or concerns without using derogatory language. I also use reframing statements in the second sense when I am working with the parties during the proposal-swapping stage of the mediation of a personal injury case. Let me give you an example of the latter from the mediator's second private session with the plaintiff:

> M: Well, John, their next move matched their last. They moved to $51,000.
>
> P: I can't believe it. What are they thinking!? This case is worth at least $90,000. There's no way I'll take $51,000. Tell them that I can't and won't accept it. There's no way I'm going to $51,000.
>
> M: $51,000 isn't a number that will work for you and isn't in the range you can settle the case in?
>
> P: Hell, no! I can't figure why he'd have the nerve to send over a number like that. That's insulting and it's a waste of time. I can't take $51,000!
>
> M: So you can't come close to their number? This isn't in the kind of range you were trying to communicate to him?
>
> P: Not at all. He's just not getting it.
>
> M: So, what kind of number could you give the defendant in return that would continue to communicate the range of settlement you think is appropriate?

The mediator's summary accurately captured the lawyer's decision that he would not settle the case for $51,000. As the exchange moved along and the lawyer continued to dwell on how inadequate the defendant's offer was, the mediator began to frame his summary in terms that suggested the language of communication. By the end of the exchange, the mediator framed his summary not in terms of the defendant's proposal but in terms of something over which the plaintiff had control, the plaintiff's range of settlement. The mediator's summary, and eventually his question to the plaintiff, was framed to lead the plaintiff to consider what he and his lawyer would do next.

> **■■■■■**
>
> Summaries and questions that are framed in the language of communication can lead a party to abandon conversation about how badly the other side is acting and to think, instead, of a proposal that will accomplish his objective of settling the case within an appropriate range.

Without such an intervention, the party may, and often does, become stuck in an endless diatribe about the other party's behavior. While this type of response from the mediator has the effect of leading the party into a different avenue of conversation, and is therefore suggestive, it does not force him to make a particular proposal. In fact, a reframing response typically stimulates discussion about the many choices the party has and, thus, increases his range of options.

Generate Options through Brainstorming

Much of the work I do in the civil trial court context helps the parties navigate the difficult, proposal-swapping stage of traditional bargaining (the "used-car sale stage" of the mediation process). The parties usually have difficulty achieving their objective of settling their case in this stage, because they choose to make proposals that discourage movement from the other side. My aim at that point in the process is to help them create new options that will encourage the other side to move and create a real chance to settle the case.

To help them create new options, I usually fall back on the time-honored technique of brainstorming. Brainstorming is one of the basic techniques taught in Mediation Training 101. It is a conversation in which the participants think up, invent, and create new options to solve a problem. The important limitation on that activity—and the one that makes it "brainstorming" as opposed to mere conversation—is that the participants may not critique the options they create during the conversation.

■ ■ ■ ■ ■

Critiquing usually turns a conversation about new ideas into one about evaluation and, as a result, shuts down creative processes. Most people don't invent very well when they are also evaluating. In addition, critiquing in a group setting tends to shut off the participation of the person being critiqued. Most people don't continue to invent ideas when they are being told that their ideas aren't workable. So, the important limitation to remember about brainstorming is that inventing is OK and critiquing is not.

When a participant or team of participants reacts to another side's proposal with anger, frustration, or resignation, I often slip into a brainstorming conversation with them. My aim in starting the conversation is to increase their range of options so that they are not stuck with the one they came up with while in a reactive state. The structure of that conversation is the structure of brainstorming:

- Refrain from critiquing their initial proposal or chastising them for making it.
- Identify the initial proposal as "an option" or possibility, thus implying that their initial option is a choice and that there are other options to be considered.
- Ask for other things the party can say or do and identify the idea as "a possibility."
- Continue to ask for other possibilities.

■ ■ ■ ■ ■

Eventually, of course, the conversation will turn to the important subject of evaluating options generated through the brainstorming process. A critique of these new options for movement will involve a discussion of the advantages and disadvantages of each option in accomplishing the objective of the negotiator at that stage of the process. I often begin such a critique with a question that is framed in terms of the language of communication.

M: Which of these possibilities helps you convey the messages you're trying to send?

or

M: What proposal can you make now that will keep the process going and continue to educate the other side about the proper range of settlement?

That kind of question often leads to a discussion about the nature of the negotiation process itself and the way in which proposals can be understood as communication devices and the flow of proposals as an educational process. The idea that negotiation can be an educational process is often new and intriguing to both experienced and inexperienced negotiators.

When brainstorming occurs in the context of a private session in which there are one or two participants, it does not look or sound like brainstorming in the context of group facilitation. It is more conversational in tone. I generally don't have a conversation about rules; I don't usually get out a flip chart (although I have used a chart with great effectiveness); and I don't strictly enforce the rule against critiquing. I convert the rules of brainstorming into the structure of our conversation and formulate my questions with that structure in mind. There is an example of such a conversation in Chapter 6, Scenario #4.a.

Make Observations and Suggestions about the Negotiation Process

A reality of civil trial court mediation is that the parties get stuck on one way of behaving during the proposal-swapping stage of traditional bargaining and they can't think of other ways of responding.

The parties become so paralyzed by their frustration with the other side that they don't have an idea of how they can go forward other than the way they initially reacted—by low- or high-balling, walking out, or making the other negotiator bid against himself.

In that case, I may offer an observation about the progress of the negotiation as a way of opening a discussion about the choices they have; or I may offer a suggestion about how they can respond as a way of putting options on the table when they can't think of other proposals to make.

■■■■■

The first type of suggestion is often not recognized by the participants as a suggestion. It is a suggestion that is inherent in the choice of words I make in either a summary statement or a question. If the suggestion is contained in a summary statement, it is a reframing statement, which I wrote about earlier. If the suggestion is made in the choice of words for a question, the suggestion is often called a presupposition.

Let me give you an example of the former. In Scenario #4.g., Chapter 6, I am working with a defendant's claims representative who is irate about the plaintiff's proposal and says:

D: My suggestion is that you go back in there and tell him I'm disgusted or angry—whichever you think is best— but I'm packing my bags here. After that, if they don't give us something that justifies our attention, then we're gone.

M: So, the first option that comes to your mind to deal with the situation is to . . .

D: Is to leave.

■■■■■

The summary statement that the mediator makes is framed in such a way that it presupposes a fact to be true and thereby suggests a certain course of action. In this example the fact presupposed is that there is more than one option to consider. The suggestion implied by the presupposition is that we will talk about more than one option. If direct questions about additional options do not stimulate parties to think of new options, reframing statements can subtly lead clients to topics they might not think of on their own.

An example of a question that contains a presupposition is found in a private session with the plaintiff when the mediator asks:

M: What result do you want to achieve with this number?

The presupposition in this question is that the party is trying to accomplish something with the formulation of his proposal. To deal with the question on its own terms, the client must now talk about his intentions for the proposal. He will have to talk about what he is trying to accomplish with his proposal and that is a subject he may never have considered.

■■■■■

This subtly introduces a new topic. Many negotiators have thought they were not doing anything in their bargaining other than trying to get the top dollar. They have always thought they were "just swapping numbers" and have not given thought to the communication that goes on within that process. Negotiators have even said to me outright, "What do you mean 'accomplish'?" That kind of response opens the door for me to make an observation about negotiations in general, or that negotiation in particular, and to suggest options for the client to consider.

As the transcripts contained in Chapter 6 reveal, I make an abundance of observations and suggestions during the proposal swapping that occurs in traditional bargaining. An example occurs again in Scenario #4.b.

P: Oh, I think if we got to that number, we could settle the case. But they're not showing us they have that in mind. They're showing us they're headed to 25 or 30.

M: That's always the problem—where are they headed? . . . Now, I would make this observation, and that is that they're $105,000 away from $125,000 and you're $100,000 away at $225,000. If you look at it that way, they may be signaling something entirely different from what you're picking up. They may be saying they could go to the middle. I don't know. [OK.] Do you and your lawyer want to talk in private about where you are and where you'd like to be at the end of the day and what you might do next?

■ ■ ■ ■ ■

The mediator's observation about the defendant's movement suggests a different meaning than the plaintiff had come up with on his own. It serves as a suggestion that he pay attention to the movement of positions over time, that he concentrate on where the positions will be at the end of the day, and that he think about whether one's movement can be a predictor of that party's final range or number. In many of the observations I make and questions I ask, I am trying to suggest to the parties that they concentrate on the number they want at the end of the negotiation in order to lead them to consider a plan for their movement for the remainder of the negotiation.

Another example of making an observation occurs in Scenario #23.

M: Well, my observation is that it's been harder and harder for you to make new moves as we've gone along. [Yeah.] And we're still a long way apart. And I'm assuming that where they are with their numbers is affecting your thinking about what you should do? [Yeah.] And I'm also assuming that because they're so high in your estimation it's keeping you from doing what you could do to settle the case?

D: Well, I think that's fair to say.

> ■ ■ ■ ■ ■
>
> In making observations, I convey something I've learned about the problems of traditional bargaining. Often, the net result of that communication is to suggest that they think about those problems too. Of course, if they don't want to talk about those subjects, then I don't force them to. However, my experience is that most people are fascinated by the subject of movement, once they've been introduced to how it can be perceived as a form of communication, and that they are pleased to have new options to think about.

An example of a suggestion also occurs in Scenario #24. In that example I outline a plan for negotiating the remainder of the case. The suggestion was made at the request of the client for help in figuring out what to do next and my suggestion was something the client hadn't thought of. My aim in making suggestions is to expand the range of options for the client's consideration while leaving the client free to accept or reject the suggestion. An example of the client rejecting a suggestion occurs in Scenario #6 in Chapter 6.

Some time ago, I was conducting a mediation in a medical malpractice case in which the plaintiff made a first offer of $875,000. Before the mediation session, the defense lawyer moved the court to dispense with mediation, thinking that there was no way the case would settle. The judge denied his motion, so we scheduled the conference. The lawyer's pessimism about settlement increased after hearing the plaintiff's first proposal. He and I had the following conversation in my first private session with the defense team:

> D: Andy, as you probably know, this is a physician approval policy, and we can't even make an offer unless he's agreed to it, and as of now, he hasn't authorized us to pay one cent on this claim. (The doctor was present and listening to this conversation.)
>
> M: So, you haven't decided that you're going to make any offers today at all?

D: That's right. Now we're here in good faith to do whatever we can do today and we haven't decided not to pay any money—but we've not heard a number until now and that number won't work at all.

M: They're way out of the ballpark with that number?

D: It's not so much that it's out of the ballpark; it's just not the kind of number we'd ever consider. I mean, Dr. Jones feels strongly about this case and doesn't believe that he ought to even be here. [Dr. Jones talks here about the facts of the case as he sees them and the things he will say at trial that contradict the plaintiff's version of the facts. Then the defense lawyer comes back into the conversation.] So, you can tell there are some strong feelings on this side of the table and we're never going to pay the kind of money they're talking about.

M: I certainly hear the determination you have about the facts and the outcome of the case. [Uh-huh.] I also hear that paying a small amount of money to get rid of this case is not outside the realm of possibility.

D: You see, I can't even talk to Dr. Jones about that kind of money. Now don't get me wrong, we're here to listen and work and do something if it's possible, but I can't even talk with Dr. Jones about that number. Listen, if we had a number that represented what we'd lose as a result of preparing and trying this case, then I'd have to sit down with Dr. Jones and talk about the costs of trial and about how taking two or three weeks out of his practice would translate into a lot of money. But I can't even talk to him at that figure.

M: So, where they are now is keeping you from having a conversation that you could have under other circumstances?

D: Sure. I can't even talk with him at that figure!

M: Well, that leaves us with quite a conundrum then. I mean, we're trying to negotiate this thing with one arm tied behind our backs.

D: Yeah, you're right. It's a difficult situation, but I can't even have a conversation with him unless they would be down in a range in which it would make sense for us to at least consider a settlement based on costs.

M: [long pause] Well, I can see several ways you could have that conversation and . . .

D: What do you mean?

M: Well, one way would be to have a heart-to-heart talk right now about what kind of money you think he should be concerned about if the plaintiff offered it. And then you automatically have a negotiating range for today.

D: Uh-huh.

M: I mean, suppose you decided that it would cost you $30,000 to try this case—and that doesn't even take into account the doctor's losses from closing up his practice for several weeks—then you would have a negotiating range of $0 to $30,000 to work with it. That's at least theoretically a possibility?

D: Well, yeah . . . .

M: And then you could work within that range and see if the plaintiff is willing to see it your way and get the message that you don't have much money to work with. [Gesturing to signal, "That's one idea."] And they won't have to bid against themselves. I'm just trying to open up the possibilities . . . .

D: Yeah. I see your point. Yeah, maybe . . . . [At that point the claims representative, who was attending the conference by speakerphone, said to me, "Andy, let us have a few minutes together."]

The defense team talked together for a while without me and then called me back into the room. Here's what the lawyer and I said.

D: Andy, what we'd like for you to do, and I want you to get the wording of this just right, is tell them that if they will come to $200,000, we'll make an offer of $50,000. It's very important that you get that right. We're not making an offer, but we will go to $50,000, if they get to $200,000.

M: So, you're trying to communicate that the negotiating range for you in this case is between $50,000 and $200,000? [Yes.] And that if, in their heart of hearts, they can't get between those numbers to settle the case,

> there's not much reason to talk any more, because this case won't settle for you above $200,000?

D: Right, you've got it. Thanks.

I proceeded to the plaintiff's room and delivered the proposal. We had already discussed the case in some detail, but the proposal produced another round of conversation about the merits of the case. At the conclusion of that session, the plaintiff's lawyer gave me the following proposal.

P: Our next number is $825,000 which is $50,000 down from where we were; that matches their movement of $50,000. In addition, we need to tell you that we can't get to $200,000, ever. That's not really even close to something we'd consider.

As you might predict, this settlement conference was terminated shortly thereafter with the plan that I would report an impasse to the court. Was this conference a success? In my opinion it was. The parties were able to communicate enough about their ranges of settlement that they were confident the case would not settle. They didn't just guess at that conclusion or stop negotiating because they were frustrated with the movement of the other. They actually communicated enough information about what numbers would not settle the case to lead them to a reasonable conclusion that the case would not settle.

I tell this story to demonstrate how a mediator can use observations and suggestions to good advantage—and to suggest that the key to making observations and suggestions is the attitude with which the mediator conveys them. Much of my tone and demeanor in this scenario is lost in print. However, it was clear to the parties that I was only making a suggestion for their consideration and that they were free to accept or reject it—or not even talk about it at all. What is especially interesting to me about this example is that the defense came back with a proposal that I had not thought of or suggested. They clearly were free to accept or reject my suggestion and, in fact, they didn't adopt mine as their own.

I should quickly add here that the use of suggestions can be overdone. If the mediator makes suggestions to the parties on every round of the negotiation, he will leave the impression that he believes he is the only one in the room who knows how to negotiate. To experienced negotiators, the overuse of suggestions is unwelcome and, even, obnoxious.

■■■■■

The subject of whether or not the mediator should make observations or offer suggestions is a topic of great debate among mediators around the country. I, for one, believe that mediators serve a useful and proper function by offering suggestions as long as two conditions are present. The first is that the parties have been given a chance to invent options and have run out of them or cannot come up with any on their own. The second condition is that the mediator offers the option, not as the one that the mediator thinks is the best, but as one more option for the parties to consider and evaluate. In other words, the mediator should not try to sell the parties on the option suggested.

When these conditions are met, is the mediator being directive by offering a suggestion? To some degree, yes, at least in the sense that a workable suggestion will have its own probative weight and will draw or direct the parties to it. But, I submit, this is a type of influence that is driven more by the suitability of the option for the parties than by the mediator's efforts to sell it.

Should the mediator make suggestions for the parties to consider? I think so. The mediator, after all, may have the clearest head of all the participants in the settlement conference and may come up with creative options that the parties are unable to invent because they are enmeshed in the controversy. I contend that making suggestions for the parties to consider and giving opinions, whether solicited or not, are two entirely different animals. As to the latter, I will have more to say in the final chapter.

Although making observations and offering suggestions are risky interventions for mediators to undertake, I undertake them nevertheless, because my clients generally benefit from them. I readily admit to the risks inherent in making such interventions and work hard to guard against directing the outcome of the negotiation and the process by which that outcome is achieved.

Summary of Chapter 5:
Tools Available to the Mediator

The tools available to the mediator to facilitate the settlement of civil litigation are familiar to most mediators. They include the use of the following:

- Open-ended questions, throwaway questions, and questions containing presuppositions.
- Summary statements, including the more specialized forms known as reflective responses and reframing.
- Brainstorming to aid in the development of new ideas.
- Observations about the negotiation process to open up new possibilities for understanding and movement.
- Suggestions for movement when the parties cannot create them on their own.

Responding to Recurring Problems of Movement in Traditional Bargaining: 25 Settlement Conference Clichés

6

The problems of movement I've discussed in the preceding chapters play out in court-ordered mediations throughout this country on a daily basis. This chapter identifies the many recurring situations that mediators encounter as the parties attempt to settle their cases through traditional bargaining. These are the "settlement conference clichés" of civil trial court mediation.

Each scenario identified in this chapter is an example of the many ways negotiators impede negotiations by formulating proposals in reaction to proposals they don't like. I begin each with a description and explanation, as it is important to recognize when and how the situation arises during the course of the mediation.

Many of the descriptions are followed by a hypothetical conversation between a mediator and negotiator, demonstrating how the mediator might handle the problem presented using the principles outlined in Chapters 3 and 4 and the tools discussed in Chapter 5. While most are not verbatim transcripts from actual cases, they are illustrative of the conversations I have with lawyers, litigants, and claims representatives every day of my workweek. Some of the facts in those transcripts refer to the case of "The Rear Ender," but most do not.

Scenario #1: Who Goes First? (Plaintiff)

"Who goes first?" stands for the reluctance of the claimant to make a first proposal. Based on that reluctance, the claimant declines to make a proposal and insists that the other party "go first." In this scenario, the mediator is asked by the plaintiff to get a proposal from the defense so that the claimant can react to it.

Why does this happen? The claimant knows from experience that any proposal made, any number thrown out as a first proposal, sets the upper parameter for the negotiation. In our culture, a negotiator can't go higher than a proposal he's previously made (at least not without good reason) without receiving a hostile reaction from the other side. Once a negotiator has given a number, he or she can't back up. This makes the announcement of an opening proposal an important event in the negotiation process.

∎∎∎∎∎

If negotiators have miscalculated either the value of the case or the other party's best number, and they make an opening proposal based on that miscalculation, they might sell themselves too short. In that event, they run the risk of leaving money on the table or paying too much for the claim. So, the one who goes first stakes himself out. That's true in our culture for both the claimant and the defense. As a consequence, negotiators may be reluctant to go first. They don't want to make the mistake of selling their claims short.

Here's an example of a "Who Goes First?" interaction during the mediation of Jimmy Young's case. To set the stage for you, let me explain that a general session has been held with the parties and their lawyers. Both parties explained their positions and asked a number of exploratory questions of each other.

The mediator is now engaged in a private session with Jimmy Young and his lawyer. The mediator, Young, and his lawyer have had a detailed discussion about the claimant's view of the case. In fact, the mediator now knows in a general way what Young's lawyer thinks the top and bottom ranges of a jury verdict in this case might be if the case were tried to a jury. Let's listen in:

Transcript

M: Well, Mr. Smith, are you and Mr. Young ready to make a proposal to open up the negotiations in this case? **[Question]**

P: I think we know what we'd like to get out of the case, but I don't think we're ready to make a proposal. We'd like to hear from them first. They haven't offered a dime in this case.

M: So, you're not sure it's in your best interest to start the negotiation? **[Summary]**

P: That's right. We sent the adjuster a settlement brochure a long time ago. It covered all the medical expenses and records, and we haven't heard a thing from them. We don't know whether they're interested in settling this case or not. We'd like to know whether they're going to make an offer.

M: I hear that you want them to give the first proposal today. [Pause] Tell me more about your reluctance to go first. **[Summary/Question]**

P: They haven't responded to a thing we've sent to them. I don't plan to bid against myself.

M: I understand not wanting to bid against yourself. **[Summary]** In every case, the one who goes first, whether it's the plaintiff or defendant, has some of that feeling. I would imagine that Walker will say the same thing if I go to him for the first proposal. **[Observation]**

P: Well, I don't know about that. All I know is that they haven't offered a dime yet.

M: Mr. Smith, I don't know whether the defense will offer any money today or not. I certainly didn't hear anything in the general session that sounded like they wouldn't. **[Observation]** So let me cover a couple of things with you before you make up you mind about this. The first is that I may also encounter reluctance on Walker's part to go first himself, and for the same reasons you've outlined. In addition, the normal way of proceeding, not the only way but the usual way, as you're aware, is for the party who has the burden of proof to make the first proposal. **[Observation]** What do you think the reaction will be in the other room to the notion that they go first? **[Question]**

P: I don't know, and I'm not sure that I really care. All these insurance companies act alike. They just try to stonewall deserving plaintiffs like Jimmy Young here and sit on their hands. I get tired of it.

M: Tired of them not taking more initiative? **[Reflective Response]**

P: Yeah, and I think it's time that some of us stood up to them.

M: Before you give me your final decision on this, are there other ways you could approach this dilemma? Do you have any other choices available to you? **[Question/ Brainstorming]**

P: Like what?

M: Like giving them the highest number you think a jury would return without any discounts for potential problems with liability or damages. Something like a home run number for you. **[Suggestion]**

P: That doesn't deal with them stonewalling us and not dealing with us up front.

M: It doesn't, you're right, at least not directly. But it does have a couple of advantages. It's a safe number, one that you could readily accept if they agreed to it. And given what you've told me about your range of settlement so far, you still have plenty of room to move. And, finally, it keeps us from spending a whole lot of time and energy on the problem of who goes first, which of course I'm prepared to do if that's your choice. [**Observation/Evaluation**]

P: Yeah, all those things are true—why don't you give us a few minutes to think about it.

Comment: I leave it to the reader's imagination as to the plaintiff's decision about making the first proposal. It's gone both ways in my experience. All I can ask for is that the parties work with me to create or consider some other ways of handling the situation and think about the pros and cons of each. In the scenario that follows, you should assume that the plaintiff has made the decision not to make the first proposal in the negotiation.

Scenario #2: Who Goes First? (Defense)— "I'm Not Going to Bid Against Myself"

This scenario takes place in the defense's room after Young's team insisted that the mediator get the first number of the day from the defense.

■■■■■

I should mention here that I frequently go to a private session with the defense without having a proposal from the claimant, but I do so because the plaintiff's team isn't ready to give a proposal and needs time to rethink their case or develop their first proposal. If so, I give them time to reflect and use my time in the other party's room to explore his or her thinking about the case. I try not to force the generation of proposals. I'm looking for proposals that are thoughtful ones, based on the needs of the parties, their goals and objectives, and their honest assessment of the evidence in the case.

In this scenario, the plaintiff and his lawyer have thought through the case with me, and are capable of making a proposal. However, they don't want to make a proposal because they don't want to be staked out. If the plaintiff persists in that desire after we've discussed his options, then I will proceed to the defense's room knowing that they will react negatively to the news I am bringing them.

Transcript

M: Gentlemen, I'm assuming you wanted to talk about some things in private. What have you been thinking about? **[Question]**

D: Andy, there are several things we're concerned about, but we would like to know where the plaintiff is right now. Have you got a number for us?

M: No, I don't. We talked a lot about the case and how they evaluate it, but when it was all said and done, they told me they wanted to hear from you first. They told me they hadn't heard anything since this case was filed.

D: Well, that's true. We haven't given them a number because they've never made a demand.

M: Did they send something with their settlement materials? I know that sometimes they at least state a value in the accompanying letter. **[Question]**

D: No, nothing. We haven't heard a word. And I don't have any intention of going first today. We're not going to bid against ourselves.

M: Doesn't seem appropriate to you? **[Summary]**

D: No. And he knows better than to ask us to give the first number today. What's his problem?

M: Probably the same as for you. He doesn't want to get staked out with his first number. For whatever reason he's stuck on getting something from you first. I know how your side operates and we certainly had some conversation about that, but in the end he decided to do it this way. **[Observation]** [Pause] What would you like to do? **[Question]**

D: That doesn't take long to answer. Tell him we just don't give the first number. He's the plaintiff and has the burden of proof. Tell him to go first.

M: Well, I certainly understand the drill in these things, Bill. **[Summary]** And if you decide that's what you want to do then I'll go back with that and see if we can move this negotiation off dead center. [Pause] I know all the reasons why you don't want to give them a number first—all the negative things the defense believes would happen—but would you mind giving some thought to why it might make good sense for your team to make the first proposal? **[Question]**

D: What do you mean? I don't think I've ever made the first proposal.

M: Well, are there any positive things that could happen if you made the first proposal? **[Question/Brainstorming]**

D: I don't think so. What do you have in mind?

M: Well, as you might imagine, I've had this situation occur more than once in my career. When I've thought it through with other folks, occasionally someone has decided to go first because they think that it will save time, number 1, and number 2, it will give the negotiation a more realistic start, and number 3, it might influence the plaintiff to give a more realistic first number. **[Observation/Suggestion]**

D: You mean, not go through the time and effort at the beginning dealing with a totally unrealistic range?

M: Yes, and letting the educational effect of your numbers start a little earlier. **[Observation/Reframe]**

D: What do you mean by educational effect?

■■■■■

M: Well, my view of what negotiators do with their numbers is to tell the other side where they need to be in order to get the case settled. So, with your proposals, over time, you are educating the plaintiff about where he has to be to get the case settled. If you start that effect with the first number, it sometimes has a beneficial effect on the plaintiff's first number. **[Observation]**

D: [Pause] Well, I've never thought about it that way. Why don't you let us have a few moments together.

M: Sure. And I hope you understand that I know there's no right or wrong way to do this. It's your decision entirely, a judgment call. I'm willing to spend as much time on who goes first as it takes to do this right. Thanks. [Mediator leaves, so that the defense team can talk privately about their decision.] **[Observation/Reframe]**

Scenario #3: Claimant's First Proposal Is Higher Than His Case Analysis

■■■■■

This scenario occurs at the beginning of the proposal-swapping stage of traditional bargaining. It was the first of the "clichés" I encountered in my career as a civil trial court mediator, and it alerted me to my need for additional understanding about the dynamics of money negotiations and for additional techniques to deal with them.

This interaction assumes that the claimant and I have had a thorough discussion about the merits of his claim and he is ready to make a proposal. To my surprise, the proposal is higher than the best number he will get from a jury after a full trial on the merits of the case. Remember, it's higher than the claimant's own estimation of value, not mine.

The proposal the claimant's team is about to make is a dangerous one. It will engender a predictable reaction from the defense team and will adversely affect the prospects for a successful negotiation. It will bring the negotiations to a grinding halt at the beginning of the process. The first time I encountered this event, I intuitively knew it would not be received well in the other room. After seeing it replayed over and over during the past 15 years, I am convinced that it is a disastrous move for the claimant, because it will drive the other side away from the bargaining table.

The plaintiff makes this proposal on the theory that it gives the defense a chance to pay him top dollar for the claim. At another level the plaintiff is fearful that he will be selling himself short and settling his case too cheaply. The plaintiff's lawyer may be hedging bets on his analysis of what the case is worth. Thus, in reaction to this fear, the plaintiff formulates a demand that is higher than his own case evaluation will support.

I suggest here that the mediator anticipate an adverse reaction on the part of the defense and work to help the claimant make a more thoughtful first proposal. My comments would be structured to identify the need (fear) that prompted the proposal, to invent several different options for handling the opening proposal, and to explore the pros and cons of those options by discussing the impact of each on the other team's first proposal.

Scenario #4: One Party Reacts Strongly to a Perceived Outlandish Proposal

When a mediator delivers a proposal from one side that the other side perceives as unrealistic, he or she will hear, see, and feel the reaction of the receiving party, and it will be a negative one. I've listed below some of the typical settlement conference responses one hears in this situation.

a. "I'm out of here. (This is a waste of my time)"

b. "That's insulting. Is that what they think my mama's worth?"

c. "That's insulting. Do they think I'm stupid?"

d. "I'm not going to bid against myself."

e. "OK, I'll give them as ridiculous a number as they gave me ($500)."

f. "Go tell them to give me a realistic number."

g. "I'm not even going to dignify that number with a response."

■■■■■

Those responses have one thing in common: They are based on a perception that the proposal conveyed by the mediator is "out of the ballpark" of settlement. As I described in previous chapters, an out-of-the-ballpark proposal will routinely produce a dramatic, and often angry, reaction from the party receiving the proposal.

Typically, this type of reaction comes from the defense, because the defense is the first party to receive a proposal during the negotiation. But we also hear this reaction from members of the claimant's team. It occurs when the defense responds to an "outlandish" proposal from the claimant with an equally "ridiculous" number. When that happens, the plaintiff will react with the same kind of frustration and anger displayed by the defense.

The level of reaction, shock, and hostility is often palpable in these situations. When hostile outbursts occur, it is our job as mediators to help the parties and their advisors move from a state of reactivity to a state of thoughtful decision making.

a. "I'm out of here. (This is a waste of my time.)"

One of the most dramatic demonstrations of the anger, frustration, or disgust generated during money negotiations occurs when a member of the defense team stands up, puts on his jacket, and packs his briefcase.

■☒■■☒

This is not an act; he really intends to leave. From his point of view, the claimant has started too high and he reacts to it emotionally. It's important for the mediator to understand what the party is experiencing at this point. When the defendant hears a proposal that is outside the ballpark of settlement, he immediately concludes that the case won't settle. He also jumps to the conclusion that the mediation is, therefore, a waste of time. His experience of the negotiation at this point in time now has an emotional component, because the plaintiff is "wasting" the defendant's valuable time.

Here's how a conversation might go in a private session between an adjuster who is reacting in such a fashion and a mediator who is using the principles we've discussed thus far. We will not be using Young's case in this example.

Transcript

M: Well, Tom, I'm sorry I was so long in there.

L: You *were* in there a long time!

M: You know, it takes a while for them to get oriented. The plaintiff isn't as experienced a negotiator as you are and hasn't seen as many of these cases. But, I think we had a good, productive session. **[Observation]** [OK.] Is there anything you would like for me to know about your thinking that you didn't tell us in the general session? **[Question]**

L: I'd just like to hear what planet they're on.

M: Well, they're on the $100,000 planet.

L: That's not in my solar system.

M: OK. [Pause] So, they're way out of the ballpark?! **[Summary]**

L: Yeah, it makes no sense. If that's what they think this case is worth, it's a waste of time to be here. And I just don't want to respond.

M: Well, your solar system, give me some idea of what you're thinking that is. **[Question]**

L: This is the typical low impact, soft tissue case that's— she does have some stuff beyond soft tissue, but that's healed; she's out of work for a month; she's lost a couple thousand dollars. As we see it, it's $10,000, $12,000, $15,000 max.

M: OK, then that's a real difference. The world views here aren't the same. **[Observation/Summary]**

L: And there's no way in the world, in this county—I mean a home run for him is probably $15,000, $16,000. We think it's $10,000. Maybe $20,000 is his runaway jury verdict. If something happens and everything goes right for them, then it may be $15,000 to $20,000.

M: OK. So it must be discouraging to you then to hear a number like $100,000?! **[Reflective Response]**

L: For them to start at $100,000. I don't want to bid against myself in this situation. You can tell him to come back with something realistic and we'll deal with it. But that's just—it shows such a lack of understanding that it's difficult to imagine we can do anything with it.

M: Well, I take it you think he needs to be educated about the proper range of settlement in this case, then?! **[Summary/Reframe]**

L: Oh yeah, go in and tell him that he ought to be asking for $10,000. Just take a zero off his original figure and he'll be fine.

■■■■■

M: Here's my difficulty in this situation, Tom. If he's given me a number and I go back in there without another number from you and ask him for a new number, I'm going to hear from him what I've heard from you: "I'm bidding against myself." **[Observation]** So, I'm just wondering whether that's our only option; are there other ways that we can approach this problem that would get us moving forward? **[Question/Brainstorming]**

L: What other options do you think I've got?

M: Well, I don't know. I've figured that you have a number . . . .

L: I'm tempted to say I think $100,000 is ridiculous; here's $50 or $100 or $500.

M: Well, that's an option. What's the positive side of that? **[Question]** [Pause] It tells him that you and he aren't in the same arena. **[Mediator suggests a positive.]**

L: That he needs to come way, way down. A positive thing is that you get to work on the situation some more. And that I'm not just leaving.

■■■■■

M: Yes, all of those things. And frankly Tom, it does give me a number from you that I can take into the other room. At least I'm not going to hear that I came back in without a proposal. So, it has that as a positive. **[Suggestion]** Are there some other options? **[Long pause]** Let me ask you a question. If he had been more realistic—like $30,000—what do you think your proposal would have been? **[Question]**

L: I probably would have started around $5,000. I mean, we want to settle the case. I'm interested in getting this done and we understand the medicals are around $3,000 and there are lost wages—I'm prepared to start around the special damages and that's a little less than $5,000.

M: So you came here to deal. I mean, you've got money; this isn't a zero case?! **[Summary/Question]**

L: Oh, no. We came here to try to settle the case.

M: So, you could say, number one, I don't like your number, give me a new number. There are some positive and negative things about that. You could say, number two, $50 or $100. Three, you could do what you would have done if they had been more reasonable. So, there are a lot of options. **[Summary/Reframe]** I'm just wondering what has the most positives and the fewest negatives? **[Question]**

L: Well, having calmed down a little bit, I guess—and since it's early in the situation, I'm tempted to go ahead and say what I would have said in the first place.

M: And that was $5,000? **[Summary]**

L: $5,000. And let him deal with that and see what his next move is. If it's $99,000, you can tell him—

M: Well I'd rather deal with that if it comes up. **[Suggestion]**

L: If it's $95,000 you can tell him—

M: You won't like that?! **[Summary]** [L shakes his head, no.] So, I take it that you not only want me to give him a number but you want me to give him a flavor of this conversation, that his numbers are way out of the ballpark, as far as you're concerned?! **[Summary/Suggestion]**

L: Sure.

M: Well, you said a very interesting thing to me, that a homerun is $15,000 or $20,000. Is that private information for here, or is that something I can communicate to him, so that he will understand your ballpark better?! **[Question]**

L: If there's something he wants to tell me I'm ready to hear it, but it seems like a straightforward case to us. There're no aggravating factors. It was bright daylight.

There was no drinking. Our insured doesn't wear tattoos or offending body jewelry. The defendant made a mistake and he hit the poor woman and we're sorry and she wasn't hurt that badly, and she's recovered, and there just doesn't seem to be anything here to justify paying a whole lot of money.

M: So you don't mind my being specific about your out-of-the-ballpark numbers? **[Summary]**

L: And you can tell him that if there is something that makes this a $100,000 case, then send it over . . . .

M: So, you're here to learn if there's something to learn?! **[Summary]**

L: Sure.

M: All right, I'll be back as soon as I can. [Mediator departs to return to a private session with the plaintiff.]

■ ■ ■ ■ ■

Comment: Notice that the evaluation part of the process—what comes after the process of brainstorming has produced a number of options—appears to be non-existent at certain points in this conversation. The mediator didn't have to ask a number of pointed questions about advantages and disadvantages. The claims representative did the evaluation for himself in his head and didn't need to go through that part of the process. The mediator chose to forego that part of the discussion because it was evident that it wasn't needed.

Notice also that when the adjuster asked a direct question, the mediator answered him directly. I suggest that a direct answer, or a statement to the effect that you will shortly answer a direct question, is the best strategy for mediators in most circumstances. Failure to respond directly is experienced by most people as evasion or manipulation and is, therefore, off-putting.

b. "That's insulting. Is that what they think my mama's worth?"

The phenomenon we heard in the defense's room also occurs in the claimant's room when the mediator returns with a "low-ball" proposal. The claimant or claimant's lawyer, hearing a proposal that hardly appears to be a legitimate effort to settle the case, may erupt with emotional outbursts. It sounds and feels very much like the eruption that occurred in the other room, but there are slight differences to which we should attend.

The claimant's outburst may have the quality of the "they're wasting my time" reaction we just heard from the defense. However, the claimant generally experiences an out-of-the-ballpark proposal as personally insulting. It has the quality of a personal offense.

■■■■■

Claimants are not seasoned negotiators of personal injury claims, although their lawyers may be. They have experienced a personal trauma—the loss of a hand, a ruptured disc, a closed head injury resulting in cognitive deficits, the loss of a loved one. They see this negotiation in very personal terms, and, thus, their experience of the negotiation will be a personal rather than a business experience. Therefore, claimants will "take the negotiations personally" and will react with negative language when they feel hurt or slighted.

A "low-ball" proposal, intended by the defense to send a message that the claimant is "out of the ballpark," is not heard by the claimant as the defense intended. It is heard and experienced as a personal affront. As we listen to the following conversation in the claimant's room, we hear a subtle difference in the reaction of the plaintiff, as compared to the adjuster, to an "out-of-the-ballpark" proposal. In this scenario, the mediator is meeting with the plaintiff's team in private session for the third time in a wrongful death case.

Transcript

M: I talked to the defense and they've got a new number. You may not perceive much movement here but they've gone to $20,000. So, we've still got a pretty big gap here.

P: Well, I think you can just stop the process now. We're clearly not doing anything here. They clearly don't understand this; they don't understand the loss, or anything. So that's enough for us.

M: I've heard you talk about your mama a lot; she sounds like a lady worth knowing. I do understand your loss and I want you to know that. I'm assuming the numbers you're hearing just don't match up to your experience of her and your loss of her. **[Summary]**

P: Yeah. It's just like buying a car or something that's just too overwhelming—they're making it into a commercial thing and that's just not why we're here. She was an older person and she never was employed outside the home. She had a lot more years as a grandmother and a mother and being killed in an automobile accident wasn't the way she was supposed to go. And so that doesn't say anything to us about what we're doing here. We'd rather take it in front of a jury and let them decide. The defense is just too cold-blooded.

M: You know I've heard a lot of people say the same thing, "This feels like a car sale," this process of going back and forth with numbers trying to settle the case. **[Observation/Summary]**

P: Well, that's the way it sounds to me right now and they might do this all the time but we only had one mother. This is the only time we'll be in this situation and we don't like it. They're looking at a file and we're looking at a life that was lost.

M: And you're probably right; they are looking at a file— but, one thing I haven't heard in the other room is any negative remark about your mother or your family. **[Observation]**

P: Well, that's not the way it's being received.

M: I hear that. The numbers speak to you of discount . . . [Pause] disrespect? **[Reflective Response]**

P: It speaks to the impersonality of it. It's an accountant asking what's the least they can get out with in this case. Instead of doing what's right. We're not asking for somebody to sell their house, mortgage their house. We're asking an insurance company to pay the policy that they wrote on the driver who did this.

M: [Long pause] Well, I think you're probably right. They're looking at this as just one more case. And while they may like you and your family, they're only going to pay so much money today. **[Observation]** [Long pause] And I know you're hurt and probably discouraged by their number? **[Reflective Response]**

P: Uh-huh.

M: I wish I knew how much money they have and that we didn't have to go back and forth with numbers all afternoon. I know the process itself is demeaning to you, but I just haven't been able to figure out how to do this differently. [Pause] I don't know what their best number is today and they aren't going to tell me. I don't know whether their $20,000 is on the way to $25,000 or whether their $20,000 is on the way to $100,000. I don't know whether they're telling you they want to settle real low or whether they're telling you they don't like how high your number is. **[Summary/Observation/ Suggestion]**

P: If they're trying to tell us they'll settle for something that's fair, we're surely willing to settle for less money than they've seen so far, but they're not indicating to us that they're even thinking about something that would be acceptable—the symbolism is that they think this is a nuisance.

■ ■ ■ ■ ■

M: Well, please don't take this as indicative of their thinking or that they've suggested this or hinted this in any way. I'm just trying to ferret out what the real problem is here. If they could get to $125,000 or $150,000 at the

> end of the day and they think that's what cases like this would bring in a typical jury verdict, taking into consideration that this is a good family person—that would be their evaluation of this case in comparison to other cases that have been tried—does that communicate the same kind of thing that $20,000 communicates to you? **[Question/Presupposition]**

P: Oh, I think if we got to that, we could settle this case. But they're not showing us they have that in mind. They're showing us they're headed to $25,000 or $30,000.

M: That's always the problem, where are they headed? **[Question]** [Pause] Now, I would make this observation, that their $20,000 is $105K away from $125K and your $225K is $100K away. If you look at it that way, they may be signaling something entirely different from what you're picking up. They may be saying they could go to the middle. I don't know. **[Observation/Question]** [OK.] Do you and your lawyer want to talk in private about where you are, and where you'd like to be at the end of the day, and what you might do next? I know you're discouraged and your reaction is to quit this process. **[Question/Summary]**

P: Yeah, that might be helpful. We'd like to get this over with, so maybe we can spend some time on that. [Mediator leaves the room, so that the plaintiff's team can have a private conversation.]

c. "That's insulting. Do they think I'm stupid?"

Mediators also hear the "It's an insult" comment from seasoned adjusters and lawyers. However, the proposal is insulting to them for a different reason than it is to the claimant. Here's their line of thought: "Because the proposal is outlandish, no one in his right mind would accept it. If such a proposal is made, then the claimant must think I'm a fool. I'm being taken for a fool. I'm being taken for an inexperienced negotiator, for a novice." So, to experienced negotiators, an outlandish proposal may also be taken personally, as an insult to their professional abilities.

d. "I'm not going to bid against myself."

I hear this response more than any of the others outlined in this chapter. What's unique about its expression at the beginning of the negotiation is that the responding party is not technically correct in using this phrase to describe the dynamics of the situation.

Bidding against oneself is a term that usually refers to the sequencing of offers. If I'm asked to give a proposal when I've heard no response from the other side to my previous proposal, I'm inclined to say, and rightfully so, "I'd be bidding against myself." It would be like saying to a car salesman, "I'll give you $25,000 for that car. No, wait a minute; I think I'll give you $30,000." It's contrary to one's pecuniary interest to negotiate in that fashion.

■■■■■

I should add here that this is a very important point for mediators to take in. No one wants to bid against themselves, and no one wants to be asked to bid against themselves. A mediator who asks a party to make a proposal in such a circumstance will lose credibility with that side instantly. This is one black-letter rule I have for myself. Never, ever, ask a party to bid against themselves. Mediators should train themselves to be able to spot subtle and not-so-subtle requests from one team for the other team to bid against themselves.

In this fact situation, the claimant is not asking the defendant to bid against himself; he is simply conveying what the defense believes is an out-of-the-ballpark, way-too-high, proposal. But the defense uses those words, "I'm bidding against myself." What leads him to do that? The plaintiff did in fact convey a proposal, so it's not technically correct to say he's asked them to bid against themselves.

The defense considers it bidding against himself because he is having the same experience he has when someone asks him to bid against himself. The proposal is so far out of the ballpark it's as if the claimant has not made a proposal at all. The defense feels like he is the only negotiator in the game.

Technically, this is more of a problem of "who goes first" than "bidding against oneself." It's as if the claimant has not made a proposal at all and the defense is being put in the position of declaring an opening number. Even if he is correct in his analysis, the mediator should not argue with the defendant about what to call this situation. What the mediator should do is to acknowledge the experience of the defendant, understand the situation from the defendant's point of view, and then help the defendant come up with additional options.

e. "OK, I'll give them as ridiculous a number as they gave me ($500)."

If the defendant's first reaction is not to pack up and walk out, it might very well be to fire back at the claimant with "an equally outlandish proposal." We hear this frequently in trial court mediations as the defendant's emotional, first response to the claimant's first offer.

Once again, this is the type of response one hears from a party who thinks the other side's proposal is "out of the ballpark." What is important for the mediator to understand about this "outlandish" proposal is that it is the defense's attempt to solve a problem; and it is the defense's attempt to communicate something very important to the claimant. The defense's goal is to communicate to the other side that their proposal is unrealistic and therefore "out of the ballpark." The difficulty is that the proposal in which he chooses to convey that message is an incomplete communication and will engender a negative response from the other side.

f. "Go tell them to give me a realistic number."

Here's a response that is particularly problematic for mediators. Once again, it's an emotional response to the other side's "outlandish" proposal. In this situation, the defense is reacting negatively, but not by formulating a proposal—even an equally outlandish one—for the mediator to convey to the plaintiff. Instead, the defense suggests, and sometimes overtly directs, that the mediator go back to the other side with no proposal at all and ask the other side for a new number. Disaster awaits the unwary mediator at this point.

If the mediator takes the party at face value and naively follows that party's suggestion, then he will be asking the other side to give a new proposal when there has been no response to their original proposal. In other words, the mediator will be conveying a request for them to bid against themselves. It is unlikely that the other side will provide a new number under these circumstances. Few people bid against themselves.

More importantly, the side being asked to bid against themselves will become resentful of any mediator who puts them in that position. The mediator runs the risk of being perceived as someone who doesn't understand the dynamics of negotiations and, therefore, runs the risk of losing the confidence of his clients.

How does the mediator handle this situation? The drill is the same as before: understand the reaction and communicate your understanding to the speaker and, then, help that side invent ways of responding that are different from the one that sends you into the other room without a counterproposal.

g. "I'm not even going to dignify that number with a response."

This is my all-time favorite response of a party who believes that the proposal from the other side is out of the ballpark of settlement. This is a statement one might hear in the early stages of a negotiation. At some point in the past, all of us have felt the way this negotiator feels and have responded in this fashion. It may be said with great disgust and anger, or with sad resignation. Either way, it represents the reluctance we've seen in the past few scenarios to engage with a party whose proposal is perceived to be out of the ballpark of settlement. If that reluctance cannot be overcome, then the negotiation will come to a rapid close. Let's listen to the mediator's first private session with the defense.

Transcript

M: So, Tom, what do you think their number is? [**Throwaway Question**]

D: You're asking me what I think the skill and wisdom of the other lawyer is? Does he have enough to ask for the right amount? I don't even want to guess.

M: You don't want to play my silly game? [**Summary**]

D: He's going to ask for $15,000—and he's way, way, way past what we can do.

M: Well, he started at $25,000.

D: Well, I overestimated his ability to do the right thing. So, you heard what I thought. I exaggerated and took into consideration what I thought was his inability to think rationally about this case and told you $15,000. He's gone to another order entirely. I figured he would be three times what's reasonable and he's gone to five times what's reasonable. So, you can tell him to take some of the air out of his balloon and when he comes down into my atmosphere, I'll respond.

M: So, he's way out of the ballpark? **[Summary]**

D: I'm not going to dignify that kind of unrealistic nonsense. If he's in there telling his client that she can have a fender bender in a supermarket parking lot and six weeks after the wreck—and "wreck" is being generous—she goes to a chiropractor and the chiro runs up $3,000 in bills, which I would bet have not been paid, and . . . the only medical report was that she had Tylenol 3 . . . and somehow she's going to get $25,000 . . . .

M: Won't happen, huh?! **[Summary]**

D: Yeah!

M: Well, I'm not worried about that happening, but I am wondering whether this negotiation is going to get off the ground. **[Question/Presupposition]**

D: My suggestion is that you go back in there and tell him I'm disgusted or angry, whichever you think is best, but that I'm packing my bags here. After that, if they don't give us something that justifies our attention, then we're gone.

M: So, the first option that comes to your mind to deal with this situation is to— **[Summary/Reframe]**

D: Is to leave!

M: To leave and not give them a number of any kind? **[Summary]**

D: Yeah. We can leave, you can leave, and three hours later, when they wake up, they can leave.

M: OK, I'll put that up on the board as option number 1. **[Summary/Reframe]** Are there any other options? **[Question/Brainstorming]**

D: Option 2 is to send you back to tell them, hey, we're still here, we're not leaving, but you've got to give us a realistic number.

M: OK, OK, we're increasing our list here. **[Reframe]** What other possibilities might there be? **[Question/Brainstorming]**

D: Tell her that we'll give her a year's supply of Tylenol 3.

M: OK, and I suppose that has some monetary value. Well, what's obvious to me is that you're expressing what happens when somebody comes in with a number that's way too big and that doesn't encourage you to get into the negotiations with them?! **[Reflective Response]**

D: Absolutely; that number is ridiculous.

M: OK, I understand that. I hear it from you and I hear it from someone almost every day of my professional life in one negotiation or another. But I also know what the likely consequence is of doing number 1, 2, or 3 of the options you've named so far, and that is we probably aren't going to get anywhere. **[Observation]**

D: And you're right. And we're here and we're dressed up. And you're right.

M: What would help them understand what the proper ballpark of settlement is in this case? **[Question/Presupposition]**

D: Well, we want to settle the case. We'd like to get rid of it. We're ready to offer some money.

M: So it's not a zero case for you? **[Summary]**

D: No, it's not a zero case. We've got expenses, she's going to get a verdict, our client ran into her, she's a nice person. There is fault. But the damages are almost nonexistent. So I'm tempted to give them $100. But I'm listening to what you're saying about the message I'm trying to send, and I'm going to say $1,500.

M: And that's a comfortable place for you? To give them an idea of where they have to be to get it settled and keep it moving forward? **[Summary/Reframe]**

D: Yes.

M: Of all the options you've suggested, that one seems to accomplish most of what you'd like to do? [**Summary/ Reframe**]

D: Yeah, and you can tell him that it came out of me kicking and screaming.

M: And I can also tell him that it's a serious part of what you have to spend? [**Summary/Suggestion**]

D: Yeah, it's not going to climb high or fast.

M: All right, I'll take it to them and we'll see what they do. [Mediator exits to the plaintiff's room.]

Scenario #5: "They're Going Backward!"

■■■■■

Among the many things a mediator needs to be aware of is the negative impact that "going backward" has on the prospects for settlement. Going backward simply means that one party makes a proposal that is higher than his or her previous proposal, if the party is the plaintiff, or lower than his or her previous proposal, if the party is the defendant. A party receiving such a proposal will become mystified, irritated, or outraged and likely will go backward as well or refuse to make further offers.

Going backward occurs frequently in the settlement of civil litigation. Occasionally it occurs because the party going backward has discovered some new fact, theory, or law that leads him or her to reassess the claim. In that event, making a proposal at mediation that is less attractive than a previous one is understandable and, when properly explained to the other side, acceptable.

Mediators should be alert to the potential negative reaction this move will engender even when it is justified. Mediators can help the moving party understand how the new proposal may generate negative reactions and encourage him or her to explain the basis for the change. When the mediator discovers that a change in case evaluation will alter a party's previous proposal, he or she should encourage the party making the proposal to inform the other party of that fact as quickly as possible, preferably before the session commences. The other side will need time to adjust to the change in evaluation, so the sooner they learn of the change, the better.

At other times, parties "go backward" either out of ignorance of the negative consequences of their doing so or because they do not remember what they previously proposed to the other side. This latter phenomenon is especially interesting to me because it occurs so frequently in the mediations I conduct.

> ■■■■■
>
> One would expect that the parties' recollection of proposals made in the past would be similar to each other's. Nothing could be further from the truth. I often find that the parties' recollections of prior, pre-mediation, oral proposals vary dramatically. One of the reasons for that has to do with the laxity with which lawyers discuss ranges of settlement prior to formal demands and offers.

Lawyers would do well not to discuss the range in which their clients would settle the case with their adversaries because it sets up expectations for settlement that may not pan out at mediation. Plaintiffs' lawyers in particular talk about case value and settlement ranges in a cavalier fashion and fail to remember what they say. The defense also engages in informal case evaluation conversation prior to mediation, but more frequently than not they record things that are said that reveal the other side's range of settlement. Thus, it is the defense side of the table that usually accuses the other side of going backward in negotiations.

Much misunderstanding and confusion are generated by informal comments about case value and settlement ranges prior to mediation. Much of the difficulty in achieving movement early in negotiations can be attributed to the perception of one side that the other party is backing up from their pre-mediation position. The other party may not have made a formal proposal at all. However, human nature is such that numbers spoken of by one person to the other are literally recorded or recorded in memory as hard and fast proposals. This phenomenon bit me once in my law practice and has bitten many of the plaintiffs' lawyers I've worked with in mediation.

Occasionally, and often enough to mention it here, a party making a proposal vehemently denies that there has been a previous lower or higher number in the past—and the other side produces a written letter enunciating the offer and the reasons for it. This is exceptionally embarrassing for the lawyer denying that an offer has been made and it can produce friction between that lawyer and his or her client. Mediators should be aware of this phenomenon and be prepared to move to the mediation-within-the-mediation that may be needed between the lawyer and client.

Going backward is not a beginning-of-the-mediation problem only. As will be discussed in Chapter 8, a personal injury case or other claim for money may produce opportunities to employ a problem-solving model of the mediation process to help the parties generate creative solutions for mutual gain. When this effort fails to produce workable solutions, as is the case most of the time, the parties will return to position-based bargaining. This is an opportunity for one party or another to "go backward" inadvertently.

In this situation, given the passage of time, the proposing party may have lost sight of his or her previous proposals. That party may indeed have gone backward inadvertently. To prevent this situation from occurring, mediators should carefully record proposals made by the parties, in all their constituent parts, and spot the problem before it occurs. To deal with it effectively if it does occur, mediators can help the parties sort out the confusion, make sure the communications between them during this difficult moment are framed to eliminate inflammatory language, and, if necessary, take the blame for the turmoil if the backward move was unintentional.

Scenario #6: A Low-Ball Proposal Is Made in Order to Send a Message But It Is Not Identified as Such

The defense believes the claimant is out of the ballpark, so they give the mediator a proposal designed to send a message to that effect. The mediator believes this is a lower-than-usual offer, but the defense has not identified it as such.

This is not a verbal cliché, but it is a cliché nevertheless. The defense team may or may not react violently to the claimant's proposal, but they clearly don't like it. However, instead of storming out of the room, or saying any of the things we have heard in the preceding paragraphs, they calmly invite the mediator out of the room so that they can have a private discussion. Upon his return, they have a proposal.

This is a variation of "OK, we'll give them an equally ridiculous number," except for the fact that the party does not say those words. Without any explanation, they simply give you a number. It's a number that you believe will be perceived by the other side as a low-ball, or it's a number that doesn't match up to their discussion of the value of the case or your own estimation of the value of the case. This happens a lot in the trial court mediations I conduct.

Sometimes I just take their proposal, even if it does appear to me to be a low- or high-ball, go back to the claimant's room to deliver it, work with them to come up with a response, and let the proposals unfold naturally until it is clear that movement will occur or that an impasse will develop. At other times, I follow my intuition and engage in a more detailed discussion like the one in the previous scenario as soon as I'm aware of my own reactions to the proposal. Those decisions are dependent on many factors and are not the focus of this discussion.

Scenario #7: "They're Just Not Here in Good Faith"

One of the reasons we did not make it a requirement of North Carolina's court-ordered mediation program that the parties "negotiate in good faith" is that it is too easy to accuse another person of negotiating in bad faith. I hear it said frequently in mediations that so-and-so "isn't bargaining in good faith." What does that mean? Is there an objective standard for good-faith negotiating?

■■■■■

The phrase "negotiating in bad faith" is usually accompanied by one of the other clichés we discussed in Scenario #4 and it signals that the speaking party believes the other party is "out of the ballpark." In other words, the speaker doesn't like the other side's number; the other party is not in a range that he likes or wants to negotiate in. It turns out that "negotiating in bad faith" often means "They're not doing what we want them to do" or "They're not negotiating in a range that's worth our time or effort."

What does the mediator do in response to an accusation of bad faith? Sometimes nothing, particularly if it's going to embroil the mediator in an argument with the speaker. Sometimes we can just let it pass and deal with the speaker in terms of one of the clichés discussed in Scenario #4. At other times we can deal with it more directly, as in the following transcript.

Transcript

M: Jane, you've said that they're not negotiating in good faith. What do you mean by that? What specifically are they doing and what should they be doing? **[Question]**

D: They should be realistically looking at their case and not just putting out a number that doesn't have any basis in fact, or in what a jury would do.

M: And the number they've given doesn't have any basis in fact?! **[Summary]**

D: No, it's ridiculous. They're wasting our time.

M: They're wasting your time at this point, because the numbers they've given are out of the ballpark? **[Summary/Reframe]**

D: That's right!

M: What would you have them do? **[Question]**

D: To come up with a number that's realistic and has some basis in what a jury would do in this case.

M: OK, and what is it that you want to do to help make that happen? **[Question/Presupposition]**

D: I want you to go in there and make them negotiate in good faith.

M: You want me to go get another number? **[Summary]**

D: Uh-huh, make them negotiate in good faith.

M: All right. Suppose the same thing was being said in their room and they sent me in here and I said, "Jane, they say you're not negotiating in good faith and they want a different, more realistic number from you. What would be your response to that? **[Question]**

D: Well, I am negotiating in good faith. I gave them a number and I'm here.

M: So the other room has given *you* a number and they want you to respond to it. **[Observation]**

D: So, I guess I could just give them another number back?

M: That's one thing you could do. **[Summary/Reframe]** What else could you do? **[Question/Brainstorming]**

D: Pack my bag.

M: You could leave. **[Summary]** What else? **[Question]**

D: I could talk to them.

M: Go talk to them and have a conversation with them about where this is going? **[Summary]** [Uh-huh.] I mean, your sense right now is that you're so far apart that it's not productive to keep going like this from number to number?! **[Summary]**

D: That's right.

M: In an actual conversation, who would you like to talk with? **[Question]**

D: The lawyers.

M: Just the lawyers? OK. So that's an option. **[Summary]** What else? **[Question]**

D: Well, I think that's it.

M: OK. [Long pause] There's one other thing I think you could do, and I see a lot of people choosing this option. And that's to give them another proposal in your acceptable range of settlement and join that with a statement of where you can't go. **[Suggestion]**

D: What do you mean?

M: Well, I've heard you say that their $100,000 proposal is ridiculous and from everything else you've said about their case, I'm inferring that $50,000 is still outside the ballpark but that it might be a number that you would have expected them to start with. **[Summary/ Observation]**

D: Yeah, that's about right.

M: So you could give them a number as an offer, say something like $5,000 to $7,000 or whatever your range might be, and tell them that if they had started at $50,000 they would still be way outside the range in which you could settle the case. That's an option that works in some situations. **[Suggestion]**

D: But won't they think I would settle for just under 50,000? I don't want to suggest that.

M: You're worried about that? [Uh-huh.] I've heard that reaction from other people as well. **[Summary/Observation]**

D: Won't they think that?

M: Sometimes they do. What you could do to disabuse them of that notion is to say that's where they should have started and then continue negotiating within your range until they get the message of where they need to be to settle the case. **[Observation/Suggestion]**

D: Hmmmm.

M: So we have several options; which do you prefer? **[Summary/Question]**

D: Well I'd like to settle the case. We're here to settle the case. I've come a long way.

M: So you'd like to do something productive now. **[Summary/Reframe]** So which of those things that we've laid out would you like to do at this point? **[Question]**

D: I want to go talk to them.

M: So, you'd like to go talk to them?! **[Summary]** [Pause] One of the things I do when one side wants to talk with the other is to find out if they're willing to talk with you at this stage. Sometimes that's something they're willing to do and sometimes it's not. So, rather than just taking you in unannounced, and surprising them, which might create problems, let me have a short talk with them and see whether they'd be willing to talk. **[Suggestion]**

D: OK.

Comment: Mediators can help parties formulate proposals and messages that accurately convey the meanings the parties intend to communicate. Obviously, the offer one party sends to the other can convey a great deal about the appropriate range of settlement. At other times, the number by itself doesn't seem to suffice.

■■■■■

Sometimes when parties are stuck on one way of responding, I offer a suggestion of another approach for their consideration. One of my favorites is to find out if parties wish to add some "commentary" to their number proposal, some words that explain or convey more than the proposal can convey by itself. Many people would never think of doing that without some help.

This transcript contains such a suggestion. If a party chooses this approach, the mediator will convey the proposal of $5,000, and the words, "And the defendant can't imagine a verdict going over $50,000." Or, "They would have expected you to start with a high number like $50,000 and you've started with a number that is more than two times that."

The communication, in effect, is that "as long as you're over $50,000, this negotiation is going nowhere." This additional information may not be believed by the other party when they hear it. They may continue to negotiate in what the other side believes is a high range until the information is confirmed by the numbers they hear in succeeding rounds. Sometimes one party hears this communication as a statement that the other party can reach the number stated in his commentary. The speaker in the preceding transcript expressed concern about that expectation.

However, if the commentary is conveyed and the defendant continues to negotiate in a range that is consistent with the message, then the other side will begin to treat the stated range seriously. With concrete information about the negotiating range of the defendant, the plaintiff will either adjust his numbers downward or make a conscious decision not to get into the range at all. This approach, then, gives the plaintiff a definite range to deal with. It has the effect of defining the negotiation and, often, speeding it up and eliminating much frustration on both sides. It also gives the mediator additional opportunities to discuss case analysis more thoroughly with the other party.

■■■■■

Of course, this suggestion is only one option for the party to consider. They may like it. They may see some difficulty with it and decide not to choose it. They may see some difficulty with it and work through that difficulty with you. In such a discussion, the mediator should be candid about the potential negatives of his or her suggestion. Every option has both positives and negatives to it, and the mediator should allow the party to make the judgment call for that move as he or she deems appropriate.

In the preceding transcript, the speaker chose her own approach. Ironically, when lawyers talk face to face during the course of negotiations, they often convey more information about their negotiating ranges than they do with the mediator as an intermediary.

I like for lawyers to talk with each other directly whenever it is possible. Many laypersons aren't familiar with the candor with which lawyers speak when their clients are not present. In that setting, they may feel that they don't have to posture for their clients. They often have a bond of mutual trust that allows them to share what others might consider to be "bottom line" information without jeopardizing their negotiating positions. As a result, they may be able to come to a proposal that each of them could recommend to their clients.

One final note on the subject of carrying commentary with the proposal: As in much of our work as mediators, timing is crucial. I have found that commentary about where a party "can't go" usually is received better by the other side if it comes after a couple of rounds of negotiations, when the negotiations appear to be stalling, or when one of the parties is frustrated with the movement that is occurring.

Scenario #8: "I'm Not Going to Do Their Homework for Them" Or "Nobody Gets Free Discovery"

This settlement conference cliché was spoken by the plaintiff's lawyer responding to the defense lawyer during the general session of one of the first trial court mediations I conducted. The defense had not received and, thus, had not reviewed the plaintiff's medical records; so he asked his opponent to produce them for review during private sessions. The plaintiff's lawyer retorted, "I don't give free discovery."

■■■■■

As we have discussed, the parties to civil litigation hold tightly to the information they possess. It's their reflex to withhold. However, they are so reflexive in their withholding that they sometimes lose sight of the obvious advantage of giving information to the other side. Forwarding basic information in the form of medical records and expenses in a personal injury case is an absolute necessity if the claimant wants to settle the case. The defense simply won't pay money without documentation of the injuries and their treatment.

The work that the mediator does before the mediation session to uncover the informational needs of the parties and develop ways of meeting those needs adds great value to the negotiation process. If this reaction occurs during the mediation, the mediator should understand the basis of the reaction, interpret the needs of one side to the other, and help develop other options for responding.

Scenario #9: "It's Not the Money; It's the Principle"

If the speaker means literally what he said, the case probably won't settle without total capitulation by the other side. If a principle needs to be set in the case, the party will have to have his way completely or the case will have to be tried.

However, given the reality that many personal injury cases settle with the payment of money by an insurance company to a plaintiff, it is unlikely that the words the speaker used should be taken literally even though he or she believes them to be true.

> ■ ■ ■ ■ ■
>
> "It's the principle" usually means that the other side has offered an amount of money to settle the case that does not do justice to the loss the plaintiff has suffered—and the plaintiff takes it personally. Since this statement is about money and what it represents to the plaintiff, the mediator likely will be correct if he or she responds to it as one of those out-of-the-ballpark statements that people make when the other side hasn't offered enough money. This statement usually means that the other side's range is so far outside the ballpark of settlement that it feels personal.

Scenario #10: "We Want Them to Know We're Serious"

This is another statement that is associated with one side's thinking the other is out of the ballpark, but it is not always accompanied by strong emotion. I have heard it many times from both plaintiff and defendant teams, and it's generally stated as an explanation for why a particular party is making a small move in comparison to his or her last position or for why that party is starting with a high (or low) number at the beginning of the negotiation.

■■■■■

When I was a practicing lawyer, I knew little about the art and science of negotiation. There was nothing in our law school curriculum about the subject and I had no mentor early in my career. I look back on my negotiations during that period with amazement. Although I didn't articulate it at the time, my operating theory was: "Tell them once. If they don't get it, tell them again. And if they still don't get it, tell them louder."

I have worked with many lawyers who have the same operating philosophy. They seem to think that if they just keep making small moves the other side will come closer to them. Unfortunately, the message the other side receives is not the one intended. The message received is that the differences between the parties are too great for the case to settle. Even experienced negotiators will revert to the self-defeating habit of repeating their last position (or its equivalent, making small changes in their positions) when they become frustrated with the other side's movement.

Repeating one's position, making mini-moves, and staying high (or low) accomplishes something. It does send a message that the other side is out of the ballpark. But it also sends an inaccurate message about where the acceptable range of settlement is. It says, "Look, the range of settlement is down here." This may be inaccurate and misleading and certainly will not motivate the other side to make movement.

Repeating one's position or making small moves is more appropriate when one has reached the end of an acceptable range of settlement. In that circumstance, the negotiator accurately sends the message that the other side is out of the ballpark and that he, the negotiator, is getting near the end of his range.

Scenario #11: "We Don't Want to Move Too Fast, Too Soon"

This is a variation of "wanting them to know we're serious." In the beginning of a negotiation, people are concerned about appearing weak, appearing uncertain of their case, or appearing that they are too eager to settle. As a result, they often move in small increments, even though their negotiating range is quite large. This happens frequently when there is a significant difference in the parties' initial positions.

As we've discussed elsewhere, making small moves when one's negotiating range is comparatively large leads the other side to think the true gap between the parties is too large to bridge. Therefore, the other side makes a correspondingly small move in an effort to make the first side come closer or to preserve their negotiating position if the case doesn't settle. This type of movement usually breeds impasse, unless the mediator can help the parties rethink their strategy for movement.

■■■■■

Of course, the mediator probably will not know the negotiating ranges of the parties at the beginning of the negotiation. Therefore, the mediator should tread lightly as the parties feel each other out and should avoid offering suggestions until the parties ask for them or until they start having real difficulties with movement. Once again, if suggestions are offered, they should be offered to expand the parties' range of options. Suggestions for movement should not be made to persuade the parties to make bigger moves.

Scenario #12: "They're Just Not Getting It"

This is another variation of "We want them to know we're serious," only it occurs after several rounds of negotiation have taken place. The speaker doesn't see the other side making significant movement and gets frustrated. He wants to get the other side to move, but in his frustration he's about to make another small move or decrease the size of his move compared to his previous increments.

If the speaker is getting close to his bottom (or top) line, then this might be the right thing to do. However, if he's acting out of frustration and trying to get the other side to move further or faster, then he is about to employ a counterproductive strategy. A small move is likely to breed a small move from the other side, and the speaker's frustration will increase as an impasse appears eminent.

■■■■■

It's important to remind ourselves at this point that it's not our role as mediators to lecture the parties about their negotiation strategy. Our conclusions about their choices are our own private thoughts. But our experience with other powerful options may indeed help them accomplish their objectives. I often offer suggestions for movement in an effort to help the parties expand their range of options and make thoughtful, rather than reflexive, proposals.

The choice of what they do is entirely theirs, as are the consequences of those choices. We, as mediators, do not have to assume responsibility for the outcome of the mediation. And, out of a sense of misplaced responsibility, we do not, and should not, try to convince the parties to do what we think is in their best interest. In my experience, the line between being helpful and being pedantic or condescending in these matters can be very thin.

Scenario #13: "We're Not Going to Pay a Dime More Than the Other Companies"

One of the most vexing circumstances that civil trial court media-tors face occurs when the plaintiff names several people as defen-dants and they are insured by multiple, and usually different, insurance companies. As you might imagine, those defendants may not analyze their liability exposure in the same way.

The situation is compounded in a state like my own in which the concept of joint and several liability applies. Defendant 1, regardless of the degree of his fault, is responsible jointly with Defendants 2 and 3 for a verdict rendered in favor of the plaintiff against all defendants. There is no apportionment of the damages awarded by a jury based upon degree of fault. Defendant 1 is responsible for satisfying the entire judgment in the event the other defendants are judgment proof.

It frequently happens in the negotiation of personal injury cases that the insurer for Defendant 1 wants to pay a smaller share of settlement proposals than the other insurers. Con-versely, the other insurers want Defendant 1's insurer to pay an equal share. In fact, the other insurers generally refuse to offer more money than Defendant 1's insurer on any move throughout the negotiation.

■ ■ ■ ■ ■

"I'm not going to pay a dime more than ... " is unique among the scenarios I describe here, because it denotes two problems of movement at once. The first problem is getting any proposal at all from the defendants. The dispute among the defendants about their relative responsibility for the injuries makes it difficult for any of them to make their first proposal. If a proposal is generated from the group of defen-dants, then it is usually lower than any of them would have made if they were solely liable.

The second problem is a consequence of the first. The no proposal or low proposal from the defendants makes it difficult to generate movement in the negotiation between the plaintiff and the defendants. We have already seen how difficult the negotiation between a plaintiff and a single defendant can be. The plaintiff thinks the defendant is negotiating in a range that's too low and vice versa. The plaintiff's perception is heightened when there are multiple insurers with differing assessments of exposure, because those assessments result in a lower-than-usual number for the defendants' proposal. We often hear something like this in the defendants' private session:

"We think a proposal of $40,000 would be a good starting point today if we were all on the same page—that's $10,000 a piece. But since George here is just going to pay $5,000 this go around, that's what we'll chip in. Not a dime more."

That kind of thinking, of course, leads to a starting proposal of $20,000 instead of $40,000. Imagine the reaction in the plaintiff's room! It'll be very hard to keep this negotiation going under these circumstances. And that's quite ironic. The very circumstance that many plaintiff lawyers think works in their favor at trial—multiple defendants pointing the finger of liability at each other—works against the prospects of settlement. It makes it harder to generate realistic proposals from the defense side of the table when the defendants do not perceive the same degree of responsibility for causing the injuries at issue.

What can the mediator do to help out in this situation? I can tell you what to try, but I must quickly say that it frequently doesn't change the negotiating posture of the defendants. The reflex to offer "not a dime more" than the next fellow is exceedingly strong and ingrained in the culture of the insurance industry. Here are some pointers, however, for your consideration:

- Understand the dilemma of each of the defendant groups.
- Promote discussions about the concept of joint and several liability, contribution, and indemnity.
- Help the defendants understand the likely consequences of their approach. (They usually won't be able to propose enough money to interest the plaintiff in settlement.)
- Help the defendants focus on their own range of settlement rather than worry about what one of the other defendants is doing. (That's the only way to get up enough money to keep the plaintiff interested in the negotiation or interested in settlement.)
- Be patient. Don't worry about how the negotiation will turn out. Just concentrate on getting the next proposal.

■■■■■

Negotiations between insurance companies under these circumstances are exceedingly complex and often involve many layers of authority above that of the persons in attendance at mediation. Understand that there may be many private conversations between companies and between differing levels of authority within a company from which you as mediator will be excluded.

Understand also that while these discussions are taking place, the plaintiff's team is sitting in its own room wondering what is going on and whether its time in mediation is being well spent. It may be important for you to convene a smaller meeting with lawyers at this point to assess whether the mediation should be recessed or whether the plaintiff should be dismissed until a later session while the defendants sort out their differences.

Scenario #14: "But We Don't Have Any More Room to Move"

This statement often is made early in the negotiations but it does not always mean that the speaker is at the end of his range of settlement. When it is made early on, it signals the speaker's perception that the case won't settle and that he may not want to move all the way through his negotiating range to his best number.

■■■■■

I remind myself, however, that what one tells me directly or indirectly about his negotiating range may not be accurate. For that reason, I never vouch for the truth of what one side says to the other about their bottom or top lines, or anything else for that matter. Mediators must be careful not to assume too much, especially when th parties are talking about their best numbers.

Here, the speaker is saying that he has more room to move but perceives it to be miniscule compared to the gap that has to be closed to settle the claim. Thus he is signaling that he doesn't believe that it is worth his effort to continue negotiating. Negotiators don't like to get to their best numbers if, in doing so, the case will not settle; hence movement may cease altogether. At this point, mediators can help the parties see opportunities they may have overlooked, and invent new ways of handling these situations that enhance the prospects of settlement.

■■■■■

What I try to do in this circumstance is help the parties not get locked into one way of handling their situation. When a party perceives that he doesn't have much room to move, he often translates that into "I don't have any room to move." This is a mistake I see negotiators making all the time.

One of the ways mediators can help at this point is to suggest to the negotiator that a small amount of money can be chunked up into a number of small moves. By chunking his available range into small increments, the negotiator is able to keep the process moving and, at the same time, communicate to the other side that he, in fact, is negotiating within a different range than the other side. The reader will see this option played out several times in the transcripts that make up the remainder of this chapter.

Scenario #15: "They're Not Moving Fast Enough"

This statement may be said either with no emotion or with a large emotional charge. I take it to mean that the other side is much further away than the speaker's team from an acceptable range of settlement. It also signals the possibility of impasse at an early stage of the negotiation. What we're hearing is the perception of one side that the gap between the parties may be too big to close. Whether it is, in fact, too big we do not know and won't really know until later in the negotiation. But these early perceptions often drive one party or the other to quit making proposals.

The mediator can help the party slow down, create additional options, or chunk up his remaining available range into multiple moves, without getting beyond his acceptable range of settlement. The mediator may not have a good idea of what the speaker's best number is at this stage. In fact, the mediator may never know the negotiator's best number. Should the mediator ask the parties what their best numbers are? For reasons that I will state in the next chapter, I believe the mediator should not.

Scenario #16: "OK, They Moved Five, So I'll Move Five"

I hear this statement often, but it means at least two different things depending on the circumstances. The party who wants to signal that they can settle the case by "splitting the difference" may want to match the other side's last move. Matching is a signal about meeting in the middle; because, if the parties continue matching each other, they will meet in the middle. If he "moves five because they moved five" for this reason, it's a good move for him, meaning that he has clearly communicated his intentions to settle in the middle while "officially" retaining a higher number as his negotiating position.

If, on the other hand, a party matches the other party's move because he doesn't like her move, I know that trouble is just around the corner. "If she's only going to move five (meaning a very small number in his mind), then I'll just move five" (meaning, I'll show her I can play that game too). Matching in this context is not a clear signal that the parties can meet in the middle. It's a reactive move intended to communicate that the other party is out of the ballpark.

Unfortunately, this move also does not communicate clearly what the proper range of settlement is. Matching traditionally means that the best number of the party matching the other's move is in the middle. If the midpoint is different from a party's best number, then that party will not accurately convey his best number by matching the increment of the other side. The likely response from the other side is to reduce the size of his movement. And the likely consequence of these moves is that the negotiation will stall or reach an impasse.

■■■■■

So, the mediator may choose to slow the speaker down a bit, work with her, and explore whether her proposal is communicating everything she wants it to communicate. A well-formed communication will say that the other side's proposal is too high and it will accurately say something about the range in which the case can settle.

In the following transcript, I am working with the plaintiff's lawyer who has just heard from the mediator that the defendant has moved to $5,000 from $2,500. He doesn't like that move because it's not close to the plaintiff's best number of $50,000. The plaintiff made the opening proposal of $130,000.

Transcript

M: Yes, Syd, they did give me a new number. They're at $5,000 now.

D: You mean they're at $5,000?! [Yep.] Well, that's just not . . . they're just so far out of the ballpark . . . .

M: They're not where you want them to be? **[Summary]**

D: No. I need to send them a message . . . they've got to come way up. Well, since they moved $2,500, we'll move $2,500.

M: OK.

D: That's what they did.

M: So, you're telling me that your number is a communication to them, a message? **[Summary/Reframe]** [Yes.] That they're just too far out of the ballpark? **[Summary]** [Yeah.] Well . . . can I just kind of think out loud with you here?

D: Please do.

M: [Pause] I'm thinking that with a move to $127,500 you very clearly say that they don't have a clue about where they need to be to settle the case. I think you've done that very effectively. My concern is that you may not have signaled to them clearly where the proper ballpark of settlement is. Let me tell you what I mean by that. [OK.] **[Observation/Suggestion]**

Usually, when negotiators match each other, they can meet in the middle. And the middle here would be around $66,250. Now I'm not asking what your best number is; I don't need to know. But if you want to send them a message, and you can do better than that number, then you may not be sending a very clear message. You're saying on the one hand I'm going to match you. They're going to look at that and get the message that your number is around the $66,000 mark. And that may slow them up, because it's out of their range. Now if that's the message you want to send them, that makes sense to me. But, if that message is off base, I wonder whether your proposal has accomplished what you want it to accomplish? **[Observation/Suggestion/Question]**

D: Well, you mean indicating whether I'm willing to go lower than 66,500?

M: Yes, if you can go lower than $66,500 and you match them now, then I'm wondering whether you've sent them an accurate message. **[Suggestion]**

D: Yeah. Well, frankly, I was disgusted with them and their move. What do you think would be appropriate to send as the proper message, because I can go lower than that?

M: Well, as I respond to that, I'm clear that you want to tell them that they're out of the ballpark. So, whatever you do has got to send that message! **[Summary]** [Yeah.] But I don't know what your best number is and I'm not asking; so it's hard for me to answer you specifically. What I would suggest is that you say, I'm here now [gesturing to show a position]; I can go to here [gesturing to show a lower position]. And then you develop some plan for spending that money that's not dependent on how they move. That way you can respond to them and stay in control of what you're doing and . . . . **[Suggestion]**

D: Not react to what they're doing. OK, I'll go to $125,000.

M That's more in line with a plan you've developed? **[Question/Presupposition]** [Yeah.] The sum of $125,000 is still so different from where they are that it still seems to me to be telling them also that they're out of the ballpark. **[Observation]**

D: But it might prompt them to make a good move.

M: That might be one of the benefits . . . but even if they don't, you're in control of your plan and you're not reacting to what they do. You can stop, you can shorten up, and you can modify it as you wish. Does this make sense and does it help you do what you want to do? **[Observation/Suggestion/Question]** [Yes.]

Comment: If the plaintiff develops a plan of movement for the remainder of the negotiation, he or she can make each remaining move without a great deal of agony and soul-searching. On each move the plaintiff keeps the process moving, demonstrates what he or she thinks is the proper range of settlement, and continues to tell the other side that they are out of the ballpark.

Scenario #17: "This Case Isn't Going to Settle"

This statement may be spoken at any time during the course of a money negotiation. It signals the speaker's conclusion that the parties are too far apart to resolve the claim. Negotiators who believe the case won't settle will be reluctant to move through their negotiating range and get to their best number.

People simply don't want to "show their hand," their best number, under these circumstances. The tendency is to shut down, quit the negotiation, and go home. This is their reaction to the perception that the case won't settle; they see no other option than to quit negotiating. Their creative processes shut down.

The mediator can help in these circumstances. The mediator can engage the parties in a conversation that will slow them down, help them understand their own reactions and untapped power to deal with the situation, and help them create additional options for their consideration. They may still choose the first, and reactive, option as the way to handle the situation. That's their prerogative. But at least they'll have other options to consider.

Scenario #18: "Let's Cut to the Chase" (Early in the Negotiation)

Everyone has heard or said this familiar statement. Its reference is thought to be to the movie industry and the types of films that typically end with a "chase scene." It means:

- "Let's get to the real numbers and quit dancing around with proposals we both know aren't going to settle this case."
- "We all know that the real action is at the end; I'm tired of all this preliminary stuff."

or

- "Let's just give each other our best numbers and get it over."

When the expression is heard at the end of the negotiation, when the parties' positions are close, the speaker is signaling that he will "break the ice" in an effort to spare everyone the agony of making the last few small steps to close a narrow gap. In this circumstance, no real problem is presented to the mediators or the other party.

However, the expression is also heard at the beginning of the negotiating process, after the first or second round of proposals. At this point it signals either a personal dislike of the bargaining process itself or a high degree of frustration on the part of the speaker with the other party's number. If it is the latter, it heralds a real problem for the negotiations and for the mediator. When this is heard at the beginning of the process, the possibility of an impasse is real, and the mediator will have to work hard to keep negotiations going.

As with many of the scenarios in this chapter, the speaker's statement is an indication that he or she thinks the other side is out of the ballpark of settlement. Mediators can assist with this reaction by understanding, questioning, reframing, and helping to create options.

Scenario #19: "Tell Them We're Not Going Any Higher/Lower"

I know from experience that the party who makes this statement probably can go further than the proposal he's just made, particularly if it's the first time he's said it during the negotiation. The mediator must be careful, however, not to jump to conclusions about the speaker's meaning. Sometimes the speaker speaks the literal truth; it is his or her last number. Sometimes it's the speaker's way of telling the other party that he's really close to his best number; and sometimes it's a statement of frustration aimed at getting the other party to make a significant move.

■■■■■

Negotiators who say they have no more room to move, when they do have more room, in fact, create several problems for themselves. The first is that they may lose credibility with the other side. The negotiator who makes bold statements and then acts contrary to them looks foolish to the other side. The other side may not take anything he says seriously.

The second problem is that the remark is not likely to produce another number from the other side. If someone announces that he has reached his best number, and the gap between the parties is still significant, the other party is going to think that there's no purpose in giving a next number even if it represents a significant move. "Why should I give a new number, if the other side says they won't consider it?" he asks himself. So, because the statement won't motivate the other side to give a new number, a negotiator would be wise to refrain from announcing that a number "is as high/low as I'm going" unless the statement is literally true.

In the following transcript, the defense responded to the plaintiff's number of 90 with 20. The mediator has returned to the plaintiff's room for a new proposal. To my surprise, the plaintiff announces that he will move to 80, but that this is as far as he's going to move.

Transcript

M: Well, I'm not sure I understand what you're telling me when you say you won't go any further than 80. Could you tell me more about your thinking? **[Question]**

P: They're just too low. I can't settle at 20. I've got a Medicare lien to take care of and debts that need to be paid. I just can't go that low.

M: So 80 is the rock bottom and you want me to tell them that? **[Summary]**

P: Yes, I've got to have 80. Just tell them that's as low as I can go and get their best number for me.

M: What do you think their reaction to that will be? **[Question/Presupposition]**

P: Well, I don't know. I would hope that they'd put their best number on the table since we're at the end of the mediation.

M: I understand. [Pause] I will certainly help them think through the positives of putting their best number out there. But I'm pessimistic about their doing it, because you've stopped so suddenly. I'm wondering if they'll say, "What's the use? We're too far apart." **[Observation]** I notice that you didn't make any stopping noises with your last proposal, so I'm wondering if what you're about to do will accomplish what you want it to. [Pause] Of course, if 80 is your rock-bottom number, then I suppose now is the time to announce it. If for some reason it isn't, could we think about other ways of handling the situation so that they get to their best numbers? **[Suggestion/Question]**

P: Well I could do better than 80, but they're just so far away and this is taking so long that it just doesn't seem useful to keep going.

M: It sounds to me that part of the problem is that they are so far away from what you need to settle the case that you're getting frustrated with them and want to just get it over? **[Reflective Response]**

P: Yeah, that's part of it. I just don't want to waste a lot of time if the case isn't going to settle.

M: I understand that. Let me throw out an option that might help at this point, if that's OK. [OK.] One way of handling the situation is to take the available amount of room you have to work with and chunk it up into a number of pieces, representing the number of moves you're willing to make to approach your bottom line. It could be five or six or seven moves. Then on each move give them another chunk. That way the process will keep going, we'll give them a chance to come toward you with their numbers, and make the gap at the end much smaller than it is now. **[Suggestion/ Observation]**

P: Won't that take a long time? I'm really frustrated with this process.

M: Yeah, I know we've been at this a long time. **[Summary]** But, actually I think you'll find that the process will speed up by doing this. You'll have to struggle less each time you're called on to make a move and, consequently, they will too. At least that's been my experience. Of course, we haven't exhausted all the options you have. We could explore those if you like. **[Observation/Brainstorming]**

P: No, that's OK. I like what you were talking about—so, I'll move to 74 on this move and see what they do.

M: OK. And that will give you the freedom to monitor how we're doing and whether they're encouraged to make movement too. **[Summary/Reframe]**

P: Right.

Scenario #20: "Is That Really Their Best Number?"

■■■■■

I consider it an important milestone in a negotiation about money when the parties announce their best numbers to each other. Money negotiations often reach an impasse quickly, so it's a real accomplishment when the parties move all the way through their negotiating ranges. It is my hope that at least one of the parties will announce a "best number" during the negotiation, unless in the party's good judgment it will harm him or her to do so.

Inevitably, the party who hears the other side announce that a proposal is their "top dollar" or "lowest number" will wonder whether or not the speaker is telling the truth. "Should I take that seriously? I didn't want to go that low/high to settle the case, but I certainly don't want to do it if I can squeeze a few more bucks out of them. I wonder if I'd be leaving some money on the table if I accept that number." Those are some of the thoughts people have when they hear a proposal that is billed as the other party's best number.

Generally it is the mediator who is communicating the proposal as he or she shuttles from one private session to another. If that is the case, the receiving party may have a hard time judging the truthfulness of the communication. The receiving party will not have had an opportunity to hear the tone of the speaker's voice or take in his or her gestures and expressions. The receiving party may wonder whether the statement is a conscious ploy on the part of the other side or whether the other side has come to its proposal after long and difficult deliberation, perhaps even surpassing its pre-mediation bottom line.

In these circumstances, the parties frequently ask the mediator whether they should take this "best number" pronouncement seriously. Unfortunately, too many mediators answer that inquiry in the affirmative. They either naively assume that no one would give a "best number" if they didn't mean it, or they vouch for the truthfulness of the announcement with a personal belief that it is the party's best number.

Such assessments on the part of the mediator are misguided and unethical. They also interrupt a negotiation that may still have much life in it. Let's look at one of the ways this problem can unfold. The scenario that follows takes place at the end of the negotiation.

Transcript

M: Well, I took them your proposal and I have a new number. It's $16,000; and it's what I call a number with commentary. They say that's really all they're going to put on the case. So I have a number and some words that went with it. And they wanted me to communicate both things.

P: That this is their last number?

M: Yes, they said it's their last number.

P: Well, let me ask you—from talking with them—do you really think that's their best number, or will they pay more?

M: I don't know. **[Observation]**

P: Well, as you know, I was hopeful of getting a lot more than $16,000. Uh ... I don't think I can go that low. I think what I'd like to do is go back with another number. [OK.] Their number is $16,000? [Yeah.] Well let's go back with $30,000.

M: OK, so that's a move from $45,000. **[Summary/Reframe]**

P: What do you think? Is that wise for me to go back like that? I've come down $15,000 in one drop.

M: I never know what to say to that question and I'm asked it a lot. In my experience, when somebody tells me their proposal is their "best number," they could be saying several different things. Number one, that it's their best number and you need to take it seriously or number two, we're getting tired of negotiating like this—meaning, they may have some more money. "I might have a thousand or two, but the gap's too big to even think about it." Now I don't know for sure which of those things they mean. All I can do is to communicate that they're at $16,000 and that they've told me they're through, that it's their last number. **[Observation]**

P: I don't want them to leave, because I can move some more. But I don't want to move too rapidly. And you know this lawyer; you've dealt with him before. Is he likely to be telling the truth about it?

M: I don't know. Every negotiation is different. **[Observation]**

P: What would you think if I went to $25,000? Would it make any better sense to them?

M: I don't know. [Pause] I do know that when people are at their "last number," if they are going to pay more, that they'll do so if they see a smaller gap between the parties rather than a bigger gap. So the smaller you can make the gap, the more inducement for them to do something, if they've got a little more money to spend. You know, Tom, I don't know that they have any more. They've said no. And I also don't know what your limits are. **[Observation/Suggestion]**

P: Well, I'll go to $25,000.

M: OK. And that's down from $45,000, which you perceive as a big jump—it may very well communicate that you'd like to get the case settled. **[Summary/Observation]**

P: I hope that it will, because we do want to settle.

M: We'll see if it has an impact on them, or whether $16,000 is their best number as they said, or— **[Observation]**

P: Now be sure that you let us know what they say and give us the option of coming back to them.

M: I won't dismiss them, Tom. I like to be very careful here at the end. We may still have a lot of work to do at this stage, so I don't let people just get up and go when there's more work to do.

P: OK.

Scenario #21: "I Don't Have Any More Room to Move" (Statement Made When the End Clearly Is Near)

This statement makes it very clear that the speaker has reached the end of his range and that the other party will not hear another proposal from him. If so, the mediator will work with the other side helping them think through their options or helping them do a net analysis, posing the question: How does this final proposal stack up against a probable range of verdicts, taking into account the costs of litigation, the uncertainty of the outcome, and other effects of litigation on the life of the litigant?

Or, it may mean something entirely different. Frequently it signals that the speaker has a little more room to move. He may pay a little more money to close the case, but not unless he's sure it will settle the case. Again, the mediator does not know for sure whether or not there's a dime more to be offered. Sometimes the mediator has a hunch that tells her the speaker might offer a few more dollars under the right circumstances. The mediator may pick it up from the speaker's tone of voice, from the way in which the conversation unfolded, or from the use of the words "room to move."

Here's an example of what the mediator might do under those circumstances. In this scene, the mediator returns from a private session with the claimant and begins a private session with the defense lawyer and claims representative.

Transcript

M: OK, Bob, I've got another number for you. They came down to $30,000. I conveyed your $15,000 to them and they came down to $30,000. [There's a long pause. The mediator observes them looking at each other.] Any thoughts? **[Question]**

D: Well, that's just not enough. And I think $15,000 is about enough. That's it. I know I didn't tell you that last time, but we're at the end of our rope.

M: OK. [Pause] He hasn't been moving at the speed you need? **[Summary]**

D: They started too high and they've been walking too slow for us. We've been going up and up. And we're at the end of our authority. I've told my clients and they've told me that we'd rather see them in court than pay more than this. We think that's a reasonable figure; we think that's a fair figure. We think anyone in their position should be able to settle with that amount. It's certain. I think they don't recognize the risk they run and that they couldn't come close to this at trial to net what's on the table today. So $15,000 is where we're going to stop.

M: Well, I hear you. [Pause] You surprised me a little bit on that one. I hadn't heard any stopping noises leading up to this. But why don't I give you and Ann a few minutes to think about that privately. I'm assuming we're probably done with what we can do today, but I would like for you to talk about whether there's anything else we can accomplish here today. **[Observation/Suggestion]**

D: Well, I'm not sure what you're asking us to do. Once we've said it's our best number, I'm not sure what we'll be talking about.

M: That's a fair question. Let me tell you what I'm thinking. Here's something people don't often think about in the heat of negotiations and here's what I see and hear in this case. There's a gap, and it's a fairly large one given how long we've been here. He's still at a number that's twice as big as yours. You haven't been happy with him; I'm aware of that.

But I'm going to hypothesize for a minute—don't even respond to this because I'm picking a number out of the air. I'm going to guess that if it would settle the case today, that you could pay another $500, if he were close enough for that number to close it out. Again, I'm not asking you to respond to that number as right or wrong.

∎∎∎∎∎

But here's something a lot of us don't think about toward the end of a difficult negotiation. The sum of $500 doesn't look like very much. But, you know, $500 could represent five moves of $100, or four moves of $125, or even 10 moves of $50. So, people think that if they don't have much room to move, they have no room at all to move. Again, I don't know if that's your situation or not; but if it is, you could chunk your amount into an arbitrary number of moves and start moving within that very small range.

It'll keep the negotiations going, if he's got room to move, and it will consistently communicate that you're at the end of your range. Those are some of the positives to be said for a strategy like that. Perhaps there're some negatives as well. Why don't I leave the two of you to talk about those kinds of things, and see if there are options you have to work with even though you're discouraged about getting this one closed. **[Observation/Suggestion, Reflective Response]**

D: Thanks, that's helpful.

Comment: This sort of thing happens to me a lot in mediations. Having become discouraged, one team may see no other option than to quit the negotiation. The discouraged team sometimes loses its way and loses sight of the power (options) it has to effect a change in the behavior of the other side. I may suggest an option and highlight its pros and cons, so that they will have a choice of options when they thought they had none.

In one mediation I conducted several years ago, the parties stalled out at $30,000 and $15,000. The defense was ready to quit. A conversation like the one above opened up some new options for the defense. With a great deal of skepticism they offered $50 more. They did this four times, as the plaintiff dropped $15,000. The case settled. It settled because they had a little more money to spend and found a way to play it out, effectively communicating that they were at the end of their negotiating range.

Scenario #22: "I'll Go to $xx.xx, But Only If It'll Settle the Case"

This is a kissing cousin of the previous scenario. In this scenario, the speaker actually tells you that he has more room to move but is unwilling to do so unless he has the assurance that it will settle the case. Again, it's reflective of the natural tendency of negotiators not to go to their best number if the case won't settle.

■■■■■

What a conundrum! One side has a number that they're willing to pay but doesn't want to reveal it to the other side. How can the other side consider it if the number is not published? This situation can put the mediator in quite a dilemma; for, implicitly, the speaker has asked the mediator to put the other party in the position of bidding against himself. Taken literally, the speaker wants the mediator to find out whether the other side would accept their number without having offered the other side a counterproposal. This would be classic "bidding against oneself." So, understanding the negative consequences of doing that, the mediator probably should spend time with the speaker, exploring the consequences of such a move and developing other ways of handling the situation.

One of the things I try to do in this circumstance is to take myself out of the middle as much as possible and not put myself in an awkward position with the other side. I try to place the responsibility for proposal making on the party I'm working with and help him develop a definite proposal of some kind. Often that is a contingent proposal, that is, a proposal that is announced but not really "offered" unless the other side accepts it. The use of this diplomatic jargon frequently works and is indicative once again of how closely the parties guard their best numbers. Another thing that I do is to suggest that the speaker talk directly with a representative of the other side. Sometimes the speaker accepts this option because he has greater faith in his own ability to covertly convey a contingent proposal than he does in the mediator's ability.

Scenario #23: "Let's Just Go to Our Bottom Line" (Late in the Negotiation)

This is very much like "Let's cut to the chase." It represents a low level of frustration and is usually heard at a later stage of the negotiation. The frustration does not stem from the gap between the parties being very large. In fact, the speaker thinks the other side might accept his best number if they heard it. The frustration is with the process of going back and forth to get to that point. So the speaker says, "Why don't we just get there?"

This is certainly a valid way for a party to conduct a negotiation. It doesn't put the mediator or the other party in a bad position or ask the other party to bid against itself. But it does not create the most favorable condition for that proposal to be accepted or optimize the chance of success.

■ ■ ■ ■ ■

After 15 years of conducting civil court case mediations, I have concluded that we humans have a hard time making changes in big jumps. We are more comfortable making life's decisions in small, incremental steps over a period of time. We perceive that the risks are smaller if we move in small steps and that the new result will be somewhat like our last position. In other words, the new result will be close to something that's familiar to us.

In money negotiations, it has been my experience that the parties are more likely to accept a new proposal if the gap they have to jump to accept it is a small gap. The smaller the gap, the better the chances for settlement.

Sometimes, negotiators overlook this fact of human nature and, out of a sense of frustration with the bidding process, want to jump to the end quickly. Given the element of human nature that motivates us to make changes in small increments, it might be in the negotiator's interest to go slower. When the negotiator finally does reach his best number, the gap between the parties will be smaller than the one that would have been present when he first wanted to go to his bottom line. The other side is more likely to jump the smaller gap to settlement than the previous, larger gap.

The mediator can articulate this option and its rationale, so that the negotiator can evaluate whether it helps him accomplish what he wants to accomplish. Once again, the mediator is not trying to convince the negotiator to choose this approach; he is only making sure that he knows it exists and knows some of its advantages and disadvantages. The choice of options should always be left to the negotiator.

Scenario #24: "Do You Have a Suggestion?"

As the reader has surmised by this time, I think that it is permissible for mediators to offer suggestions. But the timing of the suggestion and the tone with which it is made by the mediator is crucial. As a general rule, it's best not to offer a suggestion unless asked. And as a general rule it's best to offer a suggestion as just one more idea for the parties to think about. What I am recommending is that you help the parties define their goals, create options, and evaluate whether those options help them meet their goals. Offering suggestions for consideration, rather than selling them on the right thing to do, is the difference between being facilitative and being directive.

In a medical malpractice mediation several years ago, I delivered another proposal to the defendant's team after several hours of negotiations. The defense was clearly disappointed with the proposal and out of frustration indicated to me that they didn't want to move any further. It was obvious to me that they were reacting negatively to the plaintiff's movement and that they had some movement left to make.

What they did not know was that the same phenomenon was occurring in the other room. Each was reacting to the other side's moves and each had concluded that their ranges were far apart. I didn't know whether this case had any real chance of settling, because neither side had indicated what their best numbers would be. All I knew was that both sides spent most of their time with me in private sessions complaining about how bad the other side's numbers were and creating small movements in an effort to convince (unsuccessfully) the other side to get into their ballpark. After much conversation in the defendant's room and after a long silence, the defendant's lawyer asked if I had any suggestions. Here's the transcript of that conversation.

Transcript
Mediator returns from a private conference with the claimant and enters the defense's private room with a new position of $1.7 million.

M: They gave me a new number. I took your $650,000 to them and they came down to $1.6 million.

D: Phew! Well, I can't see that. That's too much!

M: They're still way outside your range?! **[Summary]**

D: Yes, that's a lot more than what I'm willing to pay.

M: And we've been at this for a while, too! **[Summary/ Observation]**

D: Yeah. Uhh. I don't want to quit, but . . . . [Long Pause] Do you have any suggestions?

M: Well, my observation is that it's been harder and harder for you to make new moves as we've gone along. [Yeah.] And you're still a long way apart. And I'm assuming that where they are is affecting your thinking about what you should do. [Yeah.] And I'm assuming that because they're so high in your estimation that it's keeping you from doing what you could do to settle this case. **[Observation/Summary]**

D: Well, I think that's fair to say.

M: Well, let me not talk about specific numbers, let me back up and talk about where I think we are in the negotiations. It seems to me that both parties are doing the same thing. You hear a number from them; you don't like it. I don't know this for a fact, but you appear to be slowing down in your movements because you're trying to tell them they aren't moving fast enough. Then they see you staying lower than they want you to be and they say, "Golly, they're not coming up fast so maybe we should stay high."

And so, pretty soon we're stuck with this self-defeating pattern. My guess is that each side probably has more room to move but doesn't want to because of where the other side is. My guess is, and you don't have to respond to this, but my guess is that you've got some more money, and that $650,000 is not all you have to settle this case. **[Observation]**

D: Yeah, but it's pretty close.

M: I understand. [Pause] Let me make a general suggestion without getting into your specific numbers. One of the problems in negotiations is that we often react to what the other side is doing, and we try to get them into the range we want them to be. Sometimes it works, but sometimes it doesn't. And when it doesn't we get to a point where we're stuck and everyone gets frustrated.

In that case it's sometimes helpful to take a look at what money you've got left to spend. You're at $650K now and you can go to $X. I don't know what that number is and I don't need to know. That's your business. But let me pull a number out of the air; let's say you've got $200K more. Don't react to that; it's just hypothetical.

Now you could develop a plan for spending that sum, whatever it is, that could be put into operation independently of what they do—regardless of how fast they are moving, how slow they are moving—and you could build into that some safety for you, so that you could play your money out and not telegraph what your best number is, how much you have. And you could do it in such a way that, as you approach the end of your range, if this is a successful strategy, you could shorten your moves and signal to them that you're getting near the end. And so it would allow movement to occur without much dependence on what they do; it would educate them over a series of moves about the range they need to be in; and it would signal them clearly when you're getting to the end.

So, as an example, let's say you've got $200K more; you could chunk that up into 10 moves of $20K a move, or pick a number. You chunk it up in whatever way you want to. And then you could move 20, 20, 20, regardless of what they do. My guess is that this negotiation would go a lot faster. We wouldn't have these heartrending discussions about what our next number will be. We'd develop some momentum to the process, and then you have a way to signal when you're at the end, all the while disguising where your final number is. That's one possible plan. There're other ways of playing this out. You could do half now, then half of that, and so on. There're some advantages and disadvantages we could talk about, but it seems to me that there are some approaches other than what we've been doing that have some possibility of getting us off dead center. **[Suggestion/Observation]**

D: Well I'm in favor of a plan, but I think we'd have to talk about it, perhaps without you. But I could see us going 20, 20, and 20 for awhile.

M: And you could evaluate as you're going along what's working or what's not and you could adjust to meet the circumstances and see whether the plan is working for you. Of course, there's no guarantee that the other side will move at the rate you want them to. But at least we'll get out of this trap of reacting to each other and it will help you move through your range and then you could send some signals about quitting at the end of your range. You'll at least have a plan and be in control of your own movement. **[Suggestion/Observation]**

D: OK, let us think about it. Now I'm not saying we've got another 200K.

M: I understand. You've got what you've got, **[Summary]** but you can chunk that up in some appropriate number and move through your range independently of how the other side chooses to act and hopefully avoid this stalling out we're experiencing now. **[Suggestion/ Observation]**

D: OK, let us talk.

Comment: This is a verbatim account of the conversation in that case. As it turned out, the defense team started moving in $20,000 increments. The plaintiff's team was pleasantly surprised and began moving. As the defense neared the end of their range, they took the remainder of their range and chunked it again. Then they started moving in equal chunks that were smaller than the original chunks. The message was accurately conveyed that they were nearing their final numbers. No other movement problems occurred and the case settled. Not every case will settle, of course, but if the parties develop a plan for their movement from proposal to proposal, they will at least get to (or close to) their best numbers and not stall out prematurely.

Scenario #25: "Do We Have to Go Back in There with Them Again?"

The success rate for mandatory mediations in civil trial court mediations in our state is around 65 percent. The overall settlement rate is 95 to 96 percent. The parties to litigation are generally happy to resolve cases and move on with their lives. However, as much as they are happy to resolve the case, they may not be happy with each other.

This was a bit of a surprise to me in the beginning of my mediation career. It may also be discouraging to mediators who hope to improve the relationship of the participants as a result of the mediation process. As I have pointed out elsewhere, the parties to a negotiation about money often have no relationship to build or repair. Frequently they become angry with each other during the course of the negotiation simply over the fact that they don't like the positions their opponent is taking.

Hopefully, the mediator has tried to bring about good communication during the conference and has worked to build or repair the meager working relationships that exist in these cases. But at the end of a civil trial court mediation, there still may be hard feelings and animosity between the parties, particularly when the case does not settle.

At that point, I generally do not force the parties to reconvene at the end of the conference. I generally do not ask them to "kiss and make up." I wasn't in favor of that approach when I was a kid and my grandmother forced my brother and me to shake hands after brawling in the backyard, and I don't think adults respond any better to that approach.

I do ask the parties if I can help them with other business, such as streamlining their discovery process or formulating a case management schedule. And I usually encourage them to think about what impression they want to make as they leave the mediation conference. Often they choose on their own to make contact with the other side and leave the session with civil conversation. Ultimately, I am guided by their desires in the moment and don't insist that they reconvene.

■ ■ ■ ■ ■
Recurring Problems of Movement: Settlement Conference Clichés

1. Who goes first? (Plaintiff)
2. Who goes first? (Defense)—"I'm not going to bid against myself."
3. Claimant's first proposal is higher than his case analysis.

4. One party reacts strongly to a perceived outlandish proposal.

   a. "I'm out of here."

   b. "That's insulting. Is that what they think my mama's worth?"

   c. "That's insulting. Do they think I'm stupid?"

   d. "I'm not going to bid against myself."

   e. "OK, I'll give them as ridiculous a number as they gave me ($500)."

   f. "Go tell them to give me a realistic number."

   g. "I'm not even going to dignify that number with a response."

5. "They're going backward."

6. A low-ball proposal is made in order to send a message but it is not identified as such.

7. "They're just not here in good faith."

8. "I'm not going to do their homework for them." Or, "Nobody gets free discovery."

9. "It's not the money; it's the principle."

10. "We want them to know we're serious."

11. "We don't want to move too fast, too soon."

12. "They're just not getting it."

13. "We're not going to pay a dime more than the other companies."

14. "But we don't have any more room to move."

15. "They're not moving fast enough."

16. "OK, they moved five, so I'll move five."

17. "This case isn't going to settle."

18. "Let's cut to the chase." (Early in the negotiation)

19. "Tell them we're not going any higher/lower."

20. "Is that really their best number?"

21. "I don't have any more room to move." (Statement made when the end clearly is near)

22. "I'll go to $xx.xx, but only if it'll settle the case."

23. "Let's just go to our bottom line." (Late in the negotiation)

24. "Do you have a suggestion?"

25. "Do we have to go back in there with them again?"

Closing the Gap: From Best Numbers to Settlement

7

I have been using the phrases "bottom line" and "best numbers" throughout this manuscript without giving them much attention. "Bottom line" is a phrase that is common to both negotiations and casual conversation, and it is taken from the language of accounting. It is used regularly throughout negotiations to refer to the parties' final proposals.

In its literal sense, it is used for the plaintiff's final number, because that number will be the one at the bottom of the plaintiff's range at the end of the negotiation. It is frequently used for the defendant's best number, even though the defendant's bottom line will be that party's top number of the day.

■ ■ ■ ■ ■

Participants in mediation training often want to know the best way of discovering negotiators' bottom lines. They think that it is important to know someone's bottom line in order to help the parties settle their case. They are surprised to learn that I don't inquire about the parties' bottom lines and, further, that I believe it is totally unnecessary to know those numbers to work productively as a facilitator of money negotiations.

I don't ask the parties about their bottom lines for several reasons. The first is that most people resent being asked for their walk-away position. It's private information, and to reveal it to the other side would be to give away a strategic advantage. Even though the mediator is supposed to be neutral and keep confidential any private information that is learned, negotiators worry that the mediator will unintentionally let private information influence the mediation to their detriment. So, the mediator's request for bottom-line information creates an awkward situation for negotiators who don't want to be put in the position of declining a mediator's request. I don't ask for bottom lines because I don't want to create an awkward situation for my clients.

The second reason I don't ask for bottom lines is that I would not get truthful information from the party who answered my inquiry. For the reasons stated in the preceding paragraph, people will hedge their number. They'll tell me a number that they think I will find justifiable, but that gives them some "wiggle room" at the end. That's understandable to me. They worry about revealing strategic information. So they'll give me just enough information to satisfy my request, but not enough to reveal the absolute best number. Therefore, I wouldn't get accurate information if I ask for a party's bottom line.

The third reason is a kissing cousin of the previous one. I don't ask, because that number will change over time. From experience, I know that what one's bottom line at the beginning of the mediation (10 a.m.) is not the same as at the middle (2 p.m.) or at the end (3:30 p.m.).

■■■■■

People change their minds about bottom lines during the mediation process. They actually take in what is being said. They identify perceived strengths and weaknesses. They learn new information and perspectives. Team members develop common understandings of potential verdict ranges. Risk analysis takes place. In other words, they do what we ask them to do, which is to evaluate and reevaluate their case. Our work, and the mediation process, makes a difference. Our clients come to new understandings; they develop new bottom lines. Therefore, the mediator does not receive accurate information if a bottom-line question is asked during the negotiating process.

The fourth reason I don't ask is that I don't want to reinforce old positions and I don't want to create a situation in which a party has the experience of "losing face" (even to the mediator) in order to make a needed change in his position. That, of course, is one of the problems with position-based bargaining: the parties have to change positions to get the case settled and in each change there is some amount of losing face that takes place. I don't want to make that problem bigger by what I say and do.

The fifth reason I don't ask for the parties' bottom lines is that I don't want to discourage either the parties or myself. In the thousands of cases I've mediated, I've never seen an overlap in the ranges of the parties, at least not one that was articulated to me. In almost every case where money negotiations form the heart of the mediation, the parties will reach their best numbers and still have a gap between them. Why should I ask for their best numbers before they are at the end of the negotiating process, when the answers will only reveal an apparently insurmountable gap? Knowing what the gap is early in the process will only serve to discourage them and discourage or distract me.

Help the Parties Reach Their Best Numbers

■ ■ ■ ■ ■

There are really two negotiations in civil trial court mediation conferences. The first one is the negotiation that takes the parties from their starting numbers to their target or walk-away numbers. The second negotiation is bridging the gap between the parties' best numbers, which we'll discuss next. This volume has explored the impediments to settlement that keep the parties from reaching their best numbers during that negotiation and the things that mediators can say and do to keep the parties moving through their negotiating ranges.

As you help them move forward, you should be aware of an important fact of human nature, and that is that the parties will be reluctant to move to their best numbers if they think they will have a gap in their positions when their best numbers are known. This presents an important dilemma for negotiators and mediators alike. How do we help the parties move to their best numbers when they believe that to do so will not settle the case?

You should also be aware of a lesser known fact of human nature and that is that if the parties reach their best numbers and the resulting gap is small, then the parties will find a way to settle in the majority of cases. This I know from experience, and I trust that it will serve to encourage you as the parties work through their negotiating ranges.

Helping the parties get to their best numbers is the bulk of what we do as civil trial court mediators. It is a significant contribution to the settlement of a money dispute. As a mediator in money negotiations, I assist the parties by helping them formulate thoughtful movement from position to position so that they accurately communicate their ranges of settlement. As a result, the parties often develop a plan for their negotiations that is not dependent upon how the other side responds. They move through their negotiating ranges with relative ease toward their bottom lines, without the acrimony that accompanies traditional bargaining and without the premature impasses that characterize most negotiations about money.

> ■■■■■
>
> When the parties do not have a plan for their negotiations, when they struggle with their decisions about movement, and when they resist going to their bottom lines because they perceive that the case won't settle if they do, I have to work diligently with them to help them understand that there are positive reasons, as well as the negative ones they perceive, to moving to their best numbers. The negatives they think they know all too well. It helps their understanding, however, to have them articulate those reasons. Often, the consequences they name turn out to be insignificant.

The most problematic consequence I hear from my clients is that trial judges will put pressure on the parties to settle the case before trial. Many negotiators believe that the judge will be unhappy with them if they "refuse" to negotiate just before trial, so they don't go to their best numbers at mediation in order to have a little room to move in the judge's chambers. This is true enough in our judicial system that some negotiators treat it as gospel. Other lawyers tell me that judges are spending less time on settlement discussions these days on the theory that the parties have tried to settle the case through mandatory mediation. Thus, these judges do not try to engage lawyers in settlement discussions prior to trial.

> ■■■■■
>
> The positives, that the real gap between the parties may be small and that most cases will settle if the real gap is known,

are factors with which many negotiators are unfamiliar. To help the parties move through their settlement range to their best numbers, a mediator may have to provide the rationale for their movement from the mediator's own experiences in civil trial court mediations. Thus, I often talk with the parties about the countless settlements I've witnessed when the parties choose to negotiate through their ranges and reach their best numbers. Those conversations have a way of expanding the options of the parties at a stage of the negotiations when they believe they have no more options.

Bridging the Gap

■ ■ ■ ■ ■

The negotiation that bridges the inevitable gap between the parties' best numbers is the second negotiation in the trial court mediation process. If the gap is relatively small in comparison to the distance the parties have traveled to get to it, the task before the parties may be less difficult and time-consuming than the negotiation process that got them there. In most cases, this second negotiation will be experienced by the parties as an entirely new negotiation.

One of the first things I do when the parties announce their best numbers is to mark the moment as the end of a difficult process and as an opportunity to take a fresh look at the case. I ask the parties to take a break and not think about the case for a moment. I take a break myself in order to clear my thinking and orient myself to this new stage of the negotiation.

During or after their break, the parties will reassess their positions in light of the true differences between them. They will once again calculate the costs of proceeding to trial, but this time with a true understanding of how close or far apart the parties' positions are. I listen carefully for clues the parties may give about how the process can be structured for a successful conclusion.

After the break, I ask the parties in private sessions if they have generated any thoughts about the settlement process at this final stage. There is no predictable path that arises in the majority of cases and there is no magic bullet that works in all situations to close the gap between the parties. However, several approaches have worked for me over the years. Some of them include:

- Ask the parties to call their superiors or others who have real authority to settle and inform them of the parties' latest proposals. Let the decision makers know what progress has been made.
- Find out what thoughts the parties themselves have for further movement. The parties will frequently solve the problem and know what to do.
- Ask each of the parties whether they have a proposal to make. They sometimes have the energy, desire, and authority for continued negotiations.
- Find out whether they have room to move. It will help you formulate a plan if they can't invent one.
- If there is an obvious midpoint between the numbers, ask the parties in private whether they can settle at that number.
- Organize a meeting of the lawyers to talk face to face. They will frequently bridge the gap with surprisingly candid conversation.
- Develop a number (or range) that would be equally difficult for the parties to accept and then structure a way to offer it to each side.

The Silver Bullet

This last suggestion needs clarification and explanation. When the conditions are right, I offer to give each of the parties a number for them to consider as the number to settle their case. This is a number somewhere between the parties' best numbers that I believe will be difficult for each of the parties to reach. It is not a number that reflects my evaluation of the case. It is a number that has some potential of settling the case based on the negotiations they have conducted earlier in the session.

I use this technique sparingly. I do not use it in every case in which a gap exists between the parties' best numbers. And I use it only as a last resort. In other words, I use it only after everything else I mentioned on the previous page has produced no plan or proposal. And I use it only when I, in fact, have a good feel for what that number should be, based upon all that I have learned and observed during the course of the mediation. I don't automatically throw out the number that is midway between the parties, although the midpoint often is the obvious and best number to use.

I talk with the parties about this procedure and offer my number only if all of the parties agree to the procedure. I tell them that I will propose the number for their consideration and ask them not to react to it in my presence. I ask them to take at least a few moments alone, call those who will make decisions about new money, recalculate their costs and expenses, and reevaluate their goals for the litigation. I ask them to treat the number as the number that will settle the case if they agree to it. I ask them to assume that the other party has already agreed to it.

■■■■■

Finally, I pledge to the parties that I will collect their answers in private and not reveal their answers to the other side unless both sides say "yes." This is the most important feature of the technique and it must be observed religiously. Without the confidentiality guaranteed by the mediator's pledge, the parties simply will not engage in the process. My pledge assures them that they will be no worse off by considering my number and saying yes to it. They will either settle the case, reach impasse, or hear a new proposal from the other side. In other words, my pledge assures the parties that they will not be put in the position of bidding against themselves.

I write this paragraph after having talked by phone with a lawyer representing a party in the mediation I conducted yesterday. He told me that his clients would accept and settle based on the number I gave at the end of the mediation. I await the response of the opposing lawyer and have no idea as I sit here what the response will be. All I know is that the real gap between the parties is known and that one side has said yes. The prospects of settlement are much better now than when the real gap between the parties was unknown. Settlement is now a real possibility.

Summary of Chapter 7

- There are two negotiations in a case that settles through traditional bargaining. The first is the negotiation that gets the parties to their best numbers and the second is the one that closes the gap between their best numbers.

- The most difficult negotiation is the first one. The signals the parties pick up in the early rounds of negotiation frequently lead them to believe that their best numbers will not settle the case. If that belief exists, the parties will be reluctant to go to their best numbers, and they will make proposals that discourage movement from the other side.

- Treat the announcement of best numbers as an important occasion and time to take a new look at the parties' goals and objectives in light of new knowledge about best numbers. Have them take a fresh look at case analysis, costs, and lost business opportunities.

- Give the parties an opportunity to come up with ideas for movement before jumping in with an idea of your own. The parties usually know what to do.

- If you choose to intervene with a mediator's final number, do so carefully. Explain the process you envision and devise a way to guard against the parties' bidding against themselves. Create a process that they will trust.

Other Models of the Mediation Process: Their Uses and Limitations in Civil Trial Court Mediation

8

In previous chapters, I described the recurring challenges that are present for mediators and litigators alike in the settlement of cases in the trial courts of this country. They are cases in which traditional bargaining abounds and that stubbornly resist our efforts to resolve them with problem-solving techniques.

These cases pose a dilemma for mediators who have been trained to employ a problem-solving approach in their work. They also pose dilemmas for mediation trainers who draw upon the literature of mediation to construct the content of their courses—because the predominant model of the mediation process in the literature is the problem-solving model. For that reason, I have developed over the years a number of observations and tools for use in my work as a mediator in civil trial court mediation that deal with the recurring dynamics inherent in traditional bargaining. These, of course, are what I have described and summarized in this volume thus far.

At several points along the way, however, I have alluded to how the problem-solving model of the mediation process can be useful in civil trial court mediations. Two days ago, for instance, I convened a mediation in a highway construction dispute and discovered that the parties did not have enough information to make informed decisions. That mediated settlement conference quickly became a mediated discovery conference in which the parties negotiated an efficient and inexpensive way of getting the information they needed.

The negotiation in that instance was a textbook example of the use of the problem-solving model. The parties started off with statements about what they would and would not do with respect to discovery and they wound up talking about their interests, mutual and otherwise, and creating workable solutions. The problem-solving approach was especially relevant at that point in the mediation of a claim for money. So, I would like to return to that model in order to review the ways in which the problem-solving frame of reference can be helpful to mediators in civil trial court cases.

The Problem-Solving Model

The aim of the problem-solving model is to help the parties to litigation, or more broadly speaking, disputants in any kind of conflict, to move away from debating and arguing about their positions and move toward a more cooperative and creative process of problem solving. The faith in the problem-solving model is that the parties can produce creative and workable solutions for mutual gain by reframing the negotiation process from traditional bargaining to problem solving.

One of the best, and best known, explications of the model is Christopher Moore's *The Mediation Process*.[1] In it, Moore identifies and describes 12 stages of the mediation process. Whether it is found in the language of Moore's 12 stages of mediation or the more familiar six-stage formulation in many community settlement centers' courses, the phrase "stages of the mediation process" has had a prominent place in the literature of mediation. The language of "stages of the mediation process" is the language of the problem-solving model.

In the early 1980s Roger Fisher and Bill Ury in *Getting To Yes*[2] introduced the distinction between "positions" and "needs and interests" to those interested in negotiation and mediation. Since then, commentators too numerous to mention have enriched the problem-solving model of mediation by incorporating this distinction.

As anyone who has read *Getting to Yes* knows, the distinction between the positions that parties take in a negotiation or dispute and their underlying interests in taking those positions is an important one for mediators and negotiators. People engaged in arguments, disputes, and lawsuits usually put forward their positions.

"This claim is worth $100,000 and that's what I want."
"Well, I'm sorry; it's not worth that much and I'll pay you $5,000 for it."

or

"I'm not going to cook supper tonight."
"But you have to; it's your turn."

"I want it" and "You can't have it" are positions. In the civil trial court context, the plaintiff demands (that's the language the defense uses to describe the plaintiff's offer to settle) a certain amount of money. That's a position. The defense counters with its offer of a lesser amount of money. That's a position. The dispute is framed initially by the competing positions of the parties.

Fisher and Ury have helped us understand that settling a dispute by arguing about positions is a tough job. People hold on to their positions with great tenacity. If settlement occurs, it does so because the parties make a series of painful concessions and agree to a position that represents a less-than-optimal arrangement.

There is an old adage in the world of negotiation that a good settlement is one in which both parties go away unhappy. This is often true of settlements reached through traditional bargaining. We all know from experience that making concessions is a difficult thing to do. The word itself has an unpleasant sound to it, because it brings to mind an endless process of giving up. To settle a conflict through traditional bargaining someone has to move from his position; he must make a concession.

Imagine a person "taking a position." A person stands straight and tall normally, but when he's arguing and in an attacking or defending mode, he's slightly crouched, his knees are bent, his feet are set wide apart, and his hands are held forward. He has taken a stance. He has adopted a position. To reach settlement with him, we have to get him out of that position. It looks, feels, and sounds like combat. It's a struggle.

The problem-solving model is an approach that can help us move away from the struggle of traditional bargaining and move toward the more cooperative process of inventing solutions for mutual gain or satisfaction. By identifying the parties' needs and interests, goals, and objectives, mediators can help them move away from arguing about positions and move toward a process of inventing solutions that meet their needs. As a result, mediators can help the parties reframe their negotiations from position-based bargaining to joint problem solving. This is the problem-solving model of the mediation process as it has been taught for the past 25 years.

Problem Solving in Business Disputes

■■■■■

I can recount many instances when I employed a problem-solving approach in the context of civil litigation and helped the parties reach settlements with which all parties were pleased. No one went away unhappy, because their needs were met. In the following paragraphs, I will identify the types of cases, issues, and situations in the civil trial court context in which a problem-solving approach may be helpful.

I find the problem-solving model useful in business disputes in which the parties have had working relationships in the past or wish to have such relationships in the future. These are cases in which the parties' best interests may best be met not by winning a lawsuit but by getting the case settled in such a way that it honors, preserves, or enhances the parties' working relationship.

One of the most difficult business disputes to work with in mediation is the breakup of a professional relationship, such as the dissolution of a medical or legal partnership. Those disputes often have the look, feel, and sound of a marital divorce. For that reason, I often approach them as I would a family mediation and adopt a problem-solving orientation.

In those disputes, the parties have a business and personal relationship. They know each other so well and dislike each other so much that they have difficulty addressing the practical problems they face. There is often present on each side a strong sense of betrayal that produces hostile interactions during the mediation session.

In business disputes, the parties may have multiple sets of interests that make the application of the problem-solving model a perfect match. Mediators can help them focus on identifying those interests and inventing options to serve and advance them. Frequently that process leads to creative solutions and win-win opportunities for all parties.

In one contract dispute I mediated several years ago, the plaintiff and defendant were locked in protracted litigation with $7 million at stake. The contract in question defined the obligations of the parties in the operation of a certain municipal facility. The facility was owned by the city and operated by a private company. Complicating the working relations of the parties was the need of the private company for autonomy and secrecy in the accounting and billing procedures of the business. Equally important to the municipal officials involved was a need for accountability and public scrutiny of the public's business.

The first two days of the mediation were spent identifying the parties' concerns. We learned for instance that the municipality operated under a state mandate that made the facility necessary and that there were no other companies that were interested in operating such a facility. On the company's side of the ledger, we learned that the facility in question was the first and only one the company had managed and that this operation would be the foundation upon which future expansion would take place.

■ ■ ■ ■ ■

In reality, we learned that the parties needed each other. Once that realization took hold, the last several days of the mediation were spent redefining the terms of the contract, the obligations and responsibilities of certain key employees, and the procedures for financial reporting. The parties resolved their dispute by going back into business with each other.

Needs and Interests in Injury Cases: The Defense

As I have mentioned in previous chapters, the case load of civil litigation is dominated by property and personal injury cases that are based on a theory of negligence and insured by a policy of liability insurance. One of the important factors to remember about the mediation of those cases is that settlement discussions are often controlled by people who are experienced negotiators— lawyers or insurance claims representatives. They are repeat litigators. They are used to negotiating. They know the drill. They know that most of their cases will be settled for money only. They want to get down to business.

Insurance claims representatives negotiate claims every day of their lives. They settle hundreds of cases in a year, most of which are settled with claimants without lawyers, litigation, or mediation. They are swamped with cases. They don't want to waste their time in mediation if they are not going to be productive. What does a claims representative need?

The needs and interests of the insurance representatives will not be discovered in a conversation during the settlement conference itself. However, anyone who takes the time to confer with people within the insurance industry will uncover something very important about the needs and interests of claims representatives. The major need of those at the settlement conference who are associated with the insurance industry is to get the claim settled as quickly and expeditiously as possible within an acceptable range of money that has been reserved for the case by the company. In the defense's room, it is no more complicated than that.

■■■■■

Over a period of time, I have come to understand that claims representatives need to move cases. The typical claims adjuster has a need to reach a settlement that disposes of the claim, gets it off his or her desk, and gets it concluded. They have a need to "close the file." There are a couple of reasons for that. The first is that claims adjusters today are overworked, and their basket of work fills up on a daily basis. It's important for them to get claims settled so that their in-basket doesn't become overwhelming.

Secondly, insurance companies are required by law to set aside enough money to pay claims as they are filed. As long as that money is set aside, "reserved" as they say, it is not available to the company to invest. Therefore, claims representatives work in a culture where they are expected to release working capital for the company's investment purposes. And so, there is a pressing need on the part of claims representatives to move cases, manage cases, get them settled, and not waste a lot of time.

A humorous incident I was involved in years ago illustrates this point. I was asked to speak to a group of independent claims adjusters to explain the newly created mediation program for the superior courts in our state court system. After I described the success we were experiencing in the program, I spoke of an impediment to settlement that we had encountered in injury cases. It occurs in cases in which the plaintiff fears he will have future medical expenses due to his injuries and the claims representative believes there is no objective evidence to support such a fear. At the end of this description, I challenged the audience to come up with a creative way of handling the situation.

Three gentlemen in the front row raised their hands and offered an intriguing suggestion. They told the assembled group that, in the proper case, they would place an appropriate amount of money in trust for the future medical expenses of the plaintiff. Future medical expenses directly related to the accident would be paid directly to the provider. The amount in trust was capped at an agreed-upon amount and was made available for a limited amount of time, generally two to five years. If any portion of the amount set aside was not paid for related medical expenses incurred, it reverted to the insurance company at the end of the time period.

I thought this was a great example of applying a problem-solving approach to a money dispute. It appeared to be a win-win situation for everybody, and I was glad to have the suggestion. However, a man in the back row stood up and asked in an agitated manner: "But how do you close the file?" He was referring to that need, interest, goal, and objective that is the backdrop for all claims representatives and, indeed, the insurance culture in the United States: the need to move cases, to close cases, to settle cases, to get cases off the books. Humorously one of the gentlemen in the front row turned to his colleague in the back, put his hands apart as if he were holding two sides of a file and slammed his hands shut, thus "closing" the imaginary file. He closed the file simply by reframing what "closing a file" meant.

The insurance culture of the company represented by the gentlemen in the front row was very different from the culture of the company represented by the man in the back row. There was less of a need for the company in the front row to "close the file" in the usual meaning of that word. In that culture the file was in fact closed if all of the money had been paid out except for a finite sum that in a finite term could revert to the company. In the back row, however, such a solution was not workable or desirable. It did not meet that adjuster's need to close the file. His was a culture that, in my experience, characterizes most of the insurance representatives with whom I work. Few claims representatives would find the solution outlined by the gentlemen in the front row to be workable in today's insurance environment.

■■■■■

Finally, it is important to remember that most insurance adjusters do not work alone. They are employees of large corporations. They are supervised by claims managers, who are supervised by other people, who in turn report to officers of the company and boards of directors. In other words, there is a strong system of accountability and reporting in the insurance industry.

This "culture of accountability" makes it exceedingly difficult for individual claims representatives to operate as autonomously as they used to when I was settling and trying cases as a lawyer. They have to report up the chain of command to become authorized to offer money to settle a case. This reporting culture necessitates that the case be carefully worked up and documented to an extent not understood by many outside the insurance industry, and particularly by many plaintiffs' lawyers.

It is important for civil trial court mediators to understand the background and culture that insurance claims representatives operate in and bring with them to the negotiating table. Mediators should work to understand the processing needs, if you will, that claims representatives have in court-ordered mediation, so that they can respond appropriately to the defense team and help other parties be better prepared for settlement negotiations.

Needs and Interests in Injury Cases: Plaintiffs

■■■■■

Plaintiffs, claimants of all kinds, come to settlement discussions with a different background than the defense. Although their lawyers are experienced negotiators, the litigants themselves are not. They are first-time litigators. They seldom negotiate settlements of insured claims. They do not know how to evaluate injury claims. They do not know what juries typically decide in those cases and they don't know what similar cases settle for outside of litigation.

Plaintiffs have suffered injuries in traumatic events. They and their families have been personally affected by those events. They are not detached; they are often emotional about their claims. They worry about the future in a very personal way. They grapple with the effects that their injuries have had on their ability to function in the world and to engage in normal personal, family, social, or business activities. The decisions they make in the settlement conference will be ones that they have to live with for the rest of their lives. The consequences of their decisions will live on.

The lawyer-client relationship on the plaintiff's side is very different from that of the defense. Typically the plaintiff does not have as much contact with his or her lawyer as the defense does. The lawyer does not report to him about developments in the case to the extent that is expected on the defense side. The plaintiff generally is not kept as well informed about the changing value of the claim as the evidence develops during discovery.

Plaintiffs typically have high expectations for their claims. This is something that plaintiffs' lawyers often are accused of pumping up. The public perception of plaintiffs' lawyers is that they inflate the expectations of their clients. My own experience is to the contrary. Most plaintiffs' lawyers work hard to help their clients develop a realistic expectation for the outcome of their cases. Most plaintiffs have unrealistic expectations.

The dilemma that plaintiffs' lawyers face is very interesting. They work hard to bring the client's expectations into a realistic framework. However, if they do so too strenuously, the plaintiff begins to wonder whether the lawyer is "really on my side." In other words, plaintiffs' lawyers walk a fine line between educating and working with a client to develop realistic expectations and losing the confidence of their clients.

Plaintiffs sometimes wonder whether their lawyers really believe them or are fully committed to pursuing their claims. A statement by lawyers about the value of the case, based solely upon an objective reading of the evidence, is often experienced by clients as a statement about their veracity or character. This is a tension that exists in the relationship between every lawyer and every client. But it seems to be more prevalent for the plaintiff's lawyer in a personal injury case, because his inexperienced client has unrealistic expectations for the case.

Plaintiffs' lawyers also come to the conference with a culture, and it is different from that of the defense. Although their clients frequently exert tremendous control over the outcome of negotiations because of their emotional involvement in the case and their lack of experience in valuing injury claims, plaintiffs' lawyers typically make the decisions about settling the case. As a consequence, the plaintiff's lawyer does his or her work without thinking about "reporting up the line." Plaintiffs' lawyers are much more autonomous than defense lawyers, and it is they, more than their clients, who will "call the shots" at the end.

■ ■ ■ ■ ■

The plaintiffs' culture is also different in another interesting respect. In their discussions of the case, both the plaintiff and the plaintiff's lawyer will pay far more attention to the development of the liability side of their case than to the damages side. In terms of discovering their case and developing evidence and expert testimony about their case, they seem to be far more concerned with proving who was right and who was wrong than they are with proving "how much I should get."

The plaintiff's team tends to spend more time in initial private sessions talking about the evidence affecting the liability issues while the defense team tends to spend more time talking about issues affecting the measure and calculation of damages.

Plaintiffs and their lawyers are much more accepting of discussions about needs and interests than the defense. The plaintiff's team typically has not decided what its negotiating ranges will be. Plaintiffs struggle to bring their expectations in line with their lawyer's evaluation of the case. They look to the mediator for help in achieving that integration.

Well-placed questions by the mediator can initiate a needs-and-interests discussion that may produce opportunities for creative solutions, even within the context of traditional bargaining. In a preceding paragraph, I mentioned the situation in which the plaintiff worried that his injury would have lasting effects and that his health would decline over time. As a plaintiff thinks about the specter of continuing medical expenses, he may become concerned about whether the sums being negotiated will cover those future medical costs.

In the same case, however, the adjuster is looking closely at the file, sees no objective statement from the doctor about future medical care related to the injury suffered in the accident, and sees no basis at all to set aside moneys for the payment of future medical expenses. The solution of a medical needs trust comes to mind as a result of the mediator's conversation with the plaintiff about her needs. Unfortunately, as we have seen, the medical needs trust as a solution typically does not fit the insurance company culture. The medical needs trust is rarely accepted by both parties as a solution for the case.

■■■■■
Another example of how a needs-and-interests discussion can bear fruit in the plaintiff's room has to do with the manner and timing of payment of the settlement proceeds.

The mediator may learn through such a discussion that the plaintiff has very little present need for the sums being negotiated in the settlement conference. The plaintiff's income is sufficient to take care of routine needs. All medical expenses for treatment of her injuries due to the accident have been paid by a health care insurance company that has no right to recover the sums it has paid. There are no future medical expenses contemplated. There is no permanent disability that produces a monetary need. A structured settlement wherein the insurer purchases an annuity with the settlement proceeds and pays the plaintiff over time might suggest itself in this instance.

In other cases, the mediator may learn that the plaintiff has many present needs. Medical providers may need to be paid. Health insurers and other lien holders may need to be paid. Debts incurred during a period of diminished income may need to be repaid. This plaintiff has an immediate need for cash. No magic solution will appear as a result of this needs discussion. The settlement conference will proceed with traditional bargaining and payment will be made, if at all, in a lump-sum check delivered within several weeks of settlement.

■■■■■
More often than not, a needs-and-interests discussion in a case involving an insured claim will not produce the wonderful opportunity for a creative, win-win solution that mediators dream of and work to make happen. New ways of

doing things will not appear dramatically. However, discrete elements of that same case may present an opportunity for such a solution with respect to that element. I am thinking now of the subject of confidentiality, an issue for the parties that usually arises in the later stages of the negotiation when it appears that the parties might indeed settle the case.

Confidentiality Provisions in Settlement Agreements

Many people involved in civil litigation do not want the terms of their settlement made public. Therefore, one or more parties may insist upon (i.e., negotiate for) a term in the settlement agreement that requires the parties to keep confidential the terms of the settlement.

This issue usually arises late in the negotiating process. It is saved by the parties for this time in the negotiation for two reasons. The first is that in the beginning of the negotiating process, the parties are skeptical about the prospects of settlement. They don't want to spend time negotiating the issue of confidentiality when they are pessimistic about the prospects of settlement. The issue of confidentiality seems irrelevant at the beginning of the negotiation.

Secondly, the parties worry about the signals they send to each other during the mediation. They worry that they may be signaling that they are too willing to settle if they raise the issue of confidentiality in the beginning of the negotiation. They worry that they are going to be disadvantaged in their bargaining by mentioning the subject too early. Mediators need to be aware of these factors and not rush into the subject of confidentiality in the early stages of the negotiation.

Later in the negotiation, however, and well before the last stages of bargaining, the mediator might take the lead and raise the issue himself. Frequently, people who are asked to consider a confidentiality provision after they believe they have an agreement on a dollar amount feel like they've been "snookered" in their bargaining. An alert mediator can help prevent this problem in the parties' negotiations by raising the issue before the end is near.

When the issue of confidentiality comes up, it is often an emotional one. The discussion about confidentiality usually starts out the way any disagreement starts. It begins with a battle over positions. "I want a confidentiality agreement" on the one hand; "You can't have it" or "You'll have to pay for it" on the other. So the argument about confidentiality typically is approached by the parties with an exchange of positions. This is an excellent time for the mediator to flip into a problem-solving frame of reference and help the parties identify their interests and invent solutions for mutual gain.

At this point, the mediator can safely ask the typical problem-solving types of questions. What is the problem that a confidentiality agreement solves for you? What are your goals in negotiating for a confidentiality provision? How does that help you? What are the consequences of not having a confidentiality agreement in place?

And to the other side the mediator might ask, What is it about a confidentiality provision that creates a problem for you? In what ways will it hinder what you're trying to accomplish? What is it that you are trying to accomplish by insisting that there be no confidentiality provision? In other words, the mediator will try to uncover basic needs and interests and goals and objectives with respect to the issue of confidentiality.

If the parties can identify their needs, then they can start working on confidentiality as a problem to be solved rather than a battle to be fought. They may even discover that their needs and interests are simple and require little from the other side to create a solution. I am reminded of a dispute one of my colleagues mediated in which an apology was demanded by the plaintiff. It turned out that the defendant, who initially was adamantly opposed to writing an apology, was only concerned that the plaintiff would publish his written apology for the community to see. Ultimately, the defendant agreed to write an apology and place it in the custody of the defendant's lawyer. It was also agreed that the plaintiff could "visit" the apology any time he wanted.

The issue of confidentiality comes up frequently in medical malpractice cases when it appears to the parties that settlement might occur. The defense seeks it to preserve the reputation of the physician and hospital. Of course, a confidentiality provision will not eliminate the requirement of reporting a settlement by or on behalf of the physician to the national databank, nor will it eliminate the ability of health insurers to require physicians to report settlements as a part of their application for preferred provider status within that insurer's network.

Plaintiffs' lawyers often want to publicize their verdicts and settlements; therefore they resist agreeing to a confidentiality clause, believing that it will hamper that publication. Sometimes they react by demanding that the defense pay extra for the clause, and they argue that it is an item of value.

The plaintiff himself may object to a confidentiality provision out of a belief that it is his civic duty to report instances of malpractice and that he would be doing the community a disservice by agreeing to it. A mediator may assist the plaintiff in this matter by initiating a discussion with the plaintiff and his lawyer in which his sense of civic duty is weighed against the risk of losing the case at trial. During that discussion, the mediator may also make sure that the plaintiff understands an important element of human nature—that people who come into money by inheritance or chance often are surprised to find out how many of their friends and relations come calling for a bit of financial assistance. Plaintiffs may change their minds about the desirability of a confidentiality provision after such a discussion.

The confidentiality provisions I see in mediation routinely allow the physician and hospital to retain their anonymity while allowing the plaintiff's lawyer to publish the facts of the case and settlement without identifying the parties, the location of the lawsuit, and, sometimes, the amount of the settlement.

The Primary Reason to Attend to Needs and Interests in an Insured Claim

■ ■ ■ ■ ■

Dramatic, win-win solutions will seldom occur in the settlement of an insured claim. However, there are subtle but important consequences that a needs-and-interests discussion can have on a negotiation about money. On the plaintiff's side, a needs-and-interests conversation will often have a dramatic impact on the plaintiff's willingness and ability to move from one position to another or to settle the case. Generally that willingness will be greatly increased by a discussion of the plaintiff's needs.

In previous chapters, I reviewed how a discussion of case value will have an impact on the positions the plaintiff makes. Through that discussion, the plaintiff "gets in touch with the realities of his case." When people are in touch with the realities of their case, even though they may still disagree about numbers, their negotiating ranges will be affected. Generally the parties' positions will be closer together, because the lawyers on both sides of the case use the same analytical methods to value their cases.

I have discovered that a discussion of the plaintiff's needs and interests will have a similar effect from another angle. For many plaintiffs in personal injury negotiations, the money they seek in litigation is an abstraction. In fact, litigation itself is an abstract idea. Most of them have never engaged in litigation. By the time their mediation rolls around, they've had little exposure to the often demanding and demeaning experience that litigation can be. Those of us who have tried cases for a living may even enjoy the litigation experience. It can be exciting and satisfying in many respects. The experience for most litigants, however, is exceedingly different and it is described by them universally in negative terms.

Litigation is a process that extracts many costs. Litigation takes time and it costs money. The extended time it takes often creates a sense of uncertainty in the mind of the litigant, making it difficult to plan his or her life. Litigation takes time and energy to prepare for and conclude. It disrupts the normal cycles of one's life and the opportunities to concentrate on productive activities. Business and professional litigants may understand this well, but other litigants have little awareness of the realities of litigation.

■ ■ ■ ■ ■

A needs-and-interests discussion can help litigants get in touch with the realities of litigation and the realities of their lives. Well-placed questions by the mediator may turn the abstraction that is litigation into something concrete and may illuminate important personal goals and objectives that have been buried and unarticulated.

To help the plaintiff connect with the realities of his or her life, I ask questions like: What will the proceeds of settlement be used for? How will you spend the money you receive from trial or settlement? What are the actual costs you will incur as a result of these injuries? Do you have present needs or future needs? What are you trying to accomplish with this litigation? If litigation is a solution to a problem, what is the problem and what will it take to fix it?

These are important questions that litigants are seldom asked during the course of litigation. Most of their preparing for litigation is spent gathering information and discussing the value of their case. The time spent with a mediator discussing these matters will help the plaintiff develop a new awareness of what settling or concluding his litigation can mean in practical terms. That, in turn, will have an impact on the plaintiff's positions during the remainder of the mediation.

■ ■ ■ ■ ■

A discussion about the realities of one's life, coupled with a discussion of the realities of one's case, can often help a litigant achieve a new perspective about his anger and his expectations. A discussion of these realities may help the plaintiff become more practical and realistic and more amenable to the information that his lawyer tries to convey to him.

The impact of a needs-and-interests discussion with the plaintiff in a personal injury negotiation is subtle. Although it rarely produces wonderfully creative solutions, it does have a way of making the plaintiff more amenable to a case value discussion and a way of producing greater willingness by the plaintiff to move through the difficult process of making movement and concessions.

This is difficult to describe on paper, but the phenomenon I'm talking about has been repeated in hundreds of personal injury cases throughout my mediation career. Negotiations that slow down and perhaps stop altogether may be jump-started by a simple discussion about the realities of the plaintiff's life. Unrealistic plaintiffs often become realistic and amenable to bargaining if someone takes the time to discuss their life, their needs, their fears, and their circumstances.

Another benefit of the needs-and-interests discussion is that it helps the mediator establish rapport with the litigant himself. This can be crucial. The litigant usually feels out of control during the litigation process and even during the mediation itself. The mediator may be the only one in the process who expends the time and effort to talk with the plaintiff about his life and his circumstances. If that happens, a degree of rapport can develop between the litigator and the mediator that will make it possible for the plaintiff to open up to the hard realities that case analysis often reveals.

■■■■■

It is worth mentioning that initiating a needs-and-interests discussion in a claim about money must be approached carefully.

In the first place, most lawyers want to talk about the factors that affect their determination of the value of the case. They want to talk about liability and damages. Let them; follow their lead; go first with what they are most concerned with. It is important to them to analyze and evaluate the evidence in the case. It is the way they get you, the other side, and their client in touch with the realities of the case as they see them. Timing is important here. Needs and interests will probably take a backseat to case analysis until well into the conference. That's OK. It's one of the things that lawyers and their clients need to do.

Secondly, it's important to remember that in a case about money, it is difficult to frame a needs-and-interests question that doesn't sound out of place or even irrelevant. The answer to your question, "What are your interests here?" will probably be, "I'm interested in getting the most money I can from this case!" The adage that the most creative part of the mediator's job is figuring out what questions to ask is never as true as it is with a needs-and-interests discussion in the context of a claim for money.

■■■■■

One of the ways I've developed to uncover a party's needs and interests in a claim for money is unusual but illuminating. I frame a question that invites the litigant to tell me what he is going to do with the settlement proceeds when they are received. This inquiry must be handled carefully, because people generally consider the subject of finances too private to discuss with strangers.

Hopefully, by the time the mediator makes the inquiry, he or she is not a total stranger and has developed some degree of rapport with the litigant. If litigants are willing to answer the question, they will talk about the various expenses they have, the goals they have, and the problems they think the proceeds will solve. An indirect question about how the proceeds will be spent will generate more information about needs and interests than a direct question that uses the well-worn phrase "needs and interests."

The Mediation Process: The Search for a New Model

As you may know, the problem-solving model has undergone much scrutiny in the past decade and has been criticized for several reasons. One such criticism came from two of my teachers, Margaret Shaw and Patrick Phear, in an article published in *Mediation Quarterly*.[3] In that article, Shaw and Phear accurately reported that the mediation process has always been described as a model with a number of discrete stages. Mediation "is conceptualized as a linear process," suggesting "a sequence for solving the problems brought to mediation." In the problem-solving model, "mediators are encouraged to define issues and progressively resolve them one by one." Their first critique is that "the model tends to ignore the dynamic interplay between issues" and is, thus, unrealistic.

Shaw and Phear's second criticism of the problem-solving model is that it promotes positional rather than interest-based bargaining. It "encourages the mediator to frame issues continually in terms of solutions," making it "difficult to redirect the discussion in terms of the parties' needs and interests." And finally, they criticized the model because "conceptualizing the mediation process as a search for solutions encourages the mediator to actively participate and intrude his or her personal values and judgments."

Shaw and Phear wanted to reconceptualize the mediation process "as an essentially dynamic, integrated system" that not only promotes "the likelihood that mediators can help parties reach effective agreements that respond to all their needs and interests but also reinforces the importance of process rather than solutions. This systems approach to the mediation process parallels family systems theory" which views the mediation process "as a dynamic process of eliciting, understanding, and reframing information into specific details of parties' needs and interests. The emphasis is on process rather than on results, with the role of the intervener usually described as a framer of the issue parameters, or elements of the party's dispute system. As the specific details about the party's needs and interests are elicited and clarified, natural links or connections between those parameters become apparent and understandable. These links and connections, or elements of resolution, then serve, in turn, as the framework for the specific terms of the final agreement." The "parameters and details are a product of the parties' conversation, and the mediator draws those from the parties from the process of eliciting, understanding, and reframing."

■■■■■

This article was an important one in my development as a mediator. It helped me understand that there are many issues and sub-issues involved in a dispute and in the decision making of the disputants that are interrelated and not susceptible to linear resolution. The insights in this article freed me to spend more time on issue identification and on understanding the many aspects of the dispute that might be important to the parties and to the resolution of the dispute. It gave me permission to spend more time doing what I call "massaging the issues." It led me to concentrate more on eliciting, understanding, and reframing, or what I now call simply, understanding.

Other authors, most notably Robert Bush and Joe Folger, have critiqued the problem-solving model of the mediation process as well. *The Promise of Mediation*[4] by Bush and Folger also criticizes the problem-solving model as being too linear in its formulation. In their view, the problem-solving model does not conceptualize the process as a dynamic one; it focuses the parties and the mediator too early on solutions; and it tends to lead the mediator to interject his or her own solutions, values, or judgments. Bush and Folger argue instead for a "transformative orientation" to conflict.

In the transformative orientation, "the conflict is first and foremost a potential occasion for growth in two critical and inter-related dimensions of human morality. The first dimension involves strengthening the self . . . . The second dimension involves reaching beyond the self to relate to others."

"The ideal response to a conflict is not to solve 'the problem.' Instead, it is to help transform the individuals involved in both dimensions of moral growth. Responding to conflicts productively means utilizing the opportunities they present to change and transform the parties as human beings. It means encouraging and helping the parties to use the conflict to realize and actualize their inherent capacities both for strength of self and for relating to others. It means bringing out the intrinsic goodness that lies within the parties as human beings. If this is done, then the response to conflict itself helps transform individuals from fearful, defensive, or self-centered beings into competent, responsive, and caring ones, ultimately transforming society as well."

In the transformative approach, empowerment and recognition are the two most important effects that mediation can produce. Bush and Folger define empowerment in the following paragraph.

> Involvement in conflict affects everyone in similar ways. Disputing parties are typically unsettled, confused, fearful, disorganized and unsure of what to do. As a result they feel vulnerable and out of control. This is as true for "powerful" executives and officials as it is for consumers, family

members, or school children. From this starting point of relative weakness, parties are empowered in mediation when they grow calmer, clearer, more confident, more organized, and more decisive—and thereby establish or regain a sense of strength and take control of their situation.[5]

■ ■ ■ ■ ■

When I first read that paragraph, I could not conceive of its application to the mediation of a personal injury case. As the problem of movement in those cases became more apparent to me, and as I started using the principles of control theory to assist the parties, the description of empowerment in Bush and Folger's work became more relevant. Bush and Folger are correct: when an insurance claims representative or a trial lawyer packs his bags and starts to leave a settlement conference because he doesn't like the proposal conveyed by the other side, it is clear that he is "out of control," as these authors suggest. A mediator can help that person become "empowered" in that moment and regain a sense of power and control in the negotiation.

Bush and Folger describe recognition in the following paragraph:

In the heat of conflict, disputing parties typically feel threatened, attacked, and victimized by the conduct and claims of the other party. As a result, they are focused on self protection; they are defensive, suspicious, and hostile to the other party, and almost incapable of looking beyond their own needs. From this starting point of relative self absorption, parties achieve recognition in mediation when they voluntarily choose to become more open, attentive, sympathetic, and responsive to the situation of the other party, thereby expanding their perspective to include an appreciation for another's situation.[6]

There is no better example of the truth of those statements than when the plaintiff's lawyer describes the claims representative as a "heartless bean counter" or the claims representative accuses the plaintiff's lawyer of being an "ambulance chasing, bottom feeder." On rare occasions in civil trial court mediation, one party or the other catches a glimpse of the humanity of the other and recognition is achieved. Bush and Folger, and many others, remind mediators to pay attention to those moments.

■■■■■

The "promise" of mediation is that mediation can do much more than settle cases. It can empower litigants in their decision making and it can connect them with each other in recognition of their common humanity. *The Promise of Mediation* reminds us of the many-faceted nature of what is ideal in mediation and that mediation is about more than simply settling a case or finding a workable solution.

Bush and Folger clearly document the many ways in which mediators lose sight of the ideal in mediation and become directive in the mediation process. Mediators do this by interjecting their own solutions, values, judgments, and ideas about how the parties should resolve their dispute. Perhaps the most chilling portion of their work is their description of how many mediators manipulate the mediation process by ignoring concerns that the parties themselves want to discuss and by adding issues that the mediator believes are important.

Having been inspired by *The Promise of Mediation*, I must also say that the book is troubling in several respects. First, while Bush and Folger effectively argue that mediators should be facilitative rather than directive, they also argue that they should be "transformative." In the description of the transformative approach to conflict there exists a potential for mischief that is also inherent in the problem-solving model. If the problem-solving model leads mediators to focus too quickly on solutions, the transformative approach can also lead mediators to focus too quickly on transformation.

The danger in adopting a "transformative" approach to mediation is that mediators who do so may become more directive and coercive than usual. If we see it as our goal to become transformative, we may indeed begin to act as if it is our duty to muck around in the lives of our clients and to "transform them."

There is something disturbing to me about a formulation of the mediation process that has the potential to produce mediators who will become directive simply because they are focusing on the goal of transformation. A friend of mine voiced my concerns about this possibility in the movement to make transformation the goal of mediation when he said, "I think that the only people mediators should be trying to transform is themselves."

The second criticism I have of the approach that Bush and Folger advocate is that they portray it as the only approach that can accomplish the goals of mediation. While an approach to mediation that concentrates first on empowerment and recognition is an orientation that can lead to important insights and progress for the parties, it is not inclusive enough to describe, explain, and handle all the phenomena and dynamics that present themselves in the many different types of conflicts and negotiations that we find in everyday life.

The insistence on the part of Bush and Folger that use of the problem-solving model precludes a transformative orientation and vice versa simply is not realistic. The transformative orientation and the orientation of the problem-solving model, as well as the approach I have described for the mediation of claims for money in previous chapters, are useful in many situations and in many disputes, but not in others. For myself, I frequently find that I have employed all of the approaches I've mentioned in this section in different mediations and at different times in the same mediation.

Facilitating Understanding

The common thread in the criticisms of the models of mediation I've mentioned in this chapter is that each believes the ideals of mediation have been compromised by the use of certain approaches to mediation that were intended to foster those ideals. All of the criticisms focus on the tendency of mediators everywhere to become directive rather than facilitative.

■■■■■

There seems to be general agreement in the national mediation community that mediators should strive to be facilitative rather than directive in the work that we do to help people resolve their disputes. That is our goal and our ideal—to be facilitative rather than directive. If there is a description of the mediation process that will remind us of that goal and at the same time help us to achieve it, then I would advocate a model of mediation in which facilitating understanding is the key element.

A civil trial court mediation training I conducted last year for the ABA's Senior Division crystallized this notion for me. As I was describing to a room full of would-be mediators the concepts I keep in the forefront of my consciousness while mediating the resolution of civil cases, the following formulation came to mind.

■■■■■

Using the tools of the mediator:
questions, brainstorming, summarizing, reframing, observations, and suggestions.

I seek first to develop understanding:
of the case, the people, their relationships, their goals and needs, their problems, their resources, and the life and outcome they desire.

Out of which may grow:
solutions, settlements, personal growth, connectedness, and moral development.

> Before we mediators strive for settlement; before we strive for solutions; before we strive for empowerment, recognition, or transformation; before any of these, we would be well served to strive first for understanding.

That is the orientation I try to take into the mediation of civil lawsuits, even those involving claims for money and traditional bargaining. I try to understand the parties and their representatives. I strive to understand the case in all its complexities. I try to understand the needs and interests and the goals and objectives of the participants. I try to understand the difficulties and opportunities that each move in the process presents. I try to understand the wide varieties of options present in each stage of the negotiation. I try to understand what settling the case can mean for the parties and their representatives.

In your own work as a mediator, if it is the problem-solving model that provides the format for achieving that understanding, then I say employ it. If it is the transformative model that does that for you, then I urge you to use it. If it is the model for facilitating traditional bargaining described in this volume that enables you to assist others with traditional bargaining, then embrace it. Whatever formulation of the mediation process fits the case, the parties, and the moment, and develops understanding is an approach to mediation that I suggest you consider using.

Notes

1. CHRISTOPHER MOORE, THE MEDIATION PROCESS: PRACTICAL STRATEGIES FOR RESOLVING CONFLICT (San Francisco: Jossey-Bass Publishers, 2d ed. 1996).

2. ROGER FISHER & WILLIAM URY, GETTING TO YES: NEGOTIATING AGREEMENT WITHOUT GIVING IN (New York: Penguin Books, 1983).

3. Margaret L. Shaw & Patrick Phear, *New Perspective on the Options Generation Process,* 16 MEDIATION Q. (Summer 1987).

4. ROBERT A. BARUCH BUSH & JOSEPH P. FOLGER, THE PROMISE OF MEDIATION: RESPONDING TO CONFLICT THROUGH EMPOWERMENT AND RECOGNITION (Jossey-Bass Publishers, San Francisco, 1994).

5. *Id.* at 167.

6. *Id.* at 167.

Do You Have an Opinion? Ethical Standards of Conduct in the Mediation of Civil Litigation

9

A perception about civil trial court mediation exists in some circles that the lawyers and former judges who typically mediate civil cases are conducting them poorly. Civil trial court mediators are accused routinely of being directive and they are faulted for relying heavily upon the use of opinions. Critics believe that civil trial court mediators are not truly mediators; they are neutral evaluators in disguise.

I agree with the critics who suggest that there are mediators in the civil trial court arena who conduct their mediations in that fashion and who expect to give their opinions about many aspects of the case, including its ultimate outcome. I also agree that when such behavior is employed, the process should be named properly. Mediation in that form is more properly termed "neutral evaluation."

225

I am reminded again of Professor Alfini's article, *Trashing, Bashing, and Hashing It Out: Is This the End of "Good Mediation"?*[1] Professor Alfini's observations of civil trial court mediation in Florida led him to believe that the principal tools employed by mediators there consisted of rendering opinions about the value of the case and browbeating the parties to settle the case. While I suggest that hashing out the case (that is, discussing case analysis) is entirely appropriate in that context, I believe that "bashing" and "trashing" have no defensible role in mediation. That kind of behavior is not acceptable even from neutral evaluators.

I know of no trainer in civil trial court mediation who teaches students to conduct mediations in this manner. Whether those students later conduct their mediations in the nondirective manner in which they are taught is another matter. However, that question can be raised about mediators in all types of disputes and in all types of settings.

■■■■■

Mediators everywhere and in every type of dispute are inclined to be directive and must guard against the tendency to be directive whenever they conduct mediations. The problem of being directive is a universal problem in the field of mediation.

Commentators often look to the model of mediation process that mediators utilize to explain the tendency to become directive. My experience leads me to believe that mediators become directive principally as a function of human nature and as a function of the culture in which we live. We human beings tend to be directive, and our culture tends to rely upon and cultivate the use of experts and expert opinions.

Directive Behavior Takes Many Forms

Mediators produce subtle shifts in mediations when we choose to inquire about and discuss one issue versus another. Mediators often direct the parties toward the issues and concerns we care about and find important. As a result, issues and topics that the parties do not care about are added to the discussion, and issues that the parties want to discuss or resolve are often lost or relegated to inferior status. This is an insidious form of direction, because we often are not aware we are engaging in it.

Another subtle form of direction involves the shift mediators choose to make from discussion to resolution. Mediators are usually the ones who move the discussion from issues to solutions; and we generally do it too quickly. Mediation trainees do it in their first role-plays and experienced mediators do it well after their initial training.

However, the most prevalent form of direction that mediators are aware of and discuss whenever they gather at professional conferences involves the expression of opinions. I am talking about opinions of all kinds, opinions concerning:

- what is or is not proper behavior
- what is or is not an appropriate offer
- how one party should feel about another
- whether to accept an offer and settle the case
- whether the other party's offer is his best number
- whether one party is acting in good faith
- whether the parties ought to meet in private sessions
- what is a strength or weakness in the case
- the outcome of the case
- whether one side is telling the truth to the other
- how a judge will rule on an evidentiary issue.

■ ■ ■ ■ ■

It's important to distinguish behavior on the part of the mediator that is rightly called "giving an opinion" from behavior that is rightly called "offering a suggestion." While each rightly could be called an opinion depending on the tone and timing and manner of the offer, I believe that a suggestion made to give the parties an option they've not thought of on their own is an appropriate thing

> for mediators to do and is not an opinion in the ordinary sense of that word.

Such an offer may, indeed, have a directive effect. If the parties have not thought of the option for themselves and the mediator does not give the option as a suggestion, then the parties will choose some other way to respond to each other. The offer of a suggestion often results in a change in the course of action by the parties. In that sense, the expression of a suggestion is directive.

I defend the use of a suggestion if it is made when the parties have run out of options and when the mediator offers it as one more option to think about. I am opposed to the offer of a suggestion if the mediator, in making it or discussing it, tries to sell that suggestion to the parties as the best way for them to act.

In the mediation of cases involving claims for money, I often make suggestions for the parties to consider when they are formulating proposals. I do so because they become stuck on making a proposal in reaction to the other side's that will further inflame the other side or lead to premature impasse. In making suggestions for movement, I am trying to expand their range of options. I am not trying to tell them that they are wrong or that my way is the only or proper way of negotiating a settlement. The decision as to what proposal to make should be entirely their own.

The expression of an opinion is an entirely different animal. It is the mediator's own judgment of what should or should not happen in a given situation. And the question for mediators everywhere is, should we engage in opinion giving or not? Should we comment in such a way that it judges an issue?

The classic answer to this question in the community of mediation in the United States is no. Every training that I've been associated with as a student or teacher has conveyed that emphatic answer. Giving opinions is generally thought to violate the parties' right to self-determination.

■■■■■

(Parenthetically, many mediators believe, all ethical considerations aside, that the offering of an opinion is an ineffective way to convince others to change their behavior. Human beings tend to resist adopting the opinions of others as their own, particularly when those opinions are unsolicited. Even when my clients ask for my opinion on a topic of discussion, I have noticed that they tend to resist my point of view if it differs from their own and they give me many reasons why their point of view is still valid. Those of you who are parents of teenage children may know whereof I speak.)

Every statement of standards of practice for mediators of which I am aware has stated that the expression of opinions violates the right of the parties to self-determination. In 1992, the National Institute of Dispute Resolution published a booklet authored by professor Robert Bush titled *The Dilemmas of Mediation Practice*.[2] The booklet is a summary of Bush's extensive study of the values of practicing mediators in family, community center, and civil trial court contexts. At the conclusion of his booklet, Bush published a set of model standards of conduct that he believed was justified by his work. They have become widely circulated in this country and have become the framework on which the standards of conduct for many professional organizations have been built.

Professor Bush's model identified the value of self-determination of the parties as one of the values that practicing mediators believe should apply to the practice of mediation. Self-determination of the parties is also referred to as the standard that calls for nondirectedness on the part of the mediator. Bush's model standard on that subject is as follows:

Standard V: Self-Determination

A mediator shall respect and encourage self-determination by the parties . . . and shall refrain from being directive and judgmental regarding the issues in dispute and options for settlement.

A. . . . s/he shall never substitute his/her judgment for that of the parties, as regards to any aspect of the mediation.

B. . . . However, at no time shall a mediator make a decision for the parties, or directly express his/her opinion about or advise for or against any proposal under consideration.[3]

In 1997, the Dispute Resolution Commission of North Carolina, which was established to certify and regulate mediators for the trial courts of North Carolina, recommended a set of standards for certified mediators to the North Carolina Supreme Court. Those standards, which were modeled on Bush's formulation, were promulgated by the court. The wording of Standard V, Self-Determination, was identical to the wording in Bush's model.

As the practice of trial court mediation unfolded in North Carolina, the subject of opinion giving became a frequent topic of discussion among mediators and members of the Commission. Interestingly, there was complete agreement among Commission members, mediators, lawyers, and judges that mediators should never give opinions in the absence of a request from the participants. Even judges who had a keen interest in managing their dockets and therefore might be suspected of favoring aggressive tactics from mediators were opposed to mediators giving unwanted opinions.

■ ■ ■ ■ ■

However, lawyers who valued the insight and experience of well-respected mediators began to question the wisdom of prohibiting giving opinions when they and their clients requested those opinions in mediation. Please note that it was lawyers, not the mediators who worked with them, who raised the issue.

Most lawyers want to know whether there are weaknesses in their case and gaps in their evidence and they are happy to have mediators point them out. They routinely ask mediators to tell them what they think and what the other side thinks of their case. Lawyers find this helpful in settlement negotiations with their clients and helpful in trial preparation if settlement doesn't occur.

Two examples will illustrate the point I am making here about the desires of the parties for the thoughts and experience of the mediator. Several months ago, I was conducting a civil case mediation in which a law enforcement officer was being sued for an illegal search, false imprisonment, and personal injury. At one point in a private session, the defendant's lawyer said:

D: I feel pretty confident about our case and the law governing this issue, and I'm not really convinced that we're going to get close to settlement. But while we have you here, I'd like to have the benefit of your thoughts and experience in this case. Is my confidence misplaced; am I missing something here that I should be concerned about?

In a business dispute I mediated several years ago, the plaintiff's lawyer recommended in private session that his client accept the final offer of the defendant. His client looked at me and said:

P: Young man [I was 54 at the time and she was 72], do you think I ought to accept that proposal?

(I looked at her lawyer for his reaction.)

L: Go ahead; I'd be interested in your thoughts.

■ ■ ■ ■ ■

This is another aspect of the behavior of lawyers about which the public is unfamiliar. Lawyers often use settlement conferences to get a read on their case. One of the benefits of mediation to them is learning more about their case. In addition to trying to convince the other side that they are right, they also are interested in learning about any weaknesses their case may have.

In the past several years the North Carolina Dispute Resolution Commission has reviewed several complaints against mediators for violations of the standards of conduct. None of these has involved the giving of opinions. However, as commission members began to grapple with the fact that they will be called upon in the future to review complaints against mediators and possibly vote to revoke their certifications, they began to question whether Standard V, on self-determination, should be written as a blanket prohibition against the expression of opinions.

Over the past year and a half the commission has debated whether or not to modify that standard. Members were divided on the issue. Some favored acknowledging the realities of practice and wanted to modify the standard to make it less rigid. Others believed it was not necessary to change the standard and feared that changing it would encourage mediators to become more directive in their approach to mediation.

Some pointed to Bush's discussion of this subject in his booklet on ethical dilemmas and pointed out that he was the first one to raise the question as to whether the standard of self-determination was compromised when the mediator gives an opinion at the parties' request. The implication in that question was that the goal of self-determination might be served, in fact, if the mediator responded to such a request by giving an opinion.

Ultimately, the commission agreed to recommend a modification of Standard V, and the Supreme Court thereafter changed it to read in its pertinent parts as follows:

Standard V: Self-Determination

A mediator shall respect and encourage self-determination by the parties . . . and shall refrain from being directive and judgmental regarding the issues in dispute and options for settlement.

A. A mediator is obligated to leave to the parties full responsibility for deciding whether and on what terms to resolve their dispute. He/She may assist them in making informed and thoughtful decisions, but shall not impose his/her judgment or opinions for those of the parties concerning any aspect of the mediation.

B. A mediator may raise questions for the participants to consider regarding their perceptions of the dispute as well as the acceptability of proposed options for settlement and their impact on third parties. Furthermore, a mediator may suggest for consideration options for settlement in addition to those conceived of by the parties themselves.

C. A mediator shall not impose his/her opinion about the merits of the dispute or about the acceptability of any proposed option for settlement. A mediator should resist giving his/her opinions about the dispute and options for settlement even when he/she is requested to do so by a party or attorney. Instead, a mediator should help that party utilize his/her own resources to evaluate the dispute and the options for settlement.

This section prohibits imposing one's opinions, advice and/or counsel upon a party or attorney. It does not prohibit the mediator's expression of an opinion as a last resort to a party or attorney who requests it when the mediator has already helped that party utilize his/her own resources to evaluate the dispute and options. (Emphasis added.)[4]

■■■■■

The new standard allows a mediator to express opinions during a court-ordered mediated settlement conference, but only under two conditions:

- A party must have requested the mediator's opinion on some aspect of the controversy under consideration. A mediator may never volunteer an opinion or evaluation without a clear invitation to do so from a party or parties. Although the standard does not specifically say this, it follows that if one party requests an opinion and the other party does not, then the mediator may give an opinion only to the party requesting it. Of course, there is no obligation to give an opinion in the first place, and so a mediator may simply decline to answer with an opinion.

- The opinion or evaluation may be given only as a last resort after the mediator has made every effort to help the parties evaluate their case themselves and to help them use their own resources to settle the dispute or claim. Last resort means when all else has failed. This new standard points to the ideal in mediation. Mediation at its best is a facilitative rather than a directive process. This new standard encourages mediators to hold back on giving opinions, or at least not to give them reflexively. This standard encourages the time-honored practices of asking good questions, listening well, inventing new options, and keeping the responsibility for decision making on the parties themselves. Opinion giving by the mediator under this standard is a last resort only.

In conjunction with the changes to Standard V, the commission also revised Standard VI. Standard VI mandates that mediators refrain from giving legal or other professional advice while conducting a mediated settlement conference. Standard VI was revised to clarify that, in responding to a party's request for an opinion on the merits of the case or in evaluating a settlement proposal under consideration, a mediator is not giving legal advice for purposes of Standard VI as long as the mediator has complied with the conditions established in revised Standard V.

■■■■■

I would like to point out two things about the revisions that are important. The first is that the changes in Standard V make it clear that the ideal in the practice of mediation is for mediators to refrain from giving opinions. They are invited, instead, to use other tools to facilitate the resolution of a dispute.

It is clear in this formulation that the Commission is not try-ing to change the ideal for the profession. The majority on the commission believed that the new formulation is clearer and more powerful in that respect than the original. The ideal is to help the parties utilize their own recourses to explore options for settlement and to resolve their dispute. The change in the stan-dard was made solely to set the bar for discipline that might be imposed by the Commission for behavior that was clearly beyond the limits of acceptability.

■■■■■

Secondly, the change in Standard V involved a shift in empha-sis that I think was long overdue. The standard now prohibits the "imposition" of an opinion, not the expression of one. This is a fundamental shift and I think a realistic and impor-tant one. It is, after all, unrealistic to expect that a mediator can do his or her work without conveying opinions.

Of necessity, mediators influence the behavior of disputants every day of their work lives. It is simply impossible for the medi-ator not to exert some direction on the participants in mediation. In fact, mediators are employed to do just that. We are hired to enable, to empower, to facilitate. We will always influence the res-olution of disputes; it is actually part of our job description to influence our clients to use thoughtful and informed decision-making processes. We will forever be directive in at least that sense. Therefore, it seems to me that the discussion about direc-tive behavior should center on the limits of directive behavior, limits that we can try to describe in helpful and objective ways.

On first blush, it appears easy to set the limits of direction by imposing a prohibition on the giving of opinions. "Just don't do it," one might say. The problem with that notion is that most of us give opinions and simply are not aware of the way in which our opinions are expressed and conveyed. Much of the opinion giving that we do, like much of human communication, is unconscious and nonverbal.

A verbatim transcript of a mediated settlement conference may contain a question that is open-ended and well crafted. The way in which that question is asked may communicate a less-than-benign intent on the part of the mediator. The question may be asked sarcastically, or it may be asked defiantly. What is communicated by the question will depend to a great extent on the way in which it is asked. It's not so much what we say but how we say it that makes a difference.

We convey opinions about the desirability of a person or idea by our tone, volume, and cadence of speech. We convey opinions by our posture and gestures. We convey opinions by our choice of words. And we convey opinions by our choice of topics to discuss. Most of the time we are not conscious of the degree to which we convey opinions in our work as mediators and in everyday life.

In addition, we have to factor into this discussion of opinion giving a subtle fact of human interaction—and that is the fact that the participants in mediation pick up messages from us that we do not intend to convey by the content of our speech. After posing what I think is a benign, open-ended question in mediation, I sometimes hear:

"I get your point, Andy, and it's well taken. Give us a few minutes to talk alone about those problems."

"What point?" I say to myself. "I wasn't trying to make a point. I was only trying to understand the case better and help them understand it, too. I wasn't trying to make a point." The parties in mediation infer all kinds of things from what we say and do that may accurately convey our intent or not. How are we to account for this phenomenon in our standards of conduct?

■ ■ ■ ■ ■

I think our current formulation of Standard V, which makes the test of prohibitive behavior the imposition of opinions rather than the giving of opinions, is a better, although a less-objective, standard. If we are concerned in the final analysis with protecting the ability of the parties to decide for themselves in mediation, we are fundamentally concerned with the question of coercion.

The expression of opinions may have no coercive impact at all upon the parties. The opinions solicited by the participants in mediations may be just one more factor among many that help the participants resolve the case or make movement toward resolution. If the parties ask for opinions, is the expression of our opinions coercive by necessity? I think not, and it seems to me that the commission got it right when it recommended that it is the imposition of opinions rather than the expression of them that ought to be the subject of inquiry in a disciplinary proceeding. It is the imposition of opinions that should be prohibited.

Having said that, I quickly return the reader to my earlier comment that Standard V of the Standards of Conduct not only prohibits certain behavior but encourages good behavior as well. The very wording of that section points the way toward the ideal in our work as mediators, and that is to be facilitative of the parties' decision making without resorting to expressing our own opinions.

■ ■ ■ ■ ■

For myself, when I revisit the subject of ethics and the value of self-determination as it is currently formulated in North Carolina, I am not prompted to increase the use of opinions in my work as a mediator. Instead, I come away with a renewed determination to keep the outcome of the dispute and the process of decision making in the hands of the parties. I admit that I constantly struggle to keep the parties in the foreground and myself in the background. I take consolation in the fact that I am not alone in this regard; I am confident that the struggle to be facilitative rather than directive will be a struggle for mediators in all disputes of all kinds and for all times.

Notes

1. James J. Alfini, TRASHING, BASHING, AND HASHING IT OUT: IS THIS THE END OF "GOOD MEDIATION?" 19 FLA. ST. U. L. REV. (1991).

2. Robert A. Baruch Bush, THE DILEMMAS OF MEDIATION PRACTICE: A STUDY OF ETHICAL DILEMMAS AND POLICY IMPLICATIONS (Report to NIDR, 1992).

3. *Id.* at 167.

4. "Standard V. Self-Determination" of the "Standards of Professional Conduct for Mediators," adopted by the North Carolina Supreme Court (1998).

Appendix: A Record of Movement: Charting Settlement Conference Proposals

I include for the reader's clarification a record of proposals and counter proposals made by Plaintiffs and Defendants in over a hundred court-ordered mediations in the superior courts of North Carolina. (In North Carolina we call those mediations, "mediated settlement conferences.") These have been drawn from the "bid sheets" I keep in each case. They contain no identifying information such as the name of the case, the names of the parties, the type of case involved, or the county in which the case was pending.

It was in studying records such as these that I began to identify the dynamics of negotiations about money and to struggle with ways to understand and deal with them. I hope they will be helpful in giving you a picture of the used-car sale stage of traditional bargaining. Unfortunately, I am not able to identify the places in the transcripts where the parties had trouble making movement nor the interactions I had with them in an effort to assist their negotiations. A close study of the transcripts, however, will give the reader a good idea of how difficult it is to settle a case through traditional bargaining. I hope, as well, that you will take some encouragement from the fact that many cases settle even when the parties' initial positions are far apart and movement is slow to materialize.

Plaintiff	Defendant
$450,000	$50,000
$425,000	$55,000
$395,000	$60,000
$380,000	$63,000
$375,000	$68,000
$350,000	$73,000
$335,000	$78,000
$325,000	$83,000
$317,000	$88,000
$312,000	$93,000
$307,000	$98,000
$302,000	$100,000
$200,000	$120,000
RECESSED	

Plaintiff	Defendant
$1,450,000	$450,000
$1,350,000	$500,000
$1,275,000	$556,000
$1,200,000	$600,000
$1,125,000	$610,000
$1,110,000	$625,000
$1,000,000	$650,000
$940,000	$662,500
$920,000	$675,000
$905,000	$687,500
$892,000	$692,500
$875,000	$700,000 (best)
$850,000 (best)	
SETTLED $750,000	

Plaintiff	Defendant
$68,000	$47,500
$67,000	$49,000
$66,000	$50,000
$65,000	$51,000
$63,000	$51,500
$62,500	$52,000
$62,000	$52,250
RECESSED	

Plaintiff	Defendant
$59,000	$10,000
$45,000	$14,000
$40,000	$17,500
$35,000	$20,000
$32,000	$22,000
$30,000	$23,500
$28,000	$25,000
SETTLED $25,000	

Plaintiff	Defendant
$85,500	$10,400
$67,500	$15,000
$55,000	$18,000
$42,000	$20,000
$30,000	$21,000
$29,000	$23,500
$25,000	$23,500
SETTLED $23,500	

Plaintiff	Defendant
$300,000	$20,000
$250,000	$25,000
$200,000	$35,000
$175,000	$45,000
$155,000	$55,000
$148,000	$65,000
$135,000	$72,000
$128,000	
	IMPASSE

Plaintiff	Defendant
$50,000	
$42,500	$6,500
$30,000	$12,500
$25,000	$15,000
$22,500	$17,000
$22,000	$17,500
$20,000	$17,500
SETTLED $18,750	

Plaintiff	Defendant
$150,000	$30,000
$130,000	$38,000
$110,000	$43,000
$90,000	$45,000
$70,000	$46,500
$53,500	$47,500
$50,000	$48,000
SETTLED $48,000	

Plaintiff	Defendant
$2,020,702.67	$303,620.67
$1,900,000	$600,000
$1,800,000	$750,000
$1,750,000	$1,050,000
$1,690,000	$1,300,000
$1,620,000	$1,500,000
$1,600,000	
RECESSED	

Plaintiff	Defendant
$80,000	$2,500
$65,000	$3,500
$54,000	$4,500
$48,000	$5,000
$41,000	$5,500
$37,500	$6,000
$34,000	$6,500
$31,000	$7,000
	IMPASSE

Plaintiff	Defendant
$60,000	$15,000
$45,000	$17,000
$39,000	$19,000
$37,000	$20,000
$36,000	$22,000
$34,500	$23,500
$33,500	$24,500
$31,500	$25,000
$30,000	
SETTLED $25,000	

Plaintiff	Defendant
$750,000	$45,000
$600,000	$75,000
$500,000	$100,000
$450,000	$150,000 if $250,000
$250,000	$175,000
$245,000	$200,000
$240,000	$210,000
$235,000	$220,000
$230,000	$225,000
$225,000	$225,000
SETTLED $222,500	

Plaintiff	Defendant
$1,750,000	$150,000
$1,600,000	$443,000
$1,575,000	$500,000
$1,100,000	$650,000
$1,100,000	$675,000
$1,050,000	$700,000
$1,025,000	$725,000
$1,015,000	$735,000
$1,000,000	$750,000
$950,000	
RECESSED	

Plaintiff	Defendant
$270,000	$75,000
$250,000	$80,000
$220,000	$87,500
$217,500	$92,500
$190,000	$95,000
$160,000	$97,500
$150,000	$100,000
$125,000	$110,000
$120,000	$110,000
SETTLED $110,000	

Plaintiff	Defendant
$1,800,000	$200,000
$1,400,000	$300,000
$1,300,000	$375,000
$1,500,000	$450,000
$1,025,000	$500,000
$900,000	$550,000
$875,000	$575,000
$850,000	$600,000
$825,000	$625,000
$750,000	$650,000
IMPASSE	

Plaintiff	Defendant
$240,000	$60,000
$180,000	$82,500
$180,000	$92,000
$175,000	$107,000
$165,000	$117,000
$160,000	$125,000
$155,000	$135,000
$150,000	$140,000
$150,000	$145,000
$147,500	
SETTLED $147,500	

Plaintiff	Defendant
$15,000	$6,000
$13,331	$7,000
$11,000	$7,500
+ Mediator's fee	
$10,000	$7,500
+ Mediator's fee	Mediator's fee
$8,900	$8,500
+ Mediator's fee	
SETTLED $8,500	

Plaintiff	Defendant
$12,000	$1,800
$11,000	$3,000
$10,000	$4,000
$9,000	$5,000
SETTLED $7,000	
+ Mediator's fee	

Plaintiff	Defendant
$120,000	$3,000
$115,000	$3,500
$110,000	$4,000
$100,000	$5,000
$90,000	$6,000
$80,000	$6,500
$75,500	$6,750
CONFERENCE BETWEEN	
ATTORNEYS	
$40,000	$13,000
$40,000	
$26,500	$20,000
+ Mediator's fee	
$25,000	$22,500
$25,000	$25,000
SETTLED $25,000	

Plaintiff	Defendant
$35,747.48	$1,500
$30,000	$2,500
$28,000	$3,500
$19,000	$5,000
$17,000	$6,000
$16,000	$7,000
$10,000	$7,500
$10,000	
SETTLED 2 WEEKS LATER	
AT $7,500	

Plaintiff	Defendant
$100,100	$25,000
$85,000	$30,000
$75,000	$35,000
$70,000	$40,000
$65,000	$44,500
$60,000	$46,500
$55,000	$48,000
$52,000	$49,000
$51,000	$50,000
SETTLED $50,000	

Plaintiff	Defendant
$600,000	$30,000
$500,000	$36,000
$390,000	$57,000
$325,000	$69,000
$300,000	$72,000
$280,000	$77,000
$260,000	$84,000
$245,000	$86,000
$235,000	$90,000
$215,000	$93,000
$206,000	$95,000
$201,000	$97,000
$199,000	$99,000
$190,000	$100,000
IMPASSE	

Plaintiff	Defendant
$250,000	$25,000
$175,000	$37,500
$155,000	$40,000
$140,000	$45,000
$90,000	$50,000
$80,000	$60,000
SETTLED $60,000	

Plaintiff	Defendant
$69,900	$500
$10,000	$2,500
$9,000	$2,750
$7,500	$3,000
$5,000	$3,000
$4,000	$3,000
SETTLED $3,000	

Plaintiff	Defendant
$1,530,000	$250,000
$800,000	$312,000
$675,000	$438,000
$591,000	$500,000
$558,912	$525,000
SETTLED $525,000	

Plaintiff	Defendant
$69,900	$500
$10,000	$2,500
$9,000	$2,750
$7,500	$3,000
$5,000	$3,000
$4,000	$3,000
SETTLED $3,000	

Plaintiff	Defendant
$157,800	$25,000
$135,000	$50,000
$140,000	$75,000
$130,000	$85,000
$125,000	$90,000
$120,000	$95,000
$119,000	$96,000
SETTLED $100,000	

Plaintiff	Defendant
$100,000	$5,000
$80,000	$20,000
$70,000	$30,000
$65,000	$35,000
$60,000	$40,000
$55,000	$42,000
$54,000	$45,000
$53,000	$45,000 + Mediator's fee
$50,000 + Mediator's fee	
SETTLED $45,000 + Mediator's fee	

Plaintiff	Defendant
$105,000	$42,500
$95,000	$55,000
$88,000	$65,000
$85,000 or $83,000 + confidentiality	$70,000 + confidentiality
$80,000 + confidentiality	$75,000
$76,000	$77,500 + confidentiality
$78,000 + confidentiality	
SETTLED $77,500 + Mediator's fee + confidentiality	

Plaintiff	Defendant
$37,000	$10,000
$26,000	$11,000
$25,000	$11,500
$24,500	$12,000
$23,750	$12,500
$22,500	$13,000
$17,500	$13,500
$17,000	$13,750
$16,250	$14,000
$16,000	$14,000 + Mediator's fee
$15,000	$14,250 + Mediator's fee
$14,500 + Mediator's fee	
SETTLED $14,250 + Mediator's fee	

Plaintiff	Defendant
$195,000	$35,000
$185,000	$50,000
$175,000	$55,000
$165,000	$60,000
$160,000	$65,000
$155,000	$70,000
$150,000	$75,000
$145,000	$90,000
$130,000	$95,000
$125,000	$97,500
$122,500	$100,000
$120,000	$100,000
$110,000	$110,000 + Mediator's fee
SETTLED $110,000	

Plaintiff	Defendant
$100,000	$15,000
$90,000	$17,500
$55,000	$20,000
$45,000	$22,500
$35,000	$25,000
$32,500	$27,000
$31,000	$28,000
$30,000	$29,000
$29,500	$29,500
SETTLED $29,500	

Plaintiff	Defendant
$1,500,000	$100,000
$1,450,000	$200,000
$1,350,000	$250,000
$1,300,000	$300,000
$1,250,000	$350,000
$1,200,000	$400,000
$1,125,000	$450,000
$1,075,000	
IMPASSE	

Plaintiff	Defendant
$975,000	$160,000
$900,000	$225,000
$850,000	$275,000
$840,000	$305,000
$825,000	$310,000
$815,000	$350,000
$780,000	$362,500
$765,000	$375,000
IMPASSE	

Plaintiff	Defendant
$100,000	$10,000
$50,000	$15,000
$40,000	$20,000
$35,000	$22,500
$30,000	$25,000
+ Mediator's fee	
$29,000	$27,500
+ Mediator's fee	
SETTLED $27,500	
+ Mediator's fee	

Plaintiff	Defendant
$75,000	$10,000
$65,000	$14,000
$58,000	$20,000
$24,000	
SETTLED $24,000	

Plaintiff	Defendant
$800,000	$125,000
$700,000	$160,000
$650,000	$190,000
$610,000	$210,000
$570,000	$230,000
$525,000	$250,000
$475,000	$265,000
$425,000	$280,000
$400,000	$295,000
$350,000	$300,000
$315,000	$335,000
SETTLED $335,000	

Plaintiff	Defendant
$40,000	$9,000
$37,500	$9,500
$34,000	$9,900
$32,500	$10,100
$31,750	$10,750
$30,750	$11,000
$30,000	$11,500
$29,500	$11,750
$29,250	$12,000
$29,000	$12,250
$28,750	$12,500
$28,500	$12,750
$28,250	$12,875
$27,850	$13,000
$27,500	$13,100
$27,250	$13,750
$26,000	$14,000
$25,500	$15,000
RECESSED	

Plaintiff	Defendant
$147,605	$21,000
$142,500	$34,000
$99,000	$40,000
$98,500	$52,000
$97,500	$65,000
$88,000	$75,000
$78,000	$76,000
SETTLED $77,000	

Plaintiff	Defendant
$80,000	$27,500
$75,000	$29,500
$65,000	$34,000
$60,000	$41,000
$57,500	$43,000
$55,500	$44,500
$54,000	$45,500
$53,000	$46,500
$52,000	$47,000
$51,500	$47,250
$51,000	$47,500
$50,000	
SETTLED $50,000	

Plaintiff	Defendant
$150,000	$90,000
$125,000	$95,000
$124,000	$97,000
$123,000	$98,000
$122,500	$100,000
$122,000	$102,500
$121,500	$104,000
$121,000	$105,000
$120,500	
$119,500	$107,000
$119,000	$108,000
$118,500	$109,000
$118,000	$109,500
$117,750	$110,000
$117,500	$112,000
$117,000	$113,000
$116,250	$113,750
SETTLED $113,750	

Plaintiff	Defendant
$15,000	$1,183
$14,000	$2,500
$13,000	$3,500
$12,000	$4,300
$11,300	$4,500
$10,000	$5,000
$9,000	$5,183
SETTLED $5,183	

Plaintiff	Defendant
$185,000	$102,000
$180,000	$104,000
$175,000	$105,000
$171,000	$106,000
$138,000	$112,000
$130,000	$115,000
$125,000	$120,000
SETTLED $120,000	

Plaintiff	Defendant
$135,000	$17,500
$110,000	$20,000
$105,000	$28,000
$85,000	$33,000
$80,000	$36,000
$78,500	$50,000
SETTLED $50,000	

Plaintiff	Defendant
$300,000	$36,000
$250,000	$50,000
$225,000	$65,000
$200,000	$80,000
$175,000	$95,000
$150,000	$110,000
$140,000	$112,907
$137,000	$117,000
$133,000	$120,000
$130,000	$123,000
$127,000	$125,000
SETTLED $125,000	

Plaintiff	Defendant
$25,000	$2,945
$25,000	$4,000
$20,000	$5,000
$19,000	$6,000
$18,000	$6,500
$16,000	$7,000
$14,000	$7,500
$11,000	
SETTLED $9,250	

Plaintiff	Defendant
$100,000	$5,000
$70,000	$10,000
$55,000	$20,000
$35,000	$25,000
$32,500	$30,000
SETTLED $30,000	

Plaintiff	Defendant
$105,000	$15,000
$85,000	$16,000
$55,000	$17,500
$36,000	
IMPASSE	

Plaintiff	Defendant
$245,000	$120,000
$235,000	$125,000
$230,000	$130,000
$225,000	$135,000
$220,000	$150,000
$175,000	$150,000
$150,000	
SETTLED $150,000	

Plaintiff	Defendant
$100,000	
$95,000	$5,000
$85,000	$8,000
$80,000	$13,000
$60,000	$15,500
$58,000	$17,000
$35,000	$18,500
	$20,000
SETTLED $20,000	

Plaintiff	Defendant
$90,000	$425,000
$110,000	$400,000
$117,500	$360,000
$130,000	$350,000
$150,000	$340,000
———	$300,000
$175,000	$290,000
$200,000	$275,000
SETTLED $237,500	

Plaintiff	Defendant
$236,000	$25,000
$211,250	$60,000
$186,250	$70,000
$156,250	$75,000
SETTLED $75,000	

Plaintiff	Defendant
$35,000	$125,000
$25,000	$95,000
$35,000	$88,000
$45,000	$75,000
$49,000	$70,000
$50,000	$55,000
SETTLED $50,000	

Plaintiff	Defendant
$300,000	$25,000
$195,000	$40,000
	Plaintiff needs to be under $100,000)
IMPASSE	

Plaintiff	Defendant
$56,209	$15,000
$51,000	$17,000
$43,000	$19,000
$39,500	$20,000
$37,000	$22,000
$36,000	$23,500
$35,000	$24,250
$34,500	$25,000
$33,900	$26,000
$33,000	$27,000
$32,000	$28,000
$31,000	$29,000
$30,000	$30,000
SETTLED $30,000	

Plaintiff	Defendant
$50,000	$1,000
$40,000	$2,000
$15,000	$3,500
$12,000	$5,000
SETTLED $7,500	

Plaintiff	Defendant
$100,000	$2,000
$70,000	$4,000
$68,000	$10,000
$45,000	$15,000
$40,000	$15,000
$30,000	$15,000
SETTLED $22,000	

Plaintiff	Defendant
$1,400,000	$550,000
$1,380,000	$650,000
$1,360,000	$750,000
$1,340,000	$810,000
$1,330,000	$850,000
$1,320,000	$880,000
$1,315,000	$900,000
$1,300,000	$920,000
$1,280,000	$940,000
$1,260,000	$960,000
$1,240,000	$980,000
$1,230,000	$990,000
$1,225,000	$995,000
$1,220,000	$1,000,000
$1,200,000	
SETTLED $1,100,000	

Plaintiff	Defendant
$37,500	$95,000
$41,000	$91,000
$45,000	$89,000
$47,000	$86,000
$48,000	$80,000
SETTLED $65,000	

Plaintiff	Defendant
$20,927	$3,000
$18,657	$4,000
$18,000	$4,000
$9,999	$4,000
$7,500	$5,000
SETTLED $5,000	

Plaintiff	Defendant
$677,500	$157,500
$390,000	$300,000
$375,000	$325,000
$365,000	$335,000
SETTLED $350,000	

Plaintiff	Defendant
$85,000	$10,000
$75,000	$20,000
$65,000	$35,000
$60,000	$40,000
$40,000	
SETTLED $40,000	

Plaintiff	Defendant
$13,075	$1,500
$11,000	$2,500
$10,000	$3,000
$9,000	$3,500
$8,000	$3,800
$7,000	$4,100
$6,500	$4,100
$6,000	$4,800
$5,500	$4,800
$5,000	$5,000
SETTLED $5,000	

Plaintiff	Defendant
$150,000	$20,000
$125,000	$27,500
$97,000	$35,000
$95,000	$45,000
$85,000	$55,000
$75,000	
SETTLED $65,000	

Plaintiff	Defendant
$40,000	$21,000
$37,000	$22,000
$36,000	$22,500
$32,000	$23,000
$31,000	$25,000
SETTLED $25,000	

Plaintiff	Defendant
$25,000	$5,000
$15,000	$10,000
$7,000	$9,000
$8,000	$8,000
+ Mediator's fee	
SETTLED $8,000	
+ Mediator's fee	

Plaintiff	Defendant
$143,200	$17,500
$123,200	$18,500
$113,200	$27,500
$99,999	$28,500
$98,999	$33,333
$95,000	$38,100
$90,000	$42,900
$87,000	$47,500
IMPASSE	

Plaintiff	Defendant
$1,200,000	$75,000
$756,000	$125,000
$675,000	$150,000
$600,000	$175,000
$525,000	$200,000
$475,000	$210,000
$450,000	$215,000
$350,000	$225,000
$300,000	$250,000
RECESSED	

Plaintiff	Defendant
$39,600	$10,000
$35,000	$12,500
$25,000	$15,000
$23,000	$17,000
	+ confidentiality
$21,000	$19,000
+ confidentiality	
SETTLED $20,000	
+ confidentiality	

Plaintiff	Defendant
$100,000	$25,000
$90,000	$35,000
$80,000	$45,000
$75,000	$50,000
$70,000	split
$65,000	$62,500
SETTLED $62,500	

Plaintiff	Defendant
$1,750,000	$50,000
$1,500,000	$100,000
$1,200,000	$125,000
$1,000,000	$250,000
$750,000	$300,000
$700,000	
SETTLED $500,000	

Plaintiff	Defendant
$95,000	$14,000
$85,000	$17,500
$75,000	$20,000
$65,000	$22,500
$60,000	$25,000
$57,500	$26,500
$56,000	$28,000
$54,000	$29,000
$52,000	$30,000
$50,000	$31,000
$48,999	$32,000
$47,999	$33,000
$46,999	$34,000
$45,999	$34,100
$42,250	$34,200
$42,150	$34,300
$40,700	$34,400
RECESSED	

Plaintiff	Defendant
$235,000	$60,000
$180,000	$75,000
$170,000	$90,000
$155,000	$100,000
$145,000	$107,500
$140,000	$110,000
$137,500	$112,500
$135,000	
RECESSED	

Plaintiff	Defendant
$47,000	$20,000
$42,000	$22,500
$39,000	$25,000
$35,000	$27,000
$33,000	$28,500
$32,000	$30,000
$30,500	$30,000
SETTLED $30,000	

Plaintiff	Defendant
$225,000	$65,000
$220,000	$85,000
$180,000	$100,000
$165,000	$110,000
$155,000	$120,000
$145,000	$132,500
SETTLED $138,750	

Plaintiff	Defendant
$300,000	$20,000
$250,000	$25,000
$200,000	$35,000
$175,000	$45,000
$155,000	$55,000
$145,000	$65,000
$135,000	$72,000
$128,000	
IMPASSE	

Plaintiff	Defendant
$2,020,702	$303,620
$1,900,000	$600,000
$1,800,000	$750,000
$1,750,000	$1,050,000
$1,690,000	$1,300,000
$1,620,000	$1,500,000
	FINAL
$1,600,000	
FINAL	
RECESSED	

Plaintiff	Defendant
$5,000,000	$1,450,000
$4,500,000	$1,750,000
$4,200,000	$2,000,000
$3,900,000	$2,250,000
$3,700,000	$2,300,000
$3,600,000	$2,400,000
$3,500,000	$2,500,000
$3,400,000	$2,550,000
$3,350,000	$2,600,000
$3,325,000	
SETTLED $3,000,000	

Plaintiff	Defendant
$250,000	$60,000
$225,000	$75,000
$200,000	$85,000
$195,000	$95,000
$190,000	$105,000
$180,000	$110,000
$150,000	$115,000
$135,000	
SETTLED $115,000 + confidentiality	

Plaintiff	Defendant
$28,000	$7,500
$24,000	$8,000
$22,000	$8,500
$20,000	$9,000
$19,000	$9,500
$18,000	$10,000
$17,500	$10,500
$17,000	$11,000
$16,500	$11,500
$16,000	$12,000
$15,500	$12,250
$15,250	$12,500
$12,500	$12,500
+ Mediator's fee	
SETTLED $12,500	

Plaintiff	Defendant
$100,000	$15,000
$90,000	$17,500
$55,000	$20,000
$45,000	$22,500
$35,000	$25,000
$32,500	$27,000
$31,000	$28,000
$30,000	$29,000
$29,500	$29,500
SETTLED $29,500	

Plaintiff	Defendant
$172,900	$20,000
$162,900	$27,000
$140,000	$30,000
$120,000	$42,500
$115,000	$50,000
$110,000	$55,000
$105,000	$60,000
$100,000	$65,000
$99,000	$70,000
$93,000	$75,000
$93,000	$82,500
$93,000	$87,500
SETTLED $93,000	

Plaintiff	Defendant
$87,300	$10,000
$70,000	$11,000
$50,000	$11,000
$25,000	$12,000
$25,000	$13,000
$24,500	——
$19,900	$15,000
$18,750	$15,000
$15,000	
SETTLED $15,000	

Plaintiff	Defendant
$138,000	$51,000
$130,000	$51,500
$88,000	$52,500
$85,000	$53,000
$79,000	$53,500
$76,000	$54,000
$73,000	$54,500
$70,000	$55,000
$68,000	$55,500
$67,000	$58,500
$62,000	$59,000
SETTLED $60,000	

Plaintiff	Defendant
$145,000	$15,000
$99,000	$25,000
$89,000	$33,000
$81,000	$40,000
$75,000	$45,000
$70,000	$47,000
$67,500	$49,000
$66,000	$50,000
$61,000	$52,000
$57,500	$52,500
$55,000	$52,500
$53,750	$53,000
SETTLED $53,000	

Plaintiff	Defendant
$700,000	$100,000
$675,000	$125,000
$625,000	$150,000
$600,000	$165,000
$585,000	$180,000
$560,000	$195,000
$540,000	$210,000
$525,000	$225,000
$495,000	$240,000
$480,000	$250,000
$470,000	$260,000
$460,000	$265,000
$450,000	$270,000
IMPASSE	

Plaintiff	Defendant
$150,000	$20,000
$110,000	$30,000
$100,000	$35,000
$90,000	$37,000
$87,000	$40,000
$85,000	$44,000
$80,000	$44,000
$76,000	$45,000
$74,000	$46,000
$73,000	$47,000
$72,000	$48,000
$71,000	$48,500
$70,000	$49,000
$69,000	$50,000
$59,000	$50,000
$55,000	$52,500
$55,000	
SETTLED $55,000	

Plaintiff	Defendant
$49,000	$5,000
$43,000	$7,500
$41,000	$9,000
$40,000	$10,000
$25,000	$13,500
$19,250	$14,275
$17,000	$15,000
SETTLED $15,000	

Plaintiff	Defendant
$450,000	$35,000
$383,000	$50,000
$300,000	$60,000
$250,000	$100,000
$150,000	
RECESS	
SETTLED $100,000	

Plaintiff	Defendant
$300,000	$25,000
$200,000	$35,000
$175,000	$40,000
$125,000	$50,000
$105,000	$52,500
$102,500	$60,000
$77,500	$67,500
$70,000	$70,000
SETTLED $70,000	

Plaintiff	Defendant
$156,722	$40,000
$120,000	$45,000
$115,000	$50,000
$110,000	$52,000
$108,000	$54,000
IMPASSE	

Plaintiff	Defendant
$135,000	$17,500
$110,000	$20,000
$105,000	$28,000
$85,000	$33,000
$80,000	$36,000
$78,500	$50,000
RECESSED	

Plaintiff	Defendant
$106,000	$56,000
$104,000	$58,000
$102,000	$59,000
$100,000	$60,000
$91,722	
SETTLED $62,000	

Plaintiff	Defendant
$650,000	$75,000
$625,000	$110,000
$600,000	$135,000
$575,000	$160,000
$550,000	$185,000
$525,000	$210,000
$510,000	$220,000
$490,000	$240,000
$465,000	$260,000
$450,000	$275,000
$435,000	$285,000
$425,000	$290,000
$415,000	$295,000
$410,000	$300,000
$405,000	$305,000
$395,000	$310,000
$390,000	$315,000
$385,000	$320,000
$375,000	$325,000
$350,000	$350,000
SETTLED $350,000	

Plaintiff	Defendant
$33,000	$500
$30,000	$700
$21,000	$900
$19,000	$1,150
$16,000	$1,150
$13,000	$1,150
$10,000	$2,000
RECESS	
SETTLED $4,500	

Plaintiff	Defendant
$275,000	$5,000
$175,000	$7,500
$150,000	$12,500
$140,00	$20,049.05
$120,000	$23,000
$117,000	$30,000
$105,000	$31,000
$99,000	$32,000
$98,000	$37,500
$95,000	$40,000
$80,000	$44,000
$75,000	$47,500
$70,000	$48,000
$68,000	$48,500
$65,000	$49,000
$60,000	$49,750
$59,000	$50,000
$58,000	$50,250
$57,500	$52,000
SETTLED $52,500	

Plaintiff	Defendant
$35,000	$12,500
$30,000	$16,500
$27,500	$18,500
$25,000	$20,000
$24,000	$22,000
SETTLED $22,000	

Plaintiff	Defendant
$65,000	$3,000
$55,000	$5,000
$47,250	$7,000
$39,500	$9,000
$24,000	$10,500
$29,500	$12,750
$25,000	$13,750
$23,000	$14,500
$21,750	$15,000
$20,000	$15,200
$19,500	$16,250
$17,500	$16,250
$16,250	$16,250
SETTLED $16,250	

Plaintiff	Defendant
$95,000	$19,000
$87,500	$20,500
$82,500	$21,500
$77,500	$22,500
$72,500	$23,500
$67,500	$24,500
$62,500	$25,500
$59,500	$26,000
$56,500	$27,000
$51,500	$27,000
$40,000	———
$32,000	$30,000
SETTLED $32,000 +Mediator's fee	

Plaintiff	Defendant
$185,000	$102,000
$180,000	$104,000
$175,000	$105,000
$171,000	$106,000
$138,000	$112,000
$130,000	$115,000
$125,000	
SETTLED $120,000	

Plaintiff	Defendant
$60,000	$7,500
$42,000	$10,000
$36,000	$13,000
$27,000	$14,000
$25,500	$15,000
$24,500	
SETTLED $18,000 + Mediator's fee	

Plaintiff	Defendant
$25,000	$4,000
$20,000	$5,000
$19,000	$6,000
$18,000	$6,500
$16,000	$7,000
$14,000	$7,500
$11,000	
SETTLED $9,250	

Plaintiff	Defendant
$150,000	$68,000
$137,060	$75,000
$121,000	$85,000
$116,100	$90,000
$112,500	$95,000
$110,000	$98,000
$109,000	$100,000
$108,000	$101,000
$107,000	$102,500
$106,030	
SETTLED $106,030	

Plaintiff	Defendant
$40,000	$21,000
$37,000	$22,000
$36,000	$22,500
$32,000	$23,000
$31,000	$25,000
SETTLED $25,000	

Plaintiff	Defendant
$150,000	$90,000
$125,000	$95,000
$124,000	$97,000
$123,000	$98,000
$122,500	$100,000
$122,000	$102,500
$121,500	$104,000
$121,000	$105,000
$120,500	———
$119,500	$107,000
$119,000	$108,000
$118,500	$109,000
$118,000	$109,500
$117,750	$110,000
$117,500	$111,000
$117,000	$113,000
$116,250	$113,750
SETTLED $113,750	

Plaintiff	Defendant
$31,000	$5,000
$27,000	$8,000
$22,000	$11,000
$20,000	$13,000
$18,000	$14,000
$17,500	$14,500
$17,000	$14,750
$16,750	
SETTLED $15,750	

Plaintiff	Defendant
$70,000	$40,000
$60,000	$45,000
$50,000	$45,000
$49,000	$45,000
SETTLED $46,000	

Plaintiff	Defendant
$750,000	$10,000
$100,000	$15,000
$95,000	$25,000
$75,000	$26,000
$65,000	$27,000
$55,000	$28,000
$45,000	$29,000
$40,000	$29,500
$39,000	$30,000
SETTLED $33,384	

Plaintiff	Defendant
$750,000	$10,000
$100,000	$15,000
$95,000	$25,000
$75,000	$26,000
$65,000	$27,000
$55,000	$28,000
$45,000	$29,000
$40,000	$29,500
$39,000	$30,000
SETTLED $33,384	

Plaintiff	Defendant
$300,000	$36,000
$250,000	$50,000
$225,000	$65,000
$200,000	$80,000
$175,000	$95,000
$150,000	$110,000
$140,000	$112,907
$137,000	$117,000
$133,000	$120,000
$130,000	$123,000
$127,000	$125,000
SETTLED $125,000	

Plaintiff	Defendant
$100,000	——
$95,000	$23,000
$90,000	$29,000
$85,000	$32,000
$80,000	$35,000
$77,000	$37,000
$75,000	$39,000
$72,000	$42,000
$69,000	$45,000
$66,000	——
MEDIATOR SUGGESTED $55,000 TO BOTH—Impasse	

Plaintiff	Defendant
$25,000	$5,000
$22,000	$5,500
$21,000	$7,000
$18,000	$7,500
$15,000	$8,000
$10,000	$8,500
$9,500	$9,000
SETTLED $9,000	

Plaintiff	Defendant
$180,000	$92,000
$175,000	$107,000
$165,000	$117,000
$160,000	$125,000
$155,000	$135,000
$150,000	$140,000
$150,000	$145,000
$147,500	$147,500
SETTLED $147,500	

Plaintiff	Defendant
$245,000	$120,000
$235,000	$125,000
$230,000	$130,000
$225,000	$135,000
$220,000	$150,000
$175,000	$150,000
$150,000	$150,000
SETTLED $150,000	

Plaintiff	Defendant
$300,000	$7,500
$150,000	$20,000
$137,500	$25,000
$132,500	$31,000
$126,500	$37,000
$120,000	$50,000
$95,000	$55,000
$85,000	$57,500
$82,500	$60,000
SETTLED $65,000	

Plaintiff	Defendant
$100,000	$25,000
$90,000	$35,000
$80,000	$45,000
$75,000	$50,000
$70,000	——
$65,000	$62,500
SETTLED $62,500	

Index